SIDELINE CHURCH

THOMAS G. BANDY

SIDELINE CHURCH

BRIDGING THE CHASM BETWEEN
CHURCHES AND CULTURES

Abingdon Press™

Nashville

SIDELINE CHURCH:
Bridging the Chasm between Churches and Cultures

Library of Congress Cataloging-in-Publication Data has been requested.

ISBN 978-1-5018-7147-4

18 19 20 21 22 23 24 25 26 27—10 9 8 7 6 5 4 3 2 1

MANUFACTURED IN THE UNITED STATES OF AMERICA

WITH APPRECIATION

This book is the culmination of observation and reflection that has informed my previous books on church and culture:

See, Know & Serve the People Within Your Reach
Worship Ways (with Lucinda Holmes)
Spiritual Leadership
Strategic Thinking

None of this would have been possible without the gracious help and support of others. So many church leaders—clergy and lay, denominational and independent—have offered constructive critique and helpful insights along the way. My colleagues in the North American Paul Tillich Society (and the American Academy of Religion) have allowed me to test my theories about church and culture through society papers and dialogue.

I also want to thank Chuck Salter, the president of MissionInsite.com, for involving me in the development of resources for this demographic search engine, and the permission to use it in my research and writing.

I am profoundly grateful to Tex Sample, now professor emeritus from St. Paul School of Theology in Kansas City, Missouri, for his previous work on church and culture. His 1990 book *U. S. Lifestyles and Mainline Churches* provided an excellent starting place to explore change over the past thirty years.

I want to particularly thank my editor Paul Franklyn for his encouragement to bring together philosophical reflection and practical ministry, and his many suggestions that have improved these books.

Finally, I thank my wife and family for the emotional support to carry on consultation and teaching, across the country and internationally, among the full range of cultural and religious diversity, despite the stress that such personal interaction with this subject matter has entailed.

CONTENTS

FOREWORD

Tom Bandy called me on the phone, and, after the usual pleasantries, asked me if I intended to do an update of my 1990 book *U.S. Lifestyles and Mainline Churches*. I told him I had no such plans, and Tom asked if I would mind if he did something of a sequel to my book. While I had continued, of course, to study in the area, my main concentration for both research and work had been focused on justice and mass-based community organizing. In fact, I was glad that someone of Tom's background and expertise would want to pick up on where my work had been more than a quarter of a century before, and would want to follow up on it to demonstrate where lifestyle expressions are today and especially where the church is in relationship to these.

In my book I had used Arnold Mitchell's "The Nine American Lifestyles" as the basic demographic profile for an overview of the American people. I sorted these nine lifestyles into three groups of three, which I called the cultural left, the cultural middle, and the cultural right. The first of these was constituted largely of the baby boomers and their powerful ethic of self-fulfillment; the second group, with a strong ethic of achievement, represented business and professional careerists who were the dominant establishment of the society; and the third group was described as the territorial-rooted, conservative traditionalists, and largely working-class people of the United States. Even then, US lifestyles were more complicated than that, but this seemed to be a useful model at the time.

What I love about Bandy's new book is the far more careful and highly differentiated analysis he brings to US lifestyles. Working with the seventy-one lifestyle groups identified by Experian, Bandy brings a nuanced description to the people of this country and provides greater clarity about their identity, their expressed wants, needs, preferences, practices, and their religious and spiritual orientations. Basic to Bandy's work is how much more differentiated, even fragmented, our culture has become since 1990. For this reason among a good many more, we have valuable lessons to be learned from his descriptions, analyses, and recommendations.

But he does not stop there; he addresses the standing situation of the church at the present time. With its membership loss over the last fifty years, the mainline church has become the *sideline* church—and the evangelical churches, exulting in their growth back then, have now themselves entered into serious decline. Religious institutions of all kinds now face an increasingly complex and diverse culture and the challenges these represent. No end of this is in sight. Yet, into the face of this cultural situation with all its lifestyle complications, Bandy moves with suggestions for doing ministry among the large range of lifestyle groups now living in the United States. His suggestions are a treasure trove of ideas and approaches that can be studied and utilized in a great variety of church settings and new community forms.

Bandy brings to this book his rich background as theological scholar, consultant, workshop leader, and church expert. It is a privilege to read along and think with him in this valuable exercise. To be sure, some may disagree with his characterizations, his analyses, and his prescriptions, but anyone should be able to appreciate this opportunity to work with a sharp mind, an informed docent, a seasoned consultant, and a person of vital faith. I know of no book or resource that does what Bandy provides for us in these pages.

—*Tex Sample, PhD, Robert B. and Kathleen Rogers Professor Emeritus of Church and Society, Saint Paul School of Theology, Leawood, KS*

i

PREFACE

In 1990, Tex Sample wrote a book entitled *U.S. Lifestyles and Mainline Churches*. The book was intended to help Protestant churches become more relevant to cultural diversity, but it did much more than that. It revealed the growing crack between established churches of all kinds and the changing, fracturing, multiplying societies around them. The book was a best seller among Protestant church leaders, and for a time influenced many churches to adapt ministries to changing circumstances.

This book, *Sideline Church*, is a second installment, so to speak, almost thirty years later. The crack revealed in 1990 has now widened into a chasm. And this has provoked a different title. In the past, "mainline" usually referred to churches that were part of larger denominations, in contrast to independent churches. Christians consciously thought of themselves as not only members of a congregation, but loyal to a larger denomination or tradition. That identification has become so weak, that I now consider "mainline" to refer to any established institutional church, regardless of denominational or independent status. People are increasingly alienated from *any* institutional church that once considered itself a significant influence on community and culture. There really isn't a "mainline" church anymore (liberal or evangelical). Most churches are now out of the *mainline* and are now on the *sideline*. Churches observe cultural change, but don't really influence it, and often don't care to participate in it.

Most churches today are like spectators at a football game. They watch. They may sing songs or shout encouragement, or they may shout criticisms and lament mistakes. Occasionally churches will leave their seats to get a hot dog with their friends . . . or quarrel with their enemies. Occasionally there is a "wave" as sections of the Christendom stadium rise to their feet to celebrate their particular denomination or tradition. Occasionally there is a movement to exponentially increase the number of fans. Occasionally the fans attempt to influence the owners about who can or cannot play for the team, or influence the coaches about what plays do or do not work. Often there are angry confrontations as liberals and conservatives, or this coalition and that coalition, shout insults at one another across the stadium.

The point, however, is that they are not players anymore. They are spectators. Indeed, churches become so preoccupied with what is going on in the stands that they pay less and less attention to the game. For better or worse, society moves on. They cheer and boo as some churches or church members leave their seats and change sides. They project their own hopes and fears on individual players who become proxy representatives for a particular cause or policy.

If we were to reverse the metaphor and pretend that the spectators were actually players, we might see the game descend into chaos and become a brawl. Even more obvious, however, would be the empty stands. Fewer and fewer people will be watching. The very spectacle of Christians brawling with each other has lost appeal. Nobody will buy tickets. The media won't bother to cover the game.

Of course, not *all* churches are sidelined. And having said this I can mentally picture church leaders grasping at the straw, reassuring themselves that I am certainly not talking about *their* church. Megachurch leaders are particularly prone to this self-deception because they seem so big. How could they be so big if they weren't so relevant? But look again. The megachurch memberships are remarkably homogeneous by race, age, income, family status, marital status, and language. Yes there are program options. But the membership of the megachurch located on the beltway of the city does not even come close to mirroring the demographic and lifestyle diversity of the city itself. Indeed, its very location on the beltway suggests a church on the sidelines of the city, its penetration into demographic diversity limited to offsite outreach away from the "home" campus.

Not *all* churches are sidelined, but the congregations that aren't tend to be smaller, nesting in the unique culture of a neighborhood or a particular public. There they will influence individuals for a lifetime, and not merely increase adherents in a temporary burst of "city-reaching" that will be forgotten in another ten years as cultural diversity relentlessly expands and overwhelms church institutions. They will focus on local, municipal, and sometimes state policy-makers, changing society from the bottom up, rather than lobbying national or international governments to change society from the top down.

Tex Sample explored a crack between church and culture in 1990. But this book is intended to explore the chasm between churches and cultures today. Many churches will never be able to cross that chasm, and already we see the closure of churches accelerating in every denomination and tradition (liberal and evangelical) and the overall aging and declining numbers of church membership. Churches that had a window of opportunity to change in 1990 have seen that window close over the last thirty years, and they simply do not have the critical mass of resources and volunteers to do it. And this is partly because, when push comes to shove, privilege reduces risk and many churches (deep in their hearts) don't want to change anyway. When it comes to change, they will always worry more about members they might lose than strangers they might bless.

Some churches can and will cross that chasm . . . or at least die trying. Those that do will discover that the key to the crossing is not dogma or ideology, or music or technology, polity or tradition, or any of the things churches debate as spectators watching the game. The key is empathy. It is empathy of the most intimate and profound kind. It is a true "heart burst" for someone other than yourself.

This book is written from a distinctly empathic perspective. It is intended to help faithful clergy and lay leaders understand the diverse public around them, and bridge the chasms of intolerance that are growing between churches and cultures today. I offer suggestions for relevant ministries, but more than this I intend to provide clues to how different people approach, or distance themselves from, religion and spirituality today. I seek insight into how they think about God in different ways, and how different motivations drive their quests for meaning and purpose.

In the chapters that follow, I explore lifestyle attitudes toward religion and preferences for ministry in three distinct groups. I describe these as the *culturally ambivalent* (chapter 1), the *culturally righteous* (chapter 3), and the *culturally passive* (chapter 5). These correspond roughly to the groups Tex Sample described in 1990 as the *culturally left, right,* and *center* (reflecting the sociological terminology at the time). I explore how these groups evolved or morphed over the past twenty-five to thirty years from a religious or spiritual point of view.

I refer primarily to my experience working with lifestyle segments, which are perhaps better described as lifestyle *portraits*. Lifestyle portraiture is a significant evolution in demographic research made possible by the digital age. Corporations such as Experian (whose terminology is used in this book) are now able to track the digital behavior of every person in America; collate the data; and create portraits that blend demographic and psychographic information. Today organizations in every sector (education, health, social service, business, entertainment, technology, government, and even law and the military) use this information to anticipate behavioral patterns (lifestyle expectations and needs) to do everything from marketing to strategic planning. Churches and other religious organizations are also starting to use search engines like www.MissionInsite.com to do the same for leadership deployment, worship design, ministry planning, church planting, and more.

The descriptions and extensions of each group will be described in detail. If we were to estimate the proportions for the lifestyle representation of the three groups in the United States today, roughly 50 percent probably belong to the *culturally ambivalent* and its extreme; 30 percent probably belong to the *culturally righteous* and its extreme; and approximately 20 percent belong to the *culturally passive* and its extreme. A snapshot might look like this:

CULTURAL HABITS OF CHURCH PARTICIPATION

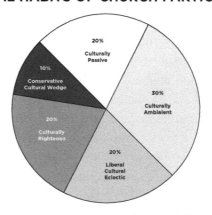

CULTURALLY AMBIVALENT:	Skeptical members, rare attenders, low commitment to Christian education
LIBERAL CULTURAL ECLECTIC:	Non-members, never attenders, periodic interest in religious issues
CULTURALLY PASSIVE:	Registered members, cyclical attenders, low commitment to adult faith formation
CULTURALLY RIGHTEOUS:	Selective members, regular attenders, high commitment to Christian lifestyle
CONSERVATIVE CULTURAL WEDGE:	Pragmatic participants, occasional attenders, high commitment to religious certainty

But I am very cautious about "snapshots" and uneasy about applying these proportions. Lifestyle attitudes toward religion are very fluid. Whether demographic diversity is studied empathically or scientifically, the general conclusions today may not fit the realities of tomorrow. In the descriptions of each cultural group, you will see footnotes that suggest why some lifestyle segments are either divided or shifting between camps.

It may be helpful, however, to observe several trends.

First, lifestyle migration is shifting more toward the *culturally righteous*. This may reflect growing dissatisfaction with religious ambiguity, and desire for religious certainty (whether or not it is real or illusory). This can help us understand why historically mainstream Christian denominations are declining faster than the evangelical denominations are declining. Both are on the sideline.

Second, a larger percentage of the *culturally righteous* gravitate toward the extremes of the *conservative cultural wedge*, than the percentage of the *culturally ambivalent* are gravitating toward the extremes of the *liberal cultural eclectic*. This may reflect the more dilettantish approach to religion of the left compared to the more constant and persistent approach to religion of the right. And it may help us understand the growth of independent churches and faith-based nonprofit advocacy groups.

Third, migration is motivated more by the rejection of one group than the affirmation of another. Migrating lifestyle segments are more like refugees fleeing to a country that they don't really understand but among whom they feel safer. They are not like intentional immigrants embracing a country about which they have done some careful research. This may mean that neither the *culturally righteous* nor the *culturally ambivalent* should count on the loyalty of migrants over the long term.

Fourth, the ranks of the *culturally passive* tend to be shrinking over time. This may reflect the anti-institutionalism of our time, or the aging of many lifestyle segments in this group. But it reveals that participation in the *culturally passive* is often just a temporary stop as people make up their minds which way to go. This helps explain why, despite every effort of *culturally passive* churches to be hospitable to visitors, the guests don't stick with that church for long.

Finally, the largest and most profound migration of lifestyle segments is the shift toward personal religion. In part this may reflect a growing dissatisfaction with the dogmatisms and pressures of all three groups, and a desire to take personal control of faith (and perhaps personal control of God). Personal religion may be a smorgasbord of consistent and contradictory values and beliefs, but at least the menu choice is *my* religious diet, and no one has the right to criticize it.

There is both danger and hope. Taken together, all these trends tend to encourage confrontation rather than conversation. The lines of separation become harder because people are often fleeing a religious point of view rather than embracing one, and so are naturally defensive about their choices. And as religion becomes increasingly personal, churches lose power to hold their loose membership accountable for their actions. That's the danger. On the other hand, migrating lifestyle segments can become natural bridges of understanding because they have experience (for better or ill) in both camps. And even as personal religion grows, so also does interest in spiritual life. The key to faith is less and less an experience of love, and more and more a quest for hope.

An empathetic perspective is different from a more academic approach. One result of the explosion of cultural diversity is that an academic perspective is no longer adequate. The academies of religion (university and seminary teachers) are also becoming sidelined by the speed, complexity, and ambiguity of cultural fragmentation. Seminary educators may protest, but occasional preaching, limited volunteer time in a few churches, and even a sabbatical year or two in a "foreign" culture is no longer sufficient to keep pace with cultural change. One reason why leaders and readers are ever more skeptical of surveys and opinion polls is that the sampling cannot contain the bubbling diversity of lifestyle voices. By the time the survey has been meticulously created and deployed, and the results collated, evaluated, and published, it is often no longer accurate.

Tex Sample wrote with a profound awareness of the limits of seeing the world through the eyes of a university professional. He writes: "University training occurs in a context of privilege. Its interest requires a life of relative leisure that provides the occasion for reflective thought, for empirical study, and for contending with an array of competing view of reality."[1]

He applies this particularly to the inability of mainline seminaries to train clergy for ministry among the "cultural right." I suggest this insight needs to be applied to the limitations of all seminaries to train clergy for ministry

---

1. Tex Sample, *U.S. Lifestyles and Mainline Churches* (Louisville: Westminster John Knox Press, 1990), 84.

among what he called the "cultural left" and "cultural middle" as well. This helps explain why so many young adults tell me they feel called into ministry but don't want to go to seminary. It's not just about accumulating more debt from higher education. It's about relevancy to the peculiar public for whom one's heart bursts. My advice is all about empathy. Immerse yourself in culture(s). Immerse yourself not just in the mystery of God and the mystery of a human being but in the unique mysteries of God's multiple ways to be relevant to a multitude of different kinds of human beings.

The development of detailed "Lifestyle Portraits" by companies that track digital information about individual and household behavior pattern provides more opportunity for "empathy" than merely tracking statistical changes in demographic trends. It is now possible to explore lifestyle preferences and empathize with the psychological and spiritual motivations that lie behind them, using sophisticate search engines like www.MissionInsite.com.

From twenty-five years as a consultant to religious and nonprofit organizations and coach to local and regional church leaders, I'm also convinced that this kind of research must be tested and nuanced through years of personal experience with each lifestyle segment, in different regions of the country, across cultural contexts and religious traditions. And then tested again with church leaders and nonprofit practitioners. And tested again with a theology of culture, which provides a filter to interpret the diverse assumptions and motivations of different groups of people as they quest for God or simply search for meaning and purpose in their life contexts.

Thankfully, Tex Sample provides helpful ways for the reader "to really empathize with the working class," which is the focus of his 2018 book *Working Class Rage: A Field Guide to White Pain* (Abingdon Press). This advice applies to all lifestyle segments where your heart bursts for God's justice. Work indigenously.

Really listen for the way in which different people think, the way people live, and how they identify the priorities in their lives. Listen to how they express themselves, and explore the hidden but all-important nuances of their daily lives. Look behind dogmas to discern passions. Look beyond ideologies to discern core values and bedrock beliefs.

Explore the "barrel" or "bucket" that contains a host of stories, ideas, proverbs, images, concepts, and categories that are unique to every lifestyle segment in America. Do not just try to "understand," but try to see, touch, taste, smell, and hear what happens, and what people hope or fear *might* happen, in their daily lives.

Discern circles of cooperation, or how groups interact or fail to interact with each other. I describe this as "influence mapping." See how different groups of people influence the thinking and behavior of other groups of people . . . regularly or occasionally . . . and how this influence does or does not occur.

Demographic research and reflection provides a kind of foundation for further listening. We cannot stop there. We must immerse ourselves in culture, and the mysteries and complexities of being human, in order to finally bridge the chasms that separate cultures and churches today.

Chapter 1
THE
CULTURALLY AMBIVALENT

Whatever happened to the cultural left?

One of the casualties from the exploding lifestyle diversity in North America is the habit of generalizing behavior based on age. We used to speak with such confidence about "Builders," "Silents," "Boomers," "Busters," and "Millennials." But age-based generalizations are becoming less and less meaningful. "Generations" has been replaced by "lifestyles," and the "lifestyle portrait" has become the primary unit of demographic generalization. These are circles of cooperation or peer groups with shared or compatible behavior patterns that are revealed by the digital footprint people leave behind them on a daily basis.

This complexity is most obvious among the generation we once called "baby boomers." As this book appears, "baby boomers" are between fifty-one and sixty-five (some say seventy) years old. We once tried to divide this group into "first wave," "middle wave," and "late wave" boomers, usually based on the theory that progressive "waves" of boomers were generally less successful and affluent. All that makes no sense today . . . and certainly does not help the church understand their diverse needs and different motivators for their quest for God. "Spirituality" is very much alive for this generation, albeit in a wide variety of forms, among which the church is now a minority interest.

In 1990, baby boomers were clearly associated with what Tex Sample called the "cultural left." They revealed an overall cultural shift from the security and self-denial of their parents and grandparents, to the desire for self-awareness and self-fulfillment that is most often associated with their culture. Some were more socially conscientious; some were more relativistic and mystical; and some were more egotistical and flighty. In truth, all boomers revealed these three aspects in their lives, but as they grew older they generally shifted from the first, through the second, to the third aspect.

Many boomers have lived all their lives with an approach/avoidance attitude toward the church. At first, the church was part of the institutional culture against which they rebelled; and later there was some renewed interest in contemporizing church practice and widening theological engagement with other religious traditions. After the turn of the millennium, however, baby boomer participation in the church began to drop alarmingly.

There are two major reasons why.

First, the attitude of self-denial central to their parents and grandparents remained the norm of church life. This tension for boomers was most visible when it came to stewardship and volunteerism. The church continued to expect members to give their money and time out of a sense of duty, assuming that self-sacrifice was its own reward. Boomers, however, need to receive something more in return (e.g., new and deeper friendships, personal growth, mystical illumination, personal involvement in ministry and mission, satisfaction in seeing the community or world change for the better). Boomers wanted to designate money to mission, and churches wanted them to underwrite unified operational budgets. Boomers wanted to get personally involved in doing mission, and churches wanted them to trust denominational agencies and professional missionaries.

Second, the loyalty and respect their parents and grandparents automatically gave to clergy remained the expectation of denominations. The church continued to assume that seminary training, ordination, advanced academic degrees, and experience climbing the career ladder of the institutional church were still adequate for the credibility and competency of the church. Boomers, however, became increasingly skeptical of church leadership. For one thing, the quality of clergy leadership seemed to go down, even as seminary enrollments dropped and ordination candidates became increasingly older and starting ministry as a second or part-time career choice. For another thing, the credibility of clergy among other professional sectors (e.g., health, counseling, social service, nonprofit administration) was declining, even as clergy spent more time attending denominational meetings.

Today there is a renewed exodus of baby boomers from the church and institutional religious organizations in general, as they migrate to alternative spiritualties, to nonprofit agencies, or simply into general self-absorption.

One result is that the church is losing an important pool of lay leadership for boards and ministry teams. Another result is that the church is losing traction as the social conscience of the community. For many boomers, the church is on its own little island of self-absorption, and the world is looking to other institutions and leaders to address injustice, poverty, famine, climate change, and a host of other social ills.

Yet the boomer search for justice and quest for God has become ever more frustrating. Many of the institutions and leaders to whom they turned have all proven to have "feet of clay." Boomers became ever more depressed that the progress they anticipated, and the vision of a better world that they imagined, hasn't materialized. Indeed, they worry that things are actually getting worse. In a sense, they must fend for themselves.

Even in 1990, there was still a general sense of self-confidence and group identity among baby boomers. They were left of center in almost every way. They were economic and social liberals, skeptical Christians, upwardly mobile households, and generally optimistic about progress. Even if they were frustrated with leaders in every public sector, they did not doubt that they could lead themselves. Whatever the measure of success (career, affluence, influence, education, local savvy, or global awareness), they were okay.

Thirty years later this has been replaced by cultural ambivalence. They are conflicted about ideology, vague about spirituality, stalled in financial growth, and dubious about progress. The local community is beyond their control and the global village is beyond their understanding. They are not only unsure if they are successful, they are no longer clear how to measure success. In 1990, to the extent that mass group psychology applies, baby boomers could say yes or no with confidence, and the marketplace would shape itself around their preferences. Now as they age out of consumption or become displaced and redundant by economic and technological disruptions, all most boomers can say with confidence is "maybe," and the marketplace no longer shapes itself around their preferences.

THE GROWING DIVERSITY OF BABY BOOMERS

The baby boomer generation has fractured into approximately twenty-seven distinct lifestyle segments today. Any unified self-awareness as a "cultural left" is gone. Any given boomer lifestyle segment often feels even more estranged from generational kin than from groups in other generations. Now we can identify at least five distinctly different baby boomer groups, plus two additional baby boomer groups among African Americans and multicultural people.

Aesthetes, Idealists, and Intellectuals: Thriving . . . but increasingly depressed[1]

This first group of baby boomers is most clearly the remnant of what was once the "cultural left." They tend to be urban and urbane people. Some live in the suburbs, but within easy driving distance of the city. They prefer churches with a strong social conscience that are often reaching out in the city for racial and gender equality, economic parity, and human rights. Most live in urban neighborhoods, either in condominiums, apartments, or renovated older homes. They prefer similar churches with a strong social conscience.

Essentially, they believe in reasonable religion, from a privileged (educated) perspective, that shapes a better world. Some still see church participation as the right thing to do (which is much the same attitude that leads them to join service clubs). Others see religion as an eccentric habit with limited benefits (like free weddings and immediate caregiving).

The ideological points of view have fragmented in this remnant of the cultural left. They may describe themselves as "liberal" (perhaps voting Democrat) or "conservative" (perhaps voting Republican), and increasing numbers would describe themselves as "free thinkers" (often identifying as an independent voter). What they share in common is a commitment to action and a desire to encourage positive social change. For example, they all want to participate in churches with a strong social conscience and community outreach that addresses quality of life or human potential. But they *may not* join churches that are aggressively affirming of gay rights. Most say that they would like to attend a truly biracial church . . . but they can't find one . . . and in truth they may not want one. They are clear in their opposition to what might be called "structural" racism, but often unclear or unaware of deeper "systemic" racism.

---

1.   Many groups mentioned are included in (but not limited to) lifestyle segments currently identified by Experian as C11 *Aging of Aquarius*, E19 *Full Pockets Empty Nests*, and K40 *Bohemian Groove*.

The churches that capture their attention may be denominational or independent, but they are congregations that self-identify as countercultural toward "consumer society." This opposition may be ironic, because many in this group are discriminating and well-informed consumers. They have strong moral convictions, but are risk averse and believe in morality with minimum sacrifice. They are often opinionated, and occasionally iconoclastic, but generally resist accountability for church membership or spiritual life.

This paradox in their behavior may be rooted in the contrast between their rebellious youth and their conformist maturity. Their goal is to live a "balanced life" that manages diverse commitments to God, church, family, friends, and self. Note that commitment to God is not the same as commitment to church. They feel that they meet God through each of the other four things. Meeting God in loving relationships, nature, or self-improvement is often more profound than meeting God at church. Indeed, the obligation to church is wearing thin. They are (still) annoyed by bureaucracy, resentful of hierarchy, and impatient with triviality.

Their decision to participate in a church today is more often determined by aesthetics and intellectual stimulation. They go to church because of the architecture, visual and dramatic arts, or quality of music (of any genre, but particularly classical, jazz, or cultural mosaic). Today they are less likely to volunteer for soup kitchens and more likely to sing in choirs. The fiercest arguments are not about theology but about renovations or musical instrumentations.

And they go to church because of the intellectual stimulation. They value profound sermons; historic—even ancient—traditions; higher biblical criticism; interfaith dialogue; and opportunities for serious and well-informed conversation. And they value introspection, guided meditation, and personality inventories. Some may be religious dilettantes, but most consider themselves deeply spiritual.

They also go to church because of the pastor, and a change in pastoral relationship can cause them to come closer or drift further away. They gravitate to pastors who are visionaries . . . relentless futurists . . . with strong management skills to get things done. The pastor needs to be a "relevant" theologian. He or she should not be dogmatic, and need not be systematic or historically grounded, but must be able to apply theology to particular world events, social causes, and interfaith dialogue. The classic caregiver or enabler—a role typical of most pastors with basic degrees from seminary—

turn them away, and the postmodern pilgrims who practice extreme account-ability frighten them.

Men and women in this group have often enjoyed careers with signifi-cant influence and authority. They deeply believe that they can control their own destiny through hard work and an independent spirit, and they project this assumption on churches and church leaders. Positively, they can lead churches in rigorous prioritization and policy development. Negatively, they can undermine the authority of clergy and indulge in micromanagement. They can strongly support outreach, and rigorously align budgets to achieve outcomes that change the world. They can also espouse idiosyncratic theo-logical views that differ from church tradition.

The *aesthetes, idealists, and intellectual* boomers in this group seem to have chronic depression or disillusionment. The ideals of their youth have not been fulfilled in adulthood. In many ways, they feel that the world situation has stayed the same or even gotten worse. The networks and movements that they once espoused have lost momentum. Looking for new allies and power bases, some turned back to the church in the late 1980s and 1990s, but are increasingly disappointed in the church in the new millennium.

Movers, Shakers, and Entitled: Privileged . . . but losing confidence[2]

The second group of baby boomers took another path. They are not the rebellious radicals of their youth, do not feel guilty about it, and are very comfortable with their wealth and power. Many are among the most affluent and influential people in the country. Like most boomers, they received a ba-sic liberal arts education (and have some familiarity with literature, philoso-phy, history, and the arts), but then went on to specialize. Unlike the previous group, their studies and careers were in business, finance, law, and media . . . and perhaps even entertainment and sports. Some rose in the corporate world, and some rose through entrepreneurship.

These mature, influential, and successful singles and couples live in pres-tigious suburbs and comfortably secure communities, often near major cit-ies or power centers like Washington DC, New York, San Francisco, and

---

2.   Many groups mentioned are included in (but not limited to) lifestyle segments cur-rently identified by Experian as A01 *American Royalty*, A02 *Platinum Prosperity*, or C13 *Silver Sophisticates*.

Orlando. Some may live downtown in fashionable, high-security high-rises, with convenient access to major airports. Many are already involved with philanthropic organizations that keep them well informed but do not require much personal presence.

In the past, "movers and shakers" would naturally participate in a church simply because it was culturally normative (i.e., "the right thing to do"). Today it isn't "natural" anymore, and participation in a church is a deliberate choice. If they participate in a church, there are conditions that determine their choice.

First, the church must be prestigious and their participation must entail privileges. They tend to gravitate to large churches, with beautiful landscaping, excellent facilities and technologies, large staff, excellent resources, and big visions. They can be very generous to the church, but they want to have significant influence on policy and personnel. Although their attendance may be sporadic, they demand immediate attention in a crisis.

In this group, some rely on digital technology and some do not. The church needs to have an excellent website and e-communication, but not necessarily a digital worship alternative. Wherever these people are, and whatever they are doing, they expect to be kept informed. And they expect to reach church leaders from any location (from the golf course, a board room, a cruise, or exotic locations) without bothering with answering machines, bureaucracy, or staff vacations.

Second, the church must preserve, honor, and belong to a tradition. Usually, this is the tradition in which they were raised (Catholic, Protestant, Evangelical, or Orthodox). Some people in this group have retired and relocated to warmer climates, but they look back to the church from which they came as the norm for a good church. A significant number of people in this group are Asian (along with some Europeans and South Americans), which means that the church probably reflects the cultural mores and speaks a second language other than English. Regardless of ethnicity, people in this group respect a church that is open to multicultural and global realities.

Third, the church must be theologically and ideologically moderate. True, these baby boomers may be passionate liberals or conservatives, but they are not extremists. They are typically rationally reserved, think before they act, and evaluate risks. Most of these people have been successful because they understand how to build and sustain teams. They tend to be peacemakers among internal factions, and reconcilers who avoid denominational schisms.

These boomers expect the church to be entrenched in networks: political, nonprofit, and corporate; local, national, and global. They understand that collaboration gets things done, and are more interested in talking with people than judging them. Dogma should not get in the way of harmonious fellowship, open-minded education, and mission impact.

Fourth, the church must be well organized and efficient in ministry. The vision must be clear, the strategic plan must be well conceived, the outcomes must be measurable, and the staff (and volunteers) must be accountable. The vision must stretch their imaginations, but ultimately seem doable. Waste (time, money, volunteer energy) is unacceptable, and impact must be significant and far-reaching.

The boomers in this group tend to favor hierarchy over consensus. Assuming that the pastor and leaders are credible, they prefer the rapid decision making of a board room over the slow decision making of a church council. Unlike the previous group of boomers, people in this group do not tend to micromanage. They prefer clear purposes and boundaries for action, letting staff and leaders get results any way they can.

Given these conditions, it becomes clear why many churches today have a hard time reaching many of these people. They do not honor the "divine right" of these boomers to shape vision and policy; they do not really cherish the traditions from which they came; they are too extreme (liberal or conservative) and exclusive; and they are badly organized and inefficiently managed.

Some churches find it even harder to reach these movers and shakers as boomers. Declining Protestant churches often discriminate against them precisely because of their wealth. It is not just that they fail to honor their sense of privilege, but that they pre-judge and dismiss them out of hand. Pentecostal churches are often too unstructured and unpredictable, too vague about tradition and vision, and too lax about accountability.

Some churches have been more effective reaching these boomers. Independent evangelical churches may not have the same sense of institutional tradition, but they are often more classically Christian and heterogeneous than traditional institutions. And they are better organized and more efficient in mission. Roman Catholic and Orthodox churches can reach them, provided that they are large enough, entrepreneurial enough, and positioned to network with other sectors beyond the ecclesiastical hierarchy.

Boomers in this group have had big ambitions for themselves, and they tend to gravitate to churches with big, bold visions. Like many senior managers, however, they believe the key to success lies in leadership development more than program efficiency. They may invest money for outreach related to survival, health, or quality of life, but they tend to invest their *time* in outreach related to human potential. Churches that are not interested in developing human potential do not interest them. This is why churches that reach this group of boomers also tend to include affluent, upwardly mobile young singles and couples. Boomers in this group like to mentor emerging leaders; and younger generations like this are actively seeking mentoring. We are also likely to see these churches include excellent children and youth programs.[3]

Like most other boomers, much depends on the identity and function of spiritual leadership in the church. And expectations vary considerably. The oldest and most sedentary in this group (e.g., settled in planned communities related to golf, yachts, or airplanes) still prefer a fairly traditional pastor who is a blend of facilitator and caregiver. But these pastors are not bold enough for most of the others in this group. They prefer a CEO leader with strong talents in mentoring and discipleship. And the most mobile in this group (globe-trotting urbanites) tend to gravitate to the rarest of all North American spiritual leaders. These cross-cultural, multilingual, highly disciplined, and interfaith sensitive leaders are more likely found in Europe or Australia.

The inner struggle among these boomers is that their confidence is waning. They are less confident that science and education will ensure progress. They are less confident that democracy and political parties can ensure peace and raise the standard of living for all. They are less confident that prejudice, poverty, and injustice can be ultimately overcome. And they are less confident that the church as an institution is the best tactic to sustain the Christian movement. This cynicism encourages them to withdraw from macro-charities and invest in micro-charities; and to step away from large congregations and step toward small groups that share enthusiasms and practice spiritual disciplines.

Homebuilders, Health Conscious, and Content: Optimistic . . . but increasingly disillusioned

The third group of baby boomers is probably more typical of what many churches assume to be the norm for all. These are moderately successful singles and couples, retired or nearing retirement, living comfortable lives in

---

3. Today these might include Experian's categories for F22 *Fast Track Couples*, or G24 *Status Seeking Singles*, or A03 *Kids and Cabernet*.

older suburban or urban neighborhoods. This group can be a multicultural mix, and includes the emerging African American middle class or some second- or third-generation Hispanic/Latino households.[4]

Some have had white-collar careers in industry, civil service, public education, or military, most often in middle-management roles. Some have had blue-collar careers, and have risen in a company to a place of greater responsibility. Many have college, or partial college educations, and they are comfortable with traditional learning methodologies. All this means that they are comfortable with traditional consensus management and Christian education programs consistent with most traditional churches. They sit on boards, chair committees, teach in Sunday schools, and listen to expository sermons.

These people have often lived in the same place for some time. Their home is a holiday destination for their children and grandchildren. They renovate and upgrade carefully, to avoid losing memories. They collect things. They value long-term friendships and usually have many friends. They also tend to consider the church as an extension of their family. They are brand loyal to denominations. Christian holidays are family-friendly events. They are cautious about upgrading technologies and renovating church properties to avoid losing memories. They like memorabilia in the narthex. They enjoy potluck suppers and large gender and generational fellowship groups. They prefer churches with no more than 200–250 members. And when it comes to change, they will always worry more about losing members than welcoming newcomers.

These boomers have long been the backbone of many churches. They are excellent volunteers, generous givers, and committed to the long-term ministries of the church. They provide safe sanctuaries, protect human rights, and walk the second mile to help strangers in a crisis or natural disaster. They tend to be concerned about climate change, pollution, crime . . . and are willing to make personal sacrifices to protect the environment and take risks to protect the neighborhood.

Two characteristics of these boomers are particularly important to the church.

First, this group of baby boomers lives in a paradox of progressive idealism and nostalgia for the past. They can protest for social justice, yet practice

---

4.   Many groups mentioned may be included in (but not limited to) lifestyle segments currently identified by Experian as L42 *Rooted Flower Power*, H28 *Everyday Moderates*, J36 *Settled and Sensible*, D18 *Suburban Attainment*, and perhaps I32 *Steadfast Conventionalists*.

traditional social values. They can be open-minded about biblical interpretation and doctrine, but remarkably unimaginative about liturgy and remain loyal to local customs. This paradox usually leads them to dislike extremes, avoid conflicts, and protect harmony. They are comfortable with evolutionary change, provided it is persistent and productive.

The opportunity for the church is that they can build on this success. The church can encourage the progressive side of this paradox to become externally focused on the diversity of needs in the neighborhood, community, city, and region. There is enormous potential volunteer energy in this group that has yet to be motivated. In order for this to happen, the church must focus less on institutional survival and more on mission impact.

Unfortunately, the church has generally encouraged the nostalgic side of this paradox. In a sense, the church has gone too far adapting itself to this lifestyle, so that their lifestyle preferences have all too often become norms and sacred cows for the institution. As a result, the church has become more internally focused on local and denominational survival.

Second, these baby boomers are natural bridges for cross-cultural and biracial understanding. This is the group of baby boomers that includes, and usually accepts, the middle-class African Americans in their midst. They often live together in the same neighborhood. They live across the street or next door to each other; shop in the same stores; eat in the same restaurants; support the same community causes. They not only oppose "structural" racism, but are more aware of broader "systemic" racism.

The opportunity for the church is that these boomers can lead the way to create truly biracial and multicultural congregations. They have idealism for social justice and equality, the proximity to public diversity, the education to develop effective strategies, and, in many contexts, they are already interacting across racial and cultural divides in other social service, health, and educational agencies in the community. Why not in the church?

Unfortunately, the church has largely failed to become truly biracial and multicultural. Black, white, and Hispanic churches still gather separately. This makes the church an anachronism, on the sidelines. At one time, the church was a pace-setter for all other community sectors, but in this one issue of racism the church is too often a drag on the community. This is leading more and more boomers in this lifestyle group to step back. Once they were members, now they are adherents, and tomorrow they are inactive.

Ultimately, only two things will truly reenergize their flagging interest in the church. Tradition, aesthetics, intellectual stimulation, program excellence, and fellowship are not enough in the medium-sized congregation of 200–250 people that they prefer. They need a *leader* and a *cause*.

The spiritual leader may well be a seminary-trained professional, accredited by a denomination, but he or she must be spiritually disciplined. These boomers are not just tired of clergy misconduct (moral or financial), but they are put off by extreme politics, preaching rants, eccentric or erratic behavior, and ego trips. They look for a spiritual leader who intentionally models the fruit of the Spirit, stands on a classical faith, and has a big heart for the neighborhood and the city.

The cause is a sustainable outreach ministry usually targeting quality of life, health, equality and respect, justice, and economic recovery. It needs to encourage, equip, and appreciate volunteers. And it needs to be a mission over which the congregation has real control (and is not dependent on a denomination or foundation). They don't need big, bold visions; but they do expect to trust and be trusted.

If the previous group of mover-and-shaker boomers is increasingly cynical, these homebuilding boomers are increasingly disillusioned. There is a difference. Cynicism has to do with systems. Some boomers are cynical about political denominational systems, policies, and organizational effectiveness. Disillusionment, however, has to do with people. These boomers have been disillusioned by hypocritical or flawed leaders, manipulative ideologically driven factions, and unfulfilled promises. Efficiency is not the answer. Credibility is the answer.

Prayerful, Poor, and Marking Time: Trying hard . . . but increasingly frustrated[5]

The fourth group of baby boomers is often forgotten. Most people associate baby boomers with affluence, education, meaningful jobs, and influence. These baby boomers are poor, relatively uneducated, working (often intermittently) in sales and service. Many are African American. Any influence they have is collective rather than individual. Their only way to get public attention is usually through protesting.

---

5.   Many groups mentioned are included in (but not limited to) lifestyle segments currently identified by Experian as S68 *Small Towns, Shallow Pockets*; S69 *Urban Survivors*; S71 *Tough Times*; P57 *Modest Metro Means*; and K38 *Gotham Blend*.

The church remains important to this group for a variety of reasons. Many are single (widowed, divorced, or never married), and those with children have seen them move away from declining small towns and deteriorating neighborhoods to find better lives. Churches provide opportunities for mutual support and interpersonal relationships. They can also provide important outreach ministries related to health, addiction intervention, or survival.

A good number of people in this group have lived in the same neighborhood, and the same place, over time. Their church is often perceived as a key presence for social stability . . . a bulwark against any further deterioration. Members may be fractious and opinionated, but people come together in a crisis. Churches become neighborhood centers, and may house other ethnic congregations or provide space for health care and social services.

But there is more to church participation than that. The quest for God among many boomers is motivated by anxieties about emptiness and meaninglessness. These people, however, often feel trapped by circumstances (e.g., prejudice, poverty, addiction) beyond their control. Church participation can give them a sense of hope and confidence that God can break into their lives and liberate them from entrapment.

These people often struggle with low self-esteem. Church participation provides opportunities to look good, feel good, and be generous with what little they have. They often feel angry. Church participation provides them with a network for activism to vent their frustrations. They continue to pursue the social justice ideals of the cultural left.

Yet this group feels increasingly estranged from others in the boomer generation. Fifty years ago they made common cause for equal rights and economic justice. Today, the boomers in the other groups are more self-absorbed. Some have become cynical and given up the fight. The first group of boomers (*aesthetes, idealists, and intellectuals*) is more supportive, but their commitment is increasingly short term. They are active for human rights for a time . . . and then take a vacation.

This may explain why these lifestyle segments are turning to what I call the *culturally righteous* in the hope of finding partnerships for change. They may also be turning away from traditional denominational churches (mainstream and evangelical) in favor of independent or Pentecostal churches. Or they may be dropping out of church to invest their energy in local neighborhood nonprofits for health, education, and quality of life.

Expectations for spiritual leadership are similar to that of other boomer groups, but there are special considerations. First, the traditional caregivers and enablers represented in significant number by denominational clergy can struggle and burn out with this group. New seminary graduates and traditional career clergy take years to empathize with them . . . and move before that happens. The pastoral care load is heavy, staff and equipped volunteers are few, fundraising and financial management can be daunting. A CEO type of leader is most effective if the denomination can subsidize their salaries.

The challenge for the CEO leader, however, is to build credibility and not just rely on competency. People in this group are not really looking for an advocate of "Liberation Theology" (who are more likely to be appreciated by the first group of boomers: *aesthetes, idealists, and intellectuals*). A leader who can articulate basic, traditional Christian beliefs and genuinely model Christian values in daily living will gain more respect. Clergy can't commute, but need to live in the community and be seen daily. The trend is increasingly toward bi-vocational or lay pastors . . . or nonprofit CEOs who are practicing, articulate Christians.

Adapters, Adopters, and Multitaskers: Enthusiastic . . . but increasingly struggling[6]

The fifth group of boomers is probably the most cross-cultural and diverse in terms of interests and activities. They are affluent multigenerational families living comfortably and with remarkable homogeneity in suburbs that offer easy transportation to city or country, nightlife and airports, sports and entertainment venues, box stores and discount malls, organic and ethnic food markets. They are all committed to family life, but open to remarkable diversity about how that family life functions.

These boomers adapt to new cultures; adopt new technologies; and, are often juggling vehicles for multiple income earners, interests in multiple indoor and outdoor activities, and commitments to various organizations and groups. The good news for churches is that they tend to be relatively traditional about faith and doctrine and loyal to traditions and denominations. The bad news for churches is they have high expectations for quality pro-

---

6. Many groups mentioned are included in (but not limited to) lifestyle segments currently identified by Experian as B07 *Generational Soup*, C14 *Boomers and Boomerangs*, and H26 *Progressive Potpourri*.

grams, like to see a menu of worship and small-group options . . . but still tend to be occasional or intermittent in their participation.

Some of these boomers are Asian or South American, and the Caucasians usually enjoy cross-cultural friendships and spice their lifestyles with international flavors. They often bring the same expectations to churches. Many gravitate to Roman Catholic churches where the doctrine is sound but the Mass is more informal and updated. Those who connect with mainstream Protestant churches often gravitate to mega-churches offering a variety of resources and programs . . . although some get involved in innovative church plants that can combine intimacy and outreach, and worship with a kind of "structured informality."

Although the boomers in this group are positive toward the church in general, they often find it difficult to settle in one church in particular. This is because these boomer households are constantly on the move, adapting to new circumstances, seizing new opportunities, and enjoying new experiences. Yes, they do enjoy home life and many passive pursuits (e.g., reading, cooking, hobbies), but this, too, interferes with regular church participation. Established churches often cannot keep up with them. They aren't as adaptable or flexible about methods and ministries. They take too long to make decisions. Change that comes so easily to these boomers is painstakingly slow for churches. And these boomers are too busy for leadership and too impatient for committees.

Although these boomer households do participate in stewardship programs and are fairly generous financially to the unified budget of a church, their church participation tends to be in short, intense bursts of energy. Short-term commitments are the norm. They may re-up participation in a small group or outreach ministry, but they need the freedom to make a guilt-free decision to continue. Long-term educational programs and volunteer-dependent outreach ministries are difficult to manage in their busy lives.

The churches that reach them best are conservative in doctrine, moderate to liberal in social policy, and cutting-edge in technology. That combination may be difficult to find in anything except a large church with lots of options. The family may travel together to church, but worship in different venues. They value a professional ministry staff, but often want the senior pastor to be younger than the rest of the staff. Again, a difficult combination to find. English is certainly the primary language, but bilingual staff and respect for the culture of other countries significantly raises the credibility of the church. Again, a difficult combination to find. It might be easier to find a good church on the East or West Coasts, or in rapidly expanding suburbs near large and diverse cities in the Midwest.

Expectations for spiritual leadership are mixed. It is hard to imagine a single pastor can be enabler, CEO, discipler, and mentor all in one. This makes the creation of a true team imperative. The old model of professional staff deployed in traditional program silos, however, doesn't work well for them. They prefer more entrepreneurial teams that work well together, define boundaries for action, and empower staff to adapt in changing circumstances.

This group of boomers can be an incredibly rich resource of energy and enthusiasm for a church, but they are struggling more and more to find the best fit for their busy lives. The tendency of churches today, in an era of institutional decline, is to minimize risks, reward seniority, and celebrate homogeneity. That doesn't work for these boomers who take risks, reward youthful initiative, and celebrate heterogeneity.

Tranquility, Tradition, and Independence: Happy . . . but getting worried[7]

The sixth group of boomers most clearly reveals the retreat of a generation from the activism of their past. These tend to be middle- or upper-class couples and singles, primarily with empty nests, who have moved from urban settings and pressured careers to lived relaxed lifestyles in the country or small towns. They do return to the city for cultural events, museums, and concerts; but they are as likely to take a cruise trip to Europe or a weekend in Las Vegas.

It is not that these boomers have lost interest in social change. They may still join a protest if strongly motivated, and they may still follow current events. Their focus has shifted to more local issues. They care about their neighbors and local communities, and are extraordinarily generous if there is a family crisis or natural disaster. But they are less concerned about global issues (like the environment) and human rights issues. They now tend to avoid risks and radicalism, and may even feel that economic decisions of the 1960s and 1970s opened a kind of "Pandora's Box" for greater social evils, which

---

7. Many groups mentioned are included in (but not limited to) lifestyle segments currently identified by Experian as E21 comfortably established baby boomer couples in town and country communities; L41 older empty-nesting couples and singles enjoying relaxed lives in small towns; and L43 lower middle-class baby boomer households living in remote town and country homes.

may explain why many are now social conservatives and high on family values, less supportive of immigration, and resist urbanization.

They are, however, consciously spiritual people, participate in churches, and are often loyal to denominations. They like the intimacy of small-country or small-town congregations, participate in fellowship groups, enjoy pot-luck suppers, and may even commit to long-term Bible study groups or Sunday school classes. They are passionate about outreach that addresses issues of survival or human destiny. They are content with basic hospitality, as long as the welcomes are hearty and there are homemade options for refreshments. They also like the antique ethos of old churches and sanctuaries. They are *conditionally* open to new technologies, provided the heritage of the church is not too disrupted. For example, projection screens in the sanctuary are welcome to show still images and the words to hymns, but not video (which is mere entertainment). They are loathe to remodel the hospitality center if it means relocating the memorial wall or library.

The boomers in this group may well maintain church membership in their former suburban or urban neighborhood, contribute financially, and visit occasionally. But they tend to bring their more conservative expectations and risk-averse attitudes with them. This can be frustrating to urban churches because they tend to delay or block change. In a sense, if it were up to them, they would prefer not to grow a church at all, but encourage participation to decline to about 250 or fewer members so that everyone can know one another's first name. It is difficult for them to grasp the reality that such churches are no longer financially viable in the post-Christendom world.

The good news for denominations is that their expectations for clergy leadership match the existing pool of ministers who are trained as caregivers, visitors, committee organizers, traditional liturgists, and modest preachers. The bad news, however, is that many of the lifestyle segments emerging within or moving toward small towns as a result of constant urbanization are often not looking for that kind of spiritual leadership.

The dilemma for this group of boomers is that their generally happy and content lifestyles are in jeopardy. Those who are poorer and less educated feel that their middle-class status is slipping away, and their influence on church policy is waning. Those who are wealthier and better educated feel that the next generation is letting them down, and the world is leaving them behind. They are in retreat and increasingly defensive. These same attitudes are brought to the church. They may still be among the largest and most consistent donors to church budgets, but are ever more outspoken against liberal church policies, and ever more resistant to change. Beneath the happy harmony of the pot-luck supper, they are worried. And they are often getting angry.

BIRACIAL, MULTICULTURAL, AND ALTERNATIVE LIFESTYLE PERSPECTIVES

The six different baby boomer groups identified are all less homogeneous and more heterogeneous than the three groups Tex Sample identified in 1990. At that time, boomers were almost solely white; they were primarily of western European descent (with a sprinkling of east Europeans); they all spoke English as their primary (and usually only) language.

Today, some thirty years later, the baby boomer clan has become somewhat more diverse. But it is not nearly as racially and culturally diverse as the baby boomers themselves hoped in the 1960s and 1970s, nor as economically diverse as African Americans, Hispanics and Latinos, and Asian or Pacific Rim, or First Nations Indian people hoped.

African American Baby Boomers[8]

There is certainly a growing lifestyle group of middle-class African Americans, and many black leaders in education, business, health and social service, politics, and other professional groups had the opportunity to advance in status, income, and influence. But that is still a relatively small proportion of African Americans. Representation of black baby boomers in the top echelons of decision making in most sectors (including the entertainment industry, corporate business, private education, and science) is still quite disproportionate.

African American boomers are of an age when most white (albeit not all) baby boomers have achieved significant power and influence. In the larger context of the struggling middle class in general, these more educated, af-

---

8.   Many groups mentioned are included in (but not limited to) lifestyle segments currently identified by Experian as D18 *Suburban Attainment*; S68 *Small Towns, Shallow Pockets*; S69 *Urban Survivors*; S71 *Tough Times*; N48 *Rural Southern Bliss*, etc.

fluent, and influential black households find themselves plateauing in educational opportunities, potential income, and recognition. And in the larger context of anxiety over immigration and vanishing jobs, these African Americans sense that their hard-won pride and equality is once again threatened by systemic prejudice and economic abuse.

To what extent has the church helped or hindered African American baby boomers in the quest for equal opportunity, equal income, and equal recognition?

Certainly, there have been positive contributions. The former "mainstream" denominations have refocused seminary education on black history and experience, and explored distinctively black theological points of view. These denominations have also promoted black pastors to larger churches and episcopal or policy-making leadership. The former "evangelical" denominations have done this with less measurable results. Black churches have received more financial support, and have somewhat more influence on regional planning.

On the other hand, both the local and denominational churches have been remarkably disappointing as change agents in American society. Professional standards, deployment systems, liturgical practices, decision-making habits, and cultural accommodations still favor white people of European descent. Outreach and social service priorities among black lifestyle groups emphasizes survival ministries, but not human potential ministries aimed to equip and empower black Christians to take initiative in their own spiritual development.

Ironically, liberal white boomers have actually been complicit in maintaining the status quo of racial inequality. Many of the non-conformist, radical social activists of the 1960s and 1970s have matured into conformists and contented social reactionaries in the new millennium. In the past, white boomers wanted to change everything and do it *now*, in solidarity with black (and other) disempowered people. Today, it is more common for white boomers to change little and do it slowly in sympathy with their aging parents.

Among increasingly cynical black boomer Christians, this remarkable U-turn suggests that white boomers were not sincere then, and may not be sincere now, because the bottom line is that white boomers simply want to do whatever makes them feel good at the time. Among some increasingly white boomer Christians, this U-turn has generated a profound guilt complex that either generates anger at the church or motivates them to withdraw from the church altogether.

Two significant trends are apparent. First, while some large, well-resourced African American churches are growing, they tend to be distancing themselves from parent denominations (in which they feel misunderstood or under-represented), and expanding relationships with community non-profits (with whom they have shared interests around social services, security, and education). Second, while there are large white churches and large black churches, there are remarkably few instances of wholeheartedly *biracial* churches.

Hispanic/Latino Baby Boomers[9]

We are probably all aware that global mobility and accelerating immigration is rapidly changing the nature of American culture. This may be something to be feared or something to be welcomed, but it is notable how divided white baby boomers are in their reactions. Immigration in the past has primarily been about lifestyle groups that were younger, poorer, less educated, and less status conscious. In other words, they were not baby boomers.

In the twenty-first century that is changing. There is a much larger mass of older, wealthier, well educated, and status-conscious immigrants seeking a home in America. In part, these may be professionals or intellectuals fleeing persecution in their own countries. Primarily, these are business executives, researchers, educators, and health-care specialists moving to America as a desirable place to live in the global village.

Most of these multicultural baby boomers are assimilated relatively easily into American society. They share collegial respect, live side by side with other white American boomers, and share many of the same consumer priorities. These multicultural boomers are often more protective of their language and heritage than some of their poorer immigrant companions, so that their lifestyle habits still reflect ethnic origins. Indeed, their cultural priorities about food, health, family, and spirituality have influenced white boomer culture.

Their experience in the church, however, has often been less welcoming.

---

9. Many groups mentioned are included in (but not limited to) lifestyle segments currently identified by Experian as B10 *Cosmopolitan Achievers*, H26 *Progressive Potpourri*, H28 *Everyday Moderates*, I32 *Steadfast Conventionalists*, P57 *Modest Metro Means*, K38 *Gotham Blend*, etc.

Most (but not all) baby boomer Hispanic/Latino people probably identify with the Roman Catholic tradition, and for that reason find it easier to connect with the church in America. Protestants and evangelicals may not like to hear it, but the Roman Catholic tradition is still the most culturally diverse Christian tradition in America.

These boomers may be more or less active in a local parish, but they are generally confident that the church respects and even honors their cultural heritage. They regard the priest as a professional peer; they see the liturgy as a kind of cultural "common denominator" that allows Christians from all cultures to experience God on a "level playing field." They have a clearer sense of moral absolutes in the context of American moral relativism. If they do experience prejudice, these Hispanic/Latino boomers, at least, can rely on a still powerful church for both moral support and political intervention.

Their relationship to boomers from Protestant traditions, however, is more complicated. Not only are they regarded as "different" because of their religious tradition, but they are even more puzzling to white Protestants of western European descent whose churches are shaped by traditions from England, Germany, Holland, and elsewhere. Many baby boomers working in senior management and professional networks have not really interacted on a neighbor-to-neighbor basis with Hispanic/Latino people (unlike many other lifestyle segments in sales and service, health care, public education, and other sectors). Protestant clergy work effectively with Catholic priests; but "Latin" stereotypes can get in the way of cooperation between Protestant and Catholic Church boards.

It is important to understand that Hispanic/LatinX boomers have been *leaders* in their churches. And their past experience with Protestant (or Pentecostal) churches has often been adversarial. That sense of caution, or outright suspicion, comes with them as they relocate to America. And it will take more effort on the part of American Protestant churches to behave differently in order to overcome that hesitance and build unity.

Asian Baby Boomers

Church relationships among Asian baby boomer immigrants are more complicated. Some have grown up in a Protestant tradition through American missionaries, and the baby boomers among them have often served on church boards and held important lay leadership positions. Yet when they

21

try to connect with churches of the same denomination in America, they are often confused and rejected.

They are confused because the Protestant missionary tradition from their home country actually seems pure compared to the seeming cultural accommodations the same churches have made to American culture. Accountability for faith and spiritual practice is much lower.

They are rejected because the hidden elitism of the American "mother" church regards them as being less able to lead than their American counterparts in the church. Authority to influence denominational policy seems weaker and opportunities to lead seem limited.

As a result, Christian baby boomer Asians tend to gather homogeneously in communities of faith that share not only the same language and heritage but also the same doctrinal clarity and higher standard of accountability. There are Asian churches and white churches—just as there are black churches and white churches. There are very few multicultural churches, just as there are very few biracial churches. And the church in general seems content with that.

The people who are *not* content with the status quo are the children of these baby boomers. They are more likely to demand a multicultural (and biracial) church that will mirror the reality of their network of friends. The culturally homogeneous church is just not credible as a faith community anymore. And Asian boomer parents are just as perplexed by the disinterest of their children in the church as white boomer parents are with their own children.

Of course, some Asian boomers have grown up in non-Christian religious traditions. There is relatively little social pressure (at least on Asian boomers) to abandon their religious commitments or practices on the East, West, and Gulf Coasts; perhaps more social pressure in the South and Midwest. Churches often seem content to leave it at that. That might indicate profound respect for other religious traditions; but it also can indicate profound relief that they do not have to really engage the ideas and practices of other religions.

Yet there should be cause for deeper anxiety in the church about their treatment of Asian boomers in their communities. The growing number of Asian boomers in America are often not just indifferent to the church. They don't really *respect* the church. Their normative experience of the church is as an agent of colonialization. In essence, Christian missionaries said to their parents and peers: *We know God better than you do; and the world would be a better place if you agreed with us.*

This is not just an issue with more evangelical or fundamentalist churches in America. It is an issue with former "mainstream" churches (e.g., Presbyterians, Methodists, Anglicans) who have had strong missionary impact on countries since the nineteenth century. The suspicion is that protestant and evangelical churches in America are "con artists," offering radical hospitality and then making surprising demands of obedience.

By itself, this is serious enough. But Asian baby boomers today are often role models, and exercise great influence, on younger generations around them. Emerging generations embrace multicultural experience. It is not an intention but a habit. And the adversarial or colonial memories of the church reinforce the hostility of younger generations to the institutional church (although perhaps not to the Christian faith per se).

LGBTQ Baby Boomers

Thirty years ago, baby boomers typically described themselves as liberal, progressive, and inclusive. Today many boomers have become more conservative, or at the least discovered that there are boundaries beyond which they cannot go. This has become especially clear over the last thirty years with respect to attitudes toward lesbian, gay, bisexual, and transgendered people. That social justice crusade has been accelerating in recent years. Despite comparisons to the black civil rights movement starting in the 1960s, and the women's rights movement gaining momentum in the 1970s and 1980s, baby boomers have been rather ambivalent toward the LGBTQ "community."

Of course, from the point of view of lifestyle segmentation, there really isn't any particular LGBTQ "community." Instead, LGBTQ people are represented in *all* seventy-one lifestyle segments currently identified by Experian, and it is neither practical nor legal to identify them.

There is no reason to believe that LGBTQ people are represented to a greater or lesser degree in any of the six groups of boomers I have identified. Some groups are more likely to acknowledge homosexuality and advocate for LGBTQ rights (e.g., *adapters, adopters, and multitaskers* or *aesthetes, idealists, and intellectuals*); and some groups may be less likely to do so (e.g., *tranquility, tradition, and independence*). And other groups may prefer to stay out of the fight, and reveal their identities or express their views (pro or con)

23

privately among friends and trusted colleagues. Finally, African American and multicultural boomers tend to be clearly (and within churches often vehemently) conservative.

The church in America is increasingly and emotionally divided over the issue of homosexuality, and this alone has caused (and will continue to cause) schisms in denominations and splits in congregations. The emotionalism over this reveals an interesting paradox in the United States. There is the same amount of emotion among baby boomers in the church over this issue as there was among baby boomers and their parents' culture over black civil rights in the 1960s. Baby boomers were passionately united then . . . and passionately divided now.

The debate in Canada (and other Western countries) is much less emotional. Indeed, in the midst of Western culture in general, homosexuality is becoming a non-issue among boomers. Baby boomers may be pro or con, but the debate itself seems unimportant compared to the larger global issues of war and genocide, climate change, hunger and poverty. But these countries are considerably more "secular," and the church has generally lost political influence anyway. The estimate of influence is suggestive. The "heat" of the debate in America (at least among baby boomers) may not be about homosexuality at all but about the loss of political influence boomers in the church once enjoyed.

Consider several trends concerning LGBTQ persons among American churches over the past twenty years.

First, the number of traditional denominational congregations that recognize, welcome, and advocate for LGBTQ people is growing—but the total membership in those traditional churches is *not* growing. Meanwhile, participation in independent or emerging LGBTQ churches is growing. This suggests that no matter how "affirming" traditional congregations might be, they continue to be embedded in denominations divided over the LGBTQ identities. It may be more difficult for LGBTQ Christians to overcome the history of prejudice that traditional Christian denominations have displayed. The longer the denominations quarrel, the less credibility even their most liberal and affirming congregations have among LGBTQ people.

Second, the growth in both traditional "affirming" churches, and specifically LGBTQ churches, includes both gay and straight baby boomers. This suggests that those boomer groups that continue to be committed liberals and progressives are shifting their congregational (and sometimes denominational) allegiances. And this suggests that denominational schisms and congregational splits are not just about homosexuality but also about class, cultural origins, and/or track of higher education.

Third, more and more professional and corporate, affluent and successful, baby boomers are recognizing and advocating LGBTQ "alternative lifestyles." Gay pride parades are no longer stereotypical. They have become more diverse than the "carnival" and "extremist" caricature they once had. They now include modest-looking professionals, self-controlled managers, moderate political leaders . . . and more and more identifiable clergy from all denominations (including evangelical traditions). As gay marriage is legalized, churches are celebrating weddings that are not very liturgically different from traditional ceremonies. In short, LGBTQ has become mainstream, and mission-minded churches are adapting to cultural norms as they always have.

Fourth, even among baby boomers moderately or vigorously opposed to homosexuality, attitudes are softened within their own families. They may be opposed to homosexuality in principle and in public; but within their family and their home congregation remarkably tolerant of children and grandchildren who claim an "alternative lifestyle." Perhaps this seeming double standard reflects the self-centeredness of boomers who have a habit of considering themselves "exceptional."

Finally, LGBTQ Christians (and also LGBTQ people interested in spirituality) have come to discern hypocrisy and sincerity in the church in unexpected ways. There are liberal churches in established denominations that claim to be "affirming," but in fact do not include many LGBTQ people. And surprisingly, there are conservative churches in established evangelical denominations that condemn homosexuality, and in fact include practicing LGBTQ people who are unafraid to own their identity. In this sense, LGBTQ are just like any Christian or seeker looking for a "good church" or a "spiritual home." What matters may not be public policy, political posturing, or advertising. What really matters is a genuine experience of the fruit of the Spirit: love, joy, peace, patience, kindness, goodness, faithfulness, gentleness, and self-control.

The diversity among baby boomers has grown significantly in thirty years. As migrations accelerate in the future due to economic challenges and job changes, and immigration grows due to economic challenges, international conflicts, and climate change, even more diversity among those lifestyle groups whose age generally places them in the boomer category will likely increase.

THE END OF JOURNEY THEOLOGY AND THE RISE OF WANDERING SPIRITUALITY

In the 1980s and 1990s, when most baby boomers were about thirty to forty years old, theology shifted focus from dogma to journey. The "study" of theology became less of a subject and more of a constructive lifelong experiment. Systematic theology was largely abandoned, replaced by theologies of relevance (e.g., a theology of creation, or a theology of feminism, or a theology of poverty, and so on). As the ecumenical movement waned, theology was less and less a dialogue among Christian traditions; it became more and more a dialogue between Christianity, world religions, and the sciences.

For journey theology, faith was a never-ending process, and very little could be said with religious certainty. And yet there were *some* certainties.

Faith was not propositional or confessional but another word for holistic personal growth. It was a nexus of meaning that blended the rational, emotional, relational, physical experiences of the individual. Increasingly, this meant that theology was in conversation with psychology.

Faith was a profound sense of the internal (rather than external) relationships of all things, including animate and inanimate, self-aware and instinctive. Human beings, nature, and the universe itself made up of yet undiscovered elements, were all internally related to one another. The essence of the one was part of the essence of the other. Increasingly, this meant that theology was in conversation with physical and theoretical sciences.

Faith was an intuition of the unity of all religious ideas. God transcended any single description, and could be accessed through a variety of spiritual disciplines. Increasingly, this meant that theology was in conversation with other world religions, with spiritualties of native peoples, and ultimately in fantasy and science fiction.

Faith was a quest to solve existential problems like the problem of evil, the mystery of the universe, life after death, and so on. It was not a gift but a form of research. Since these were complex problems, that research was probably beyond ordinary people and needed to be done by professional experts . . .

who would then summarize and pass on their insights to reassure society. Increasingly, this meant that theology was in conversation with social services, think tanks, and nonprofit organizations.

Faith was a hidden knowledge that was accessible to human reason, and would one day be encompassed by human reason. The Bible needed to be rationally investigated, the miracles explained, the writers placed in historical context, the Old Testament edited to eliminate absurdities, and the New Testament humanized as an ethical system. Increasingly, this meant that theology was in conversation with modern historiography and cultural perceptions.

Faith was a key to unlock successful living. It was not only the power of positive thinking but also a plan to accumulate wealth, build happy marriages, raise respectful children, and rise in social status. In a sense, faith was the secret to personalizing inevitable human progress. It was a tool to get my fair share of life's benefits. Increasingly, this meant that theology was in conversation with economists, social reformers, home renovators, and life coaches.

Given these assumptions, it is not surprising that journey theology should adopt a new methodology for learning and communicating. The culture of the *word* gave way to the culture of the *experience*. Images and motion pictures, music and song became the media and the medium of choice. Certainly, baby boomers continued to read. But their reading became lighter, shorter, and supplementary to these other experiences. The books they were willing to read had fewer and fewer pages; gradually they were replaced by magazines and then blogs; and ultimately, they only supplemented what boomers saw at the movies, watched on television, or heard driving the car.

Journey theology was good for the church in many ways. It encouraged the church to awaken from its dogmatic slumber and seriously engage the contemporary world. It pushed them to separate essential faith from cultural expressions and forms of faith; and to update technology, modernize architecture, and explore new symbols. It made theological reflection interesting and relevant . . . and to some extent urgent. And it empowered laity to take initiative, be creative, question dogmas, and open their hearts and minds to the emerging heterogeneity and cultural diversity of their communities and world.

On the other hand, journey theology was hard for the church in many more ways. Confessional and Eucharistic churches could no longer assume obedience or expect weekly participation. The essentials of faith seemed to become fewer and more generalized and abstract. Appreciation for traditional technologies, facilities, and symbols became a wedge dividing older and younger generations. And it disempowered clergy and institutional religious leaders as authoritative teachers and interpreters of faith.

For some baby boomers, this shift in conversation partners led them to "*Progressive* Christianity" as a rationalized religion, freed from historical baggage and dogmatic bondage, and merged with scientific theories and psychological interpretations. But for many other boomers this shift in conversation meant that their spiritual journey carried them away from the church altogether. They found fellowship in clubs, they served the community through nonprofit social services, and they worshipped alone.

Moreover, their spiritual journey was no longer unfolding amid familiar cultural landmarks. As a group they no longer considered themselves "culturally left," and as they fragmented no one was quite sure what group culture suited them best. They had changed careers, homes, spouses, families, and friendship circles multiple times. The difference between "progress" and "regress" was blurred. Good initiative resulted in bad results; and bad results often led to unexpected benefits. But most importantly, the boomers were no longer in control.

The spiritual journey has become spiritual wandering. That wandering may mean different things to different boomers, but it is not really a journey. "Journey" implies both intentionality and accountability.

When baby boomers were younger, many were quite serious about holistic spiritual growth. They experimented with a variety of spiritual disciplines and practices. They visited different churches and religious organizations; sought conversations with different faiths and perspectives; and followed the emerging dialogue between academic theologians and scientists. Many seminaries and theological colleges reshaped curricula for the sake of second-career boomer enrollment. The goal was to "make theologians" rather than "train pastors."

When they were younger, many boomers had a strong sense of accountability for the integrity of their spiritual quest. Some compared their spiritual insights with church doctrine and practice, interacted with pastors and teachers. Some shared their spiritual insights with peer groups and opened themselves to critique and coaching. And others found ways to "reality test" their insights with life cycles and life crises, or the tensions of work, home, and play.

Both intentionality and accountability have waned in the past thirty years. What was once a quest has now (for many boomers) become a hobby; or a superstition; or a talisman to survive hard times. It is a collection of ideas, much like collections of art or coins, displayed with pride to friends and admirers. It is a memorable quotation, comforting thought, philanthropic interest, or last straw of divine predictability.

Some boomers are still passionate about faith, regular in church attendance, and eager to learn more about the Bible, or Christian tradition, or the relevance of faith to global issues. For most boomers there is no real intentionality. Theology has become a leisure pursuit, or an occasionally useful tool, or a remedy for chronic illness or temporary crisis. They are increasingly irregular about church attendance, uninterested in church institutions, and indifferent to church policies. They no longer conjure reasons not to go to church or ponder a question of faith; they have to conjure reasons why they should care about either.

Some boomers are convinced that absolute convictions and values should still shape personal lifestyles and social behavior. They accept accountability for their errors and speak prophetically to society, and they are ready to forgive and be forgiven. But for most boomers there is no longer any real accountability. No one has the right to criticize one's personal convictions or question one's personal behavior. The church should be grateful for their participation and honor their privileges, but not expect much in return in time, energy, or money. They feel no need to be forgiven, nor do they feel any compulsion to forgive. Lifestyle is more likely to shape faith; and faith is less likely to shape lifestyle.

Once there were some underlying certainties about journey theology. Today there are mostly ambiguities as baby boomers wander (with little intentionality and no accountability) among the spiritualties of the world. Baby boomers are no longer quite sure what faith is about in the first place.

For many boomers, faith is not primarily about holistic personal growth anymore. For example, faith among *Movers, Shakers, and Entitled* is often more about self-justification, survivor guilt, or postponing aging and death for as long as possible. Faith among the *Homebuilders, Health Conscious, and Content* is often more about guaranteed health or stress management. Faith among *Adapters, Adopters, and Multitaskers* is often more about finding meaningful work, careers, and financial success.

29

For many boomers, faith is not about solidarity with the poor and op-pressed, and unity with nature and the cosmos anymore. For example, among *Aesthetes, Idealists, and Intellectuals* it is often more about artistic expression, public policy, and scientific progress. Faith among the *Prayerful, Poor, and Marking Time* is often more about day-to-day survival, addiction interven-tion, and personal security. Among *Adapters, Adopters, and Multitaskers* faith is often about common social values between generations, intimacy, and re-pairing fractured marriages and families.

For many boomers, faith is not about the unity of all religions anymore. For example, lifestyles belonging to *Tranquility, Tradition, and Independence* are often cocooning around personal talismans, preserving local mores, and entrenching ideologies. Faith for the *Homebuilders, Health Conscious, and Content* is often more about therapeutic practices, family values, and bal-anced living. *Aesthetes, Idealists, and Intellectuals* and many *Adapters, Adopters, and Multitaskers* are less interested in world religions, and more interested in new religious movements.

For many boomers, faith is not about solving the big existential prob-lems of life anymore. Among *Movers, Shakers, and Entitled* it is often more about personal identity after retirement than shoring up national or personal security. Among the *Prayerful, Poor, and Marking Time* it is more about com-munity networks and programs or personal strength one day at a time. Even among *Aesthetes, Idealists, and Intellectuals* faith is less about philosophical explanations and more about openness to all perspectives.

For many boomers, faith is not primarily about understanding what really happened in the Bible anymore. For example, boomers belonging to *Home Builders, Health Conscious, and Content* and *Tranquility, Tradition, and Independence* are more interested in using the Bible to defend cultural bi-ases and promote public policies. Faith is about indisputable authority and a manual to organize daily living.

For many boomers, faith is not about success anymore. For example, among *Movers, Shakers, and Entitled* or among *Tranquility, Tradition, and In-dependence* faith is more about preservation, sustainability, and legacy. Among the *Prayerful, Poor, and Marking Time* it is a life preserver to survive, or an incentive to keep going.

Exactly what faith is varies from boomer to boomer . . . and often changes from day to day. Faith was once an adventure. Boomers may not have cap-tured it in words, and certainly avoided creeds, but faith was in their hearts and expressed in songs. Today faith is elusive. Some try to revive old dogmas; many try to place their trust in science and progress; more try to equate it with ideologies; and most simply fall back on their sense of self and individuality.

Journey theology might have been in conflict or tension with the more dogmatic, historical, and systematic theologies of established churches and denominations . . . but God was still central to their lives. Education, career, family and friends, volunteer service, and even leisure time still revolved around the quest for God. In the spiritual wandering that characterizes the religious interest of boomers today, God is no longer central but only alongside other priorities. Today when churches ask boomers to prioritize their lives, they often start by saying "God" . . . then hesitate . . . "and also health, friends, grandchildren, travel, sports, private time" and more. In other words, the primary quest of boomers is not God but self-fulfillment. If God and the church contribute to self-fulfillment, then they are interested. If God becomes too vague or uncomfortable, and if the church becomes too vague about its vision or too demanding for membership expectations, they are not interested.

Wandering spirituality means that attitudes toward faith have once again shifted. Different groups of boomers have different attitudes toward religion, which leads to different perspectives on the church.

Aesthetes, Idealists, and Intellectuals approach faith as "reasonable religion, from privileged perspective, for a better world." They expect the church to avoid mystery and miracle and explain miracles and gratuitous evil. The church should be an agent of social service. When the church gets too mysterious for these boomers, it fails to explain why good people suffer, and then it turns inward toward institutional preservation; so they often drop out.

Movers, Shakers, and Entitled approach faith as a kind of "divine right." They expect the church to honor their personal or family priorities, values, tastes, political perspectives, and status. When the church fails to prioritize their needs and opinions, or preserve their privileges, they often drop out; or a few try to impose their perspectives and status on the whole society by winning elections.

Homebuilders, the Health Conscious, and the Content view religion as one among many activities that leads to balanced living. Faith is about "taking time out to smell the roses." They expect the church to preserve harmony, encourage introspection, and generally contribute to healthy, safe, and homogeneous communities. When the church enters conflict, urges them to dialogue

31

or debate, or becomes a faction that disrupts the status quo in communities, they often drop out.

The Prayerful, Poor, and Marking Time approach religion in the hope that "prayer works." They are looking for the touch of the holy, divine intervention, and strength for tomorrow that only comes through an intimate connection with God. When the church becomes too formal, when it becomes ambiguous about the efficacy of prayer, and when it fails to establish environments where people can sense God's real presence beside them, they often drop out.

Adapters, Adopters, and Multitaskers include God among their many priorities because "participation in religion is a way to cherish the past, empower the future, and overcome generational gaps. They expect the church to continue the essentials (if not necessarily the trappings) of denominational traditions, blend worship to appeal to all tastes, and prioritize youth and young adult ministries. When the church and denomination disagree, worship fails to satisfy, and youth ministries stagnate or decline, they often drop out.

The boomers committed to *Tranquility, Tradition, and Independence* may still be among the most active church participants. After all, religion is still the "right thing to do." They believe that faithfulness means being brand loyal and cost conscious, so they tend to remain in the congregations and denominations of their parents and grandparents. If other boomers are impatient with slow decision making, these boomers prefer to slow down change. However, when the church breaks with denominational policy and practice, or denominations form unpopular public policies; and when churches fall into debt and enter reckless or unrealistic capital campaigns; they often drop out.

It probably goes without saying that these various boomer expectations of the church are unrealistic today; dissatisfied people don't drop out all at once. Most boomers understand that the church needs to change somehow. But they are less and less patient with bureaucracy, parliamentary procedure, institutional polity, and generally slow decision making. If their expectations are unrealistic and patience is thin, it is also true that churches often fail to understand their true attitudes toward religion and expectations of the church. Institutions tend to be poor listeners and intent on their top-down agendas.

Boomers are wandering. When they drop out, they explore many options. They may volunteer for a time in nonprofits, or shop for another church, or join a social or fitness club, or connect with gurus and other religions, or immerse themselves in sports and hobbies, or just spend quality time with family on Sunday mornings. These are generally short-term commitments. When boomers are bored or unfulfilled, or want to indulge in travel or other opportunities, they move on.

When churches ask boomers about what they believe, they frequently receive an enigmatic reply: *We just want to make a difference!* But this is more plea than purpose. It reveals the hidden fear that their lives really haven't made much difference; that their hopes have been disappointed; that their ideals have been distorted or lost; that progress has not really generated peace.

There are many reasons why different kinds of baby boomers are not only dropping out of the institutional church but also wandering further afield in their spirituality. But it is mainly driven by anxieties of emptiness and meaninglessness, and a quest for purpose and effectiveness. In their youth, the New Testament belief that where two or three are gathered together Christ would be there among them, generally assumed some form of classic Christian organization or dogma. When they shared faith stories in word and song about unity in love, they were assuming not only shared Western behavioral patterns and value systems but also shared beliefs about God's redemptive action in the world. Their faith journey followed a broad but still predictable, path. That may still be true for some boomers, but not for many more. Love is not limited to Western systems of values and beliefs, and may often be influenced or replaced by, Eastern or indigenous or personal interpretations of love and hope.

The good news for churches is that even though they wander far, some are still familiar with traditional Christian concepts and symbols, and many more are at least open to consider them in the wider context of spiritualties today. The challenge is to represent Christian values and beliefs in ways that truly "make a difference" in their quest for meaning and purpose, and to their goal to "make a difference" in the world.

MINISTRY AMONG AGING BABY BOOMERS

The more baby boomers wander, the harder it is for a church to attract them. Once the intentionality of journey theology is gone, the *habit* of spiritual wandering is hard to break. In the 1980s and 1990s, many churches experienced a surge in baby boomer participation. It was the result of adapting to contemporary worship and music, upgrading technologies, concentrating on interpersonal relationships, and loosening (but usually not abandoning) structures and processes. For many churches, the surge fell away due to conflicts, financial crises, and unstable leadership.

In the late 1980s, baby boomers (defined by age) tended to be alike. They had national and global sensitivities, wrestled with socialization and social justice issues, tended to be countercultural innovators, and held progressive attitudes. Since the end of the second millennium, that has changed. I have identified six distinct groups. Within each group, African American, Hispanic/Latino, and Asian multi-cultures are increasing, and within each group increasing numbers are redefining sexual identity. These trends are further transforming these groups with distinct social values and religious assumptions. Several things are clear:

First, age is no longer helpful to identify groups of people. Now that there are at least six different kinds of baby boomers, with different social priorities and religious or church expectations, the very label "baby boomer" is obsolete. Some of these "baby boomers" have little affinity for one another; and all may have more affinity with older or younger, more multicultural or eccentric, lifestyle segments.

Second, the "cultural left" that was once defined by baby boomers has fragmented, declined, and largely disappeared. The importance of social values and spirituality may continue, but they are less central to lifestyle, and are diversified and nuanced among other younger and older, richer and poorer, and often non-white lifestyle segments. Boomers today are as likely to be economic neo-liberals as they are social conservatives. They are more likely to give to universities, hospitals, public television, and political parties than they are to a religious organization.

Attitudes toward religion and church expectations among the six groups of baby boomers today are incredibly diverse. Church leaders are rightly concerned about the withdrawal of this age group from church membership and participation, but they are wrong to think that there are one-size-fits-all tactical adjustments that can turn the tide.

In an age of increasing diversity, the strategic thinking of churches should be less about tactics and more about tendencies. If a church intuits the right tendencies for the baby boomers in their community, then tactics really can vary in form and quality. You don't *have* to offer just coffee and refreshments, or just the right music and band for worship, or just the right small-group multiplication program, or just the right technology or facility.

Surveying attitudes and perspectives is the kind of psychographic research often done through surveys and algorithms based on specific questions (e.g., "Are you pro-choice or pro-life?" "Would you rather spend a quiet evening at home or go out on the town?" "Do you carefully plan each day or prefer to act spontaneously?") The results are used for marketing strategies, public policy development, and political campaigns. Churches, however, are not equipped to do such sophisticated surveys and calculations.

I find it is better for churches to reality test key tendencies among the lifestyle segments that shape either community or church cultures. These are discerned by going deeper into lifestyle portraits to understand basic attitudes or "default" dispositions that they bring to all aspects of their lives (including church involvement). The following table describes four key polarities. Lifestyle segments tend to lean toward one side of the polarity or the other in lesser or greater degrees.

Church leaders can test the accuracy of these tendencies with distinct groups in the church regarding the membership, and with social service and nonprofit partners regarding the community to get a clearer picture of the attitudes and expectations of baby boomers in both church and community.

Thirty years ago, the recipe for reaching baby boomers included minimal, general ingredients: contemporary music, experiential worship, updated technology, small groups, and marketing that emphasize opportunity rather than duty. Think of it as much the same recipe that grandma used, but with less salt and more pepper.

Today there is no single recipe. The spices are more diverse and exotic. And the strategy that reaches, blesses, and empowers some boomers will turn away and turn off other baby boomers. Even though I identify six distinct groups of baby boomers today, the diversity of expectation for Christian ministries is far greater than that. But here are some of the trends.

Boomers with *local* priorities tend to prefer slower, more caregiving worship; with more lyrical inspirational music and preaching on practical daily Christian living; and outreach that is more oriented toward health, neighbors in need, and conversion. Those boomers with *global* priorities tend to prefer faster, more educational worship; with more rhythmic inspirational music and preaching about ethics or theology; and outreach that is more oriented toward international crises, human rights, and human potential.

Extreme Priority	Extreme Priority
Local	**Global**
Neighborhood, town, and city focus	State, nation, and international focus
Family tradition, local custom	Ecumenical, interfaith, indigenous spirituality
Denominational distinctiveness	Personal religious preference
Our culture, common language, homogeneity	Multi-culture, fluency in other languages, heterogeneity
Our home and family	Our world and friends
Steadfast	**Progressive**
Conservative, cautious	Liberal and adventurous
Stability and consistency	Change and innovation
Religious tradition	Religious syncretism
Urgent about place	Urgent about time
Loyalty to principle	Loyalty to progress
Personal Fulfillment	**Social Obligation**
Entitlement and privilege	Responsibility and inclusivity
Lasting relationships	Temporary alliances
Internally focused churches	Externally focused churches
Urgent about being loved	Urgent about being right
Balanced living	Unbalanced living
Corporate	**Entrepreneurial**
Compromise and procedure	Contest and outcome
Harmony, and security	Accountability, and risk
Keeping church members	Welcoming church newcomers
Member of the team	Leader of the team
Sacrifice for the good of the organization	Sacrifice for the achievement of a cause

Boomers with *steadfast* priorities tend to prefer passive hospitality with untrained greeters and friendship circles and tasty treats; worship that reflects specific religious traditions and uses classic Christendom symbols; more ecclesiastical architecture; and modern technologies. Boomers with more *progressive* priorities tend to prefer active hospitality, with layers of trained greeters and health-conscious food choices; worship that uses interfaith symbols or relies on scenes of nature; more utilitarian architecture and postmodern technologics.

Boomers with *personal fulfillment* priorities tend to prefer worship that highlights children's stories; long-term fellowship groups and low-accountability small groups; pastors who are visitors, counselors, and caregivers; budgets that emphasize paid personnel and internal programs; and less risky strategic plans that minimize debt. Boomers with *social obligation* priorities tend to prefer worship that highlights mission stories; short-term fellowship groups and high-accountability small groups; pastors who are visionaries and CEOs; budgets that emphasize lay empowerment and external programs; and more risky strategic plans that accept higher debt.

Boomers with *corporate* priorities tend to prefer worship that is standardized and presentational; Christian education material from approved resources and denominational publishing houses, and methodologies that are more generational; large boards or councils making decisions by consensus; stewardship programs that promote unified budgets; and pastors who are enablers and mediators. Boomers with *entrepreneurial* priorities tend to prefer worship that is customized and dialogical; Christian education materials focusing on specific issues for multiple sources, and methodologies that are more intergenerational; small boards making decisions by alignment to vision; stewardship programs that promote designated giving; and pastors who engage in mentoring and discipleship.

In the past, baby boomers tended to be a demographic of peacemakers. Even though they were generally anti-institutional and countercultural in their youth, they tended to build bridges between generations, ethnicities, political parties, and Christian or religious traditions. Today many baby boomers have joined the extremism that has risen in American culture. The four tendencies I describe in the chart of extreme priorities no longer allows for degrees of preference. They have become either/or choices; there is little moderate ground in between. Similarly, the ministry options I describe have become "my way or the highway" choices. Baby boomers who dislike the tactical choices of a church are less likely to stay and work it out. And they are more likely to change churches or leave the church altogether.

There is clearly a deeper concern and more difficult challenge churches face in reaching baby boomers. It has become harder to *attract* boomers

37

because churches have confused institutional growth with a desire to *bless* boomers without any institutional expectations. Baby boomers can tell the difference. A church can adapt worship, upgrade technologies, train leaders, and elevate the quest for quality and choices in programming . . . and still not reach boomers.

The deeper concern is that aging boomers are less concerned about matching personal *needs and tastes* to church *programs and liturgies*. They are more concerned to experience divine grace that is directly relevant to the existential anxieties that drive their quests for God. And they are more open to go beyond their comfort zones if the result is an experience with the real presence of God. Thirty years ago it was generally safe to assume all or most boomers were driven by anxieties of meaninglessness and emptiness, and generally felt lost or alone. Today their existential dilemmas are nuanced in important ways. They are thriving, confident, optimistic, hard-working, enthusiastic, and generally happy . . . *but they are increasingly depressed, cynical, disillusioned, frustrated, struggling, and worried.* If churches are to reach and bless them, they need to be more intentional about addressing the unique anxieties that dominate the consciousness of each baby boomer group.

So the emphasis for effective ministry should not be on perfecting style and developing programs but on focusing the central *message* and deploying the right *leadership*. The message is no longer love but hope. Love they can get anywhere. Hope is harder to find.

The central *message* of a church needs to permeate everything the church says on Sunday, everything the church does during the week, and everything every leader models spontaneously and daringly in daily living. Moreover, the message that blesses one group of boomers may not bless another. For some, the message will be about providence, and for others it will be about trust. For some it will be about life after death, and for others it will be about justice; for some it will be about practical faithfulness, and for others it will be about unchanging ideals.

There are significant implications for preaching and worship design. I observe that the tradition of expository preaching on a set of texts following the Christian year is still interesting to *some* boomers, but even many of them realize they could gain the same insights reading by themselves and don't need to attend worship regularly to glean that information. Preaching is becoming more thematic, specific to the anxieties that dominate life, and follow the secular calendar.

The right *leadership* needs to be trained, deployed, and evaluated in ways that are credible for the specific groups of baby boomers the church seeks to bless. The key is no longer professionalism but credibility. *Some* boomers respect well-educated and certified clergy, but even they realize they can find better educated and more competent professionals in other sectors (education, health care, social service, management, and the like) to meet their needs. But it is more difficult to find role models who can be articulate about faith in a world of harsh realities, and visibly model core values in daily living.

There are significant implications for clergy and clergy deployment, but also boards and board development, and for volunteers and team leader training. Boomers sustain their interest in the church when clergy are an example of courage and hope, boards intentionally align hope to measurable outcomes, and team leaders are trustworthy and accountable for their actions.

In a sense, the challenge to the church for effective ministry among the baby boomer groups is a conflict of self-interest. The self-interests of the institution (membership, attendance, donations, volunteer energy, and institutional survival) conflict with the self-interests of boomers (status, acceptance, rewards, attention, and personal fulfillment). Both entities are motivated primarily by *self-interest*, which, as we shall see, drives emerging lifestyle segments to reject *both* baby boomers *and* churches as role models or agents of change. In this context, however, the hidden agendas of boomers and hidden agendas of church organizations are distinct. Sometimes self-interests coincide; but increasingly self-interests diverge. When baby boomers ask the church to be "externally focused," they are often asking the church to be externally focused *on them.* When the church asks boomers to sacrifice self for mission, rather than persuading with a deep mission focus on suffering people, they are often asking boomers to be "externally focused" on the institution as the primary authority and means for social service.

Some churches today are responding to the challenge by focusing solely upon the self-interest of boomers. They adapt programs and styles to accommodate the needs and tastes boomers prefer. They deploy clergy who say what boomers want to hear. They set standards for behavior and participation that are low enough for boomers to accept. But in my observation, these churches are like seeds sown in thin soil, springing up quickly and growing large, but unsustainable because they do not really address the anxieties that dominate their lives.

Effective churches, however, focus on neither the self-interest of the institution nor the self-interest of boomers. Instead, they focus on going deeper and further: *deeper* into the meaning and mystery of the Spirit, and *further* to sacrificially bless people regardless of eventual institutional commitment and regardless of boomer comfort zones. If the *message* is clear and the *messengers* are credible, baby boomers may well sustain their interest in the church in the long run.

Chapter 2

THE LIBERAL CULTURAL ECLECTIC

The emergence of the extreme left

One of the great paradoxes of the cultural left from the final quarter of the twentieth century was the combination of social consciousness and self-centeredness. In those days, boomers could be passionate about a cause one day, and remarkably indifferent to anyone other than themselves the next. The great weakness of the cultural left was their inability to sustain sacrificial commitment for very long. As boomers aged into the first quarter of the twenty-first century, this paradox could no longer be sustained.

Some boomers became even more committed to social change, and pursued careers that sacrificed affluence for social service. These boomers, primarily educated in the liberal arts, followed careers in public education and public health, social service and advocacy, and the church. Many boomers became more immersed in consumerism, and pursued careers in business, applied sciences, law, and other professions. Now in retirement, the former are less affluent, struggling to sustain middle-class status, and often wondering if their sacrifice was worth it. The latter are more affluent, struggling with their conscience, and wondering if their investment means anything.

I describe the legacy remnant of the cultural left as the *liberal cultural eclectic*. This group is not nearly as large as the boomers of the former cultural left, but they take the paradox of the cultural left to extremes. They are *extremely* conscious of social justice on the one hand, and *extremely* self-absorbed on the other. The boomers found it hard to sustain their passion for a cause longer than a few months or years, but the heirs of the cultural left find it hard to sustain their passion for a cause longer than a few days or weeks. The boomers could be *very* generous with their time and money, involved in political process, and prepared to take risks to help their neighbors or change the world. The *liberal cultural eclectic* can be *extremely* sacrificial with their time and money, and are often prepared to take *enormous* risks to help their neighbors and the world . . . but they have largely dropped out of the political process.

There is a difference between the anti-establishment attitudes of the boomers who shaped the cultural left, and the anti-institutional attitudes that shape the *liberal cultural eclectic*. The early cultural left was not opposed to organization per se. Indeed, they became excellent organizers and managers, and went on to apply those skills to business, educational reform, and politics. Some of them went on to grow large churches and lead denominations. The emerging *liberal cultural eclectic*, however, are generally cynical about organization itself. They are often ineffective managers but excellent entrepreneurs. They are unlikely to succeed as megachurch leaders, but excellent church planters and outreach specialists. The priority of the old cultural left was to reform programs and shape policies. The priority of the new *liberal cultural eclectic* is to build relationships and network constantly.

Sustainable change was always a weakness for the cultural left, because self-centeredness tended to compromise their passion for social change. Their focus on organization was a kind of compromise to hold the two sides of their paradoxical natures together. But organization leads to management; and management involves hierarchy; and hierarchy leads to competitiveness; and competitiveness measures self-worth by success; and success is defined in North America by affluence. The path to organization ultimately encouraged their self-centeredness and undermined their social conscience. Even those boomers who deliberately chose less affluent careers (e.g., public education or government service) found themselves later in life more concerned about pension plans than reform.

Their cultural heirs call this hypocrisy. Their focus is on relationships; which leads to networks. But networks lead to peer groups; and peer groups lead to comparisons; and comparisons lead to in-groups and outliers; and the tension between in-groups and outliers leads to self-promotion; and self-promotion in North America is defined by style and status. The path to relationships ultimately encourages even more blatant self-centeredness that undermines social conscience. Even those young *liberal cultural eclectics* who immerse themselves in relationships choose fitness clubs over soup kitchens, and spend Christmas vacations on a Caribbean beach with their significant others, rather than at an inner-city church with insignificant nobodies.

If the cultural left once saw itself as a movement, then it appears that the handoff of the torch to the next generation has been bobbled . . . if not dropped. The boomers of the cultural left, and the emerging generation of the *liberal cultural eclectic* don't fully understand or respect each other. The latter sees the hypocrisy in the former, and the former sees the hypocrisy in the latter, and cooperation is often difficult to establish. Each regards the other as "uncoachable," even though they still share many common values and goals. So they tend to disagree over strategy; focus on different measurable outcomes for social change; and trip over one another in political process.

This is not just a typical "generation gap." For one thing, the *liberal cultural eclectic* are not necessarily defined by age. Older people can be included in their midst, and younger people may not be included. For another thing, the gap between the *liberal cultural eclectic* and the rest of the *culturally ambivalent* cannot be interpreted as a matter of maturity. The *liberal cultural eclectic* will not "grow up" and return to the less radical ranks of the *culturally ambivalent*. If anything, they are more likely to take a 180-degree turn to migrate to the *culturally righteous*! This separation is more fundamental. It is a different perception of reality and human nature, shades of meaning and the cultural contingencies of truth. In a sense, the *culturally ambivalent* have taken modernity as far as it can go, and the *liberal cultural eclectic* are the trend setters for the post-modern world.

Nevertheless, if we draw an "Influence Map," we often see boomers of the former cultural left and younger generations of the *liberal cultural eclectic* living side by side. An "Influence Map" resembles a family tree that shows how lifestyle segments relate to each other based on three demographic polarities of age, income, and family status.[1] An "influence map," however, also shows how lifestyle segments are more likely or less likely to influence the social values, life priorities, and religious expectations of other lifestyle segments.

The family tree gathers lifestyle segments that share age, income, and family status traits into a lifestyle group. An "influence map" charts the degree of influence a lifestyle segment may or may not have on another segment. It recognizes that some lifestyle groups actually do not get along with, nor do

---

1. See, for example, the Family Tree in the *Mosaic USA E-Handbook* by Experian, page 7.

they have much influence on, other segments in the same family; and that some lifestyle segments relate better across group boundaries.

Admittedly, my notion of an "influence map" is more subjective than a family tree. Much of it comes out of my own experience observing cultural patterns and mapping lifestyle representation in communities or regions. However, I believe any church or non-profit leader who spends time not only observing the community but also immersing themselves in the community will begin to see the following patterns:

Patterns of residency: Certain lifestyle segments predictably locate themselves in proximity to other lifestyle segments. They migrate into neighborhoods *on purpose*, because they are more comfortable living near these particular people.

Patterns of socializing: Certain lifestyle segments are predictably attracted to distinct recreational venues. Successful restaurants, for example, locate and develop menus in empathy with multiple markets who share similar expectations for hospitality and environment.

Patterns of anxiety and spirituality: Certain lifestyle segments share similar anxieties about life that drive their quest for meaning; and often define expectations for worship and spiritual leadership that are even more important than preferences for style or religious tradition.

An "influence map" is certainly more fluid than a family tree." Many more psychographic factors shape and reshape the map. Church or non-profit leaders must constantly monitor, reality check, and adjust the map. However, maps like this are far more useful for strategic planning and relevant ministry than illustrations of age, income, and family status patterns.

The lifestyles represented by the *liberal cultural eclectic* tend to connect with *some* baby boomers of the former cultural left. Specifically, they tend to connect with the boomer groups described as *aesthetes, idealists, and intellectuals*; the *prayerful, poor, and marking time*; and *adapters, adopters, and multitaskers*. And they tend not to connect with *movers, shakers, and entitled*; or *homebuilders, health conscious, and content*; or *tranquility, tradition, and independence*. In addition, the lifestyle segments represented in the *liberal cultural eclectic* are more likely to value and/or accept biracial, multicultural, and LGBTQ friendships.

The eclectic heirs of the cultural left may have an uneasy relationship with baby boomers, but they do tend to live near, socialize with, and share similar values and religious expectations. Birds of a feather do tend to flock together. But who, exactly, are they? What are their potential spiritual priorities? And is there any way a church can involve and bless them?

HALLMARKS OF THE LIBERAL CULTURAL ECLECTIC[2]

The name chosen here to describe the heirs of the cultural left reveals the radical unpredictability of these people. Their *attitudes* do not always correspond to their *behavior*. This is why it is so difficult for marketers to anticipate their desires and needs. They are generally social, economic, political, and religious liberals. Indeed, they can be quite extreme liberals. However, their passions and choices can vary day to day, or situation to situation. Again and again, politicians and religious leaders expect them to show high passion for a particular cause, only to be surprised by their tepid response; or they expect them to show low interest in another cause only to be surprised by their extreme passion.

For example, both secular and religious organizations were surprised by the passionate response of the *liberal cultural eclectic* to the devastation in New Orleans caused by Hurricanes Katrina and Rita, as young adult volunteers flocked to the city. Churches were surprised by their sudden interest in spirituality as these young adult volunteers helped churches rebuild communities. Civic and church leaders were ill prepared to take advantage of their sacrificial energy. And yet, secular and religious organizations were surprised again by the seeming lack of interest caused by Hurricane Harvey in Houston and Irma in Puerto Rico.

Or, for example, liberal baby boomers in the church have been surprised by their sustained passion among their heirs for LGBTQ rights, including civil and religious sanction of gay marriages. They pushed the boundaries of advocacy further than some liberal boomers wanted to go. On the other hand, boomers have been surprised by the modest passion among the *liberal cultural eclectic* for women's rights. The feminist movement endorsed by

---

2. Many groups mentioned are included in (but not limited to) lifestyle segments currently identified by Experian as A05 *Couples with Clout* and F22 *Fast Track Couples;* family group G *(Young City Solos)* including G24 *Status Seeking Singles* and G25 *Urban Edge;* family group K *(Significant Singles)* including K37 *Wired for Success* and K40 *Metro Fusion;* family group O *(Singles and Starters)* including O50 *Full Steam Ahead,* O51 *Digital Dependents,* O52 *Urban Ambition,* O53 *Colleges and Cafes,* O54 *Striving Single Scene;* and R66 *Dare to Dream.*

liberal boomers has had somewhat less-enthusiastic support. Perhaps this is because the *liberal cultural eclectic* assume that the battle has already been won, but fail to see the actual erosion of women's rights in the new millennium.

This is what makes this group "eclectic." What they "see" and what they don't "see" is so surprising. They can "see" the macro picture of climate change, immigration abuses, or poverty and pandemic on the one hand; and yet be alarmingly myopic when it comes to "seeing" micro issues for addiction, spousal abuse, or the erosion of individual privacy. And yet even that statement is inaccurate, because what was "macro" one day becomes "micro" another day, and vice versa.

Young . . . but Not Necessarily Representative of Youth

The heirs to the cultural left tend to be "young" or "younger," in their twenties and thirties. However, the *liberal cultural eclectic* can include people in their forties if their profile largely matches certain hallmarks. Intimacy, for example, can be shared between people with significant age differences. The hallmarks of the "young" or "younger" include:

Age matters less than shared lifestyle choices;
Intersecting passions;
Multicultural values;
Certain affinities such as extreme sports and music in multiple
    genres; and
High-energy vibe.

The *liberal cultural eclectic* includes only a portion of young and younger people. They are not normative of "youth," although some may think they are. Just as a significant number of baby boomers once identified as liberal have now become conservative, so also many youth and younger people who are expected to be liberal are actually quite conservative. Yet the *liberal cultural eclectic* do reveal a distinctively youth, fresh, high-energy vibe. It is this energy that makes them such good volunteers.

It is this same energy that churches often covet for their own purposes. The problem is that most are quite alienated from the church, organized religion, and anything "religious" (e.g., dogma, liturgy, holy texts, clergy). For many in this group, spiritual truth (if there is any) is buried beneath an avalanche of hypocrisy, and to ask a church to guide them into spiritual truth is like asking buddies drinking at the bar to guide them to sobriety. It's not going to happen.

Many churches mistakenly stereotype the *liberal cultural eclectic* as "young people," and assume that traditional "youth ministries" will attract and encourage them. The traditional "recipes" that include "contemporary" worship, group intimacy, and outreach projects are rarely effective. It's not about style, friendliness, or good works. And it's not about age.

Urban and Urbane

The *liberal cultural eclectic* are primarily an urban or "urbanized" demographic. As urban people, they tend toward the largest urban centers on the East and West Coasts, or in the megalopolis Midwest including the greater Chicago area, or southern and Gulf Coast centers like Atlanta or New Orleans. They also tend to follow lines of "peri-urbanization" as major industries relocate on the perimeters of cities for cheaper land and better transportation routes and in college and university locations. They are also represented increasingly in towns and small cities (and even remote areas) because the Internet is a major method of communication, relationship, and entertainment.

This group is quite open to diversity in all its forms. Perhaps they are more likely to accept diversity because it is already there in urban and Internet environments; but it is more likely that they are *predisposed* to welcome it and thus diversity shapes their urban environments. They tend to welcome or tolerate diversity in all its forms (racial and multicultural, gender and sexuality, income, marriage and family configurations, age, occupation and education, and more). However, they tend to be markedly intolerant of late adopters of technology, social conservatives, and dogmatists or religious absolutists. And they tend to be hyper-sensitive to organizations that are perceived to be wasteful, sectarian, manipulative, or abusive to the environment.

The high concentration of *liberal cultural eclectic* in urban and urbanizing environments contrasts sharply with the inability or unwillingness of urban churches to reach and empower them. Most churches are not nearly as welcoming or friendly as this group of people seems to be. Churches tend to be homogeneous rather than heterogeneous and gather around clear affinities of race, occupation, relative wealth and status, and so on. Urban churches have often shrunk to the size of a "family church," and the self-awareness of being an in-group dramatically limits their hospitality and creativity.

Moreover, churches are perceived by the *liberal cultural eclectic* as wasteful (spending inordinate amounts of money on property maintenance); sectarian (adamant about denominational polity and practice or theological absolutes); manipulative (primarily interested in attracting members more than blessing strangers); and abusive toward the environment (predisposed to energy inefficiency). Ironically, even churches that are part of denominations that consider themselves "liberal" or "progressive" are perceived by this group as *late adopters* who think "words" are the primary method to share meaning (rather than popular music and image); and who remain social conservatives (because their claims of inclusiveness are rarely backed up by spontaneous deeds of inclusiveness and high accountability for inclusiveness); and who are dogmatic and absolutist (because the hidden assumptions of people with institutional power still dictate the boundaries for spiritual experimentation).

The urban or urbanizing ethos of the *liberal cultural eclectic* contributes to the growing gap between urban/suburban and town/rural life in America. It also contributes to the growing gap between "youngers" and "olders" in the church; and (as many baby boomers transition in both age and inclination) the increased alienation of the emerging *liberal cultural eclectic* from the cultural left of thirty years ago.

Socially Hyperactive

The *liberal cultural eclectic* are notorious for "burning the candle at both ends." They are often working multiple part-time jobs, and at the same time immersed in interpersonal activities, various entertainments, and personal passions. It is not just that they have an active night life but that night and day is a single chaos of shift work and self-fulfillment. Their remedy for fatigue and illness is not rest but the gym.

Hyperactivity, of course, includes social media. Even the least affluent in this group will own a smartphone with a multitude of apps that allow them to manage their busy lives. They keep in touch with friends hourly, and follow cultural influencers constantly.

The *liberal cultural eclectic* are known for high energy. Unlike the baby boomers of the former cultural left, they do not even try to live "balanced lives." Their lives are chronically unbalanced. They do not invest their energy in portions. They give 100 percent of the energy to every activity, even if those activities are occurring at the same time. So in practical terms, they attempt to give 100 percent energy to everything, and end up giving their complete attention to nothing. Every face-to-face conversation is accompanied by texting with someone else, somewhere else. People in this group are present and absent at the same time.

Churches generally covet their high energy, but find their short attention spans disconcerting. They are unlikely to join committees, although they may occasionally participate in short-term task groups. They have no time for meetings, little patience for bureaucracy, and no tolerance for endless announcements and chatter that often typifies traditional church worship and hospitality. Since they are constantly in multiple conversations at the same time, church people often feel they are disrespectful. And church people cannot fathom how online relationships can be as intimate as face-to-face ones.

Single and Cohabitating

The *liberal cultural eclectic* tends to include people who stay single longer and take more time to explore intimacy; and who avoid long-term relational contracts, and long for long-term interpersonal trust. Their prolonged single status is partly economic. They can't afford families. It is partly psychological. It takes them longer to mature emotionally. And it is partly egotistic. They cherish their independence and fear the limitations brought about by emotional entanglements with others.

Ironically, however, their keenness to explore intimacy and their longing for interpersonal trust often causes them to be self-absorbed, self-critical, and depressed. And it leads them to become susceptible to peer pressure, to become vulnerable to the unintentional slights and intentional slanders of others, and to having daily lives that seem to older generations unduly "dramatic" or crisis driven.

The result is that traditional churches misunderstand them, and their typical strategies to build relationships fail to connect with them. They do not look to the church for friendships, group activities, or entertainment, because they can find that in other places and at other times, where they feel more free to be themselves, with more options for communication and fun. (They *may* look to the church for opportunities to participate in teams doing social service.)

The old wisdom—let the youth wander from the church, in the full expectation that they would return to the church when they married and started families—doesn't work today. They are not likely to participate in marriage preparation counseling, having experimented long enough in relationships to believe they are already prepared. They are much less likely to return to the church sanctuary for a traditional or even "contemporary" wedding, and much more likely to simply live together and one day legalize their relationships in a civil service and big party. For a time in their life they might well ask an ordained minister to officiate a simple wedding rite in some environment outside the church building, but that time is passing quickly. The clergy no longer represent the Holy; they represent the hypocrisy of caving in to their parental or grandparental expectations.

Educated

By and large, the *liberal cultural eclectic* are educated, or at least believe in education. However, their experiences and expectations of education are quite different than for older lifestyle groups.

First, their educational history and future educational plan include less and less liberal arts studies. Most have had little formal education in history, philosophy, religion, music theory, art forms, and literary genre. Their post-secondary education has usually specialized in business, marketing or economics, applied sciences, public service, health care, or trades.

This means that much of the subtlety and layers of meaning associated with traditional worship is lost on them; and expository preaching that references literature, compares theologies, explores history and tradition, and quotes dead saints is boring to them.

Second, most people in this group do not follow the traditional pattern of four years of post-secondary education, at a single educational institution, which then leads to career. Four years of college or university education may be stretched out over a decade, shaped around the demands of jobs and relationships; or it may be condensed into a shorter, more intensive burst of energy to save money for fast-track careers. Alternatively, college and university may be deferred, or interrupted several times, in favor of travel, volunteer service, or the pursuit of particular hobbies or passions.

This means that churches can no longer expect even modest time commitments from people in this group for church participation (assuming they want to do that). The church does not have the luxury of time. They do not have a lot of time to get to know them before they move on. They are less likely to find that they are interested in any sort of "membership" in the church. Perhaps the most significant result of this shift in educational patterns is the church can no longer naively assume that their *next* church will be in the same denomination or theological tradition of their *current* church. Education in the essentials of faith, love, and hope are relevant to their mobile lives . . . but education in denominational identity, policy, polity, and practice is not.

Third, most people in this group accumulate courses from multiple institutions. They are less and less likely to select an educational institution, and more and more likely to seek a particular teacher or program in whatever institution employs the teacher or offers the program. Education is not "residential" but "mobile." And today the mobility will include distance learning or online learning.

This means that traditional programs of Christian education are less and less valuable to people in this group. Sunday school classes, Bible study, and even midweek small groups are not that important if *content* or *information* is all that matters. It is the spiritual maturity, accessibility, and mentoring ability of the leaders that counts. What people in this group value most is a high-trust, mentor-mentee relationship with a credible spiritual leader who can guide them deeper into spiritual life. It's not about theological education. It's about merging life and hope.

Finally, many people in this group are turning to alternative sources of education. Formal education is very expensive, usually entails enormous debt, and (for many) bears too little fruit. Upward mobility, once a hallmark of a career path, has become less and less likely. So, many in this group embrace and expand the apprenticeship model of the blue-collar trades, to a *peripatetic* model of learning applicable to white-collar employment. In short, they learn how to live a productive and successful life by working with multiple employers, changing jobs frequently, and searching out expertise through online blogs, talks, and podcasts.

Traditional methods used to educate clergy are becoming obsolete for the *liberal cultural eclectic*. They are less likely to attend a seminary or theological college, or they may attend part time, or they may connect with more than one institution. Increasingly, they simply find an alternative path that relies on apprenticeship experience in diverse churches, assuming leadership positions through experience rather than through academia. This does not mean that basic biblical, doctrinal, historical knowledge and pastoral training is unimportant to the group, only that such knowledge and experience is acquired in other ways.

One reason for this shift in training for spiritual leadership is that traditional theological education is simply too expensive and leads to significant debt. When that is compared to the relatively stagnant or diminishing incomes for pastors today, seminary training is financially no longer viable.

But a more significant reason for this shift in training is that people in this group seriously doubt that traditional theological training will equip them for the post-modern world of competing spiritualities, increasing mobility, and escalating insecurity. The traditional 5:1 mixture of seminary training (five parts classroom to one part fieldwork) is reversed. Their energy goes to fieldwork, which is selectively supplemented by the classroom. Many urban megachurches recognize this shift and often train their leaders from within on the job, and supplement with formal theological education.

Holistic

The *liberal cultural eclectic* approach life holistically. They are both introverted and extroverted and morph easily into different personality types. Intimacy tends to be communal, and "family" includes a wide circle of odd people and unusual networks. Privacy readily goes public; religious ideas and moral attitudes that are usually corporate are private.

People in this group avoid pigeon-holes, stereotypes, and compartments. Life and work merge together, and if they start to separate (as is typical, for example, of baby boomers) they are likely to change their lifestyle or get a different job. Local and global perspectives merge together. They readily identify with the abuses people in another country experience, and share their anger and shame. They see local solutions and magnify them to have international significance, sharing their optimism and acceptance.

Mind, body, and spirit are a single experience. Intellectual stimulus, physical fitness, emotional empathy, and spirituality blend seamlessly together. Indeed, spirituality is not "authentic" if it is not also thoughtful, physical, and emotional at the same time. People in this group are wired to be pantheists. All things are an expression of God, all people carry a divine spark within them, and all religions point to the same ideal.

Churches today also use the term "holistic," but usually in a different and limited way. Churches usually mean that a human being is only healthy if mind, body, and spirit work in harmony, and that even the smallest changes for good or ill can have global significance. They do not use the term to radically link all religious perspectives or respect the widest spectrum of behaviors; and they are generally unwilling to curb the urge to evangelize (or colonize) in what is now the "global village."

Even progressive churches (especially if they are primarily baby boomer churches) struggle to understand the *radical* holism of the *liberal cultural eclectic*. Many are still caught up in the rationalized dualism of subject/object. They generally take an ecological or scientific approach to religion, and focus on external relationships and how individual "subjects" interact with other "objects." But people in this group are generally not interested in secularizing religion, but rather in spiritualizing secularity.

The "holism" of the *liberal cultural eclectic* means that this group is remarkably open to the supernatural. There is no boundary between dimensions, and it is not difficult for them to intuit another reality beyond reality. The supernaturalism of the *liberal cultural eclectic* may not be systematic, and certainly does not suggest yet another religion, but it is revealed in their reactions to crisis, openness to chance or luck, and curiosity about the paranormal.

Chronically Undervalued

The *liberal cultural eclectic* includes lifestyle segments that feel chronically undervalued. Many of them are well educated and talented, yet they are stuck in meaningless jobs and feel they have limited employment possibilities. Some have basic and graduate university degrees, but find themselves living with their parents again, working for minimum hourly wages in food services, retail, security, and the like. Most of these jobs are part time. This means people in this group are juggling multiple part-time jobs to survive, without any pension or medical benefits.

Interestingly, the lack of meaningful, sustainable employment has created a rift between this group and the baby boomers where one might expect to be their advocates. Many boomers are delaying retirement, taking jobs for which younger people in this group are quite qualified. They may be angry and frustrated with boomers, further fracturing the unity of the former cultural left.

53

Feelings of being underrated are more profound than this. At one time, there was a correlation between education and wealth. Today, education is one of the least important requirements for the accumulation of wealth. This group is repeatedly told that patronage (i.e., "knowing the right people") is most important, followed by the ability to work with a team, and sheer luck. So these people are often torn between feelings of pride and humiliation. They are proud of their educational accomplishments, but shamed by their lack of financial success.

Even those members of the *liberal cultural eclectic* with little education feel that they have talent that is under- or unrecognized. Aside from the "shame" of seeming financial failure, they feel the stigma of being considered intellectually limited. Even when they are open to coaching and training, opportunities from the government and corporate sector are ever more limited. They feel trapped in a frustrating cycle in which employers only hire people with experience, but there are no opportunities to get experience.

In part this explains some of the behavioral characteristics of the *liberal cultural eclectic*. They tend to live large, follow fashion and technology trends, and intentionally make a statement in public. They tend to be body-conscious and impulse buyers. They tend to gamble on high-risk ventures. They often don't vote but march in protests. They often struggle to sustain long-lasting relationships even though they are surrounded by a crowd of acquaintances. This may be partial compensation for low self-esteem and a way to demand to be seen, heard, and respected.

Churches habitually undervalue people in this group as well. They are perceived as too impetuous to serve on a board, or too immature to teach a class, or too extreme to lead a team. Their life experience is often so different from the 1960s and 1970s (considered the high point of many church member memories) that they seem almost alien to the sensibilities of church veterans. The tactics of church life that members take for granted are often irrelevant and even distasteful to these people. And changing tactics in hospitality, music and liturgy, technology, symbolism, educational methodology, communication, and even fundraising and money management has to be so radical that it offends the long-time members. Churches may want to reach and encourage them, but the cost to do so is simply too high for some.

Churches that succeed in ministry among the *liberal cultural eclectic* are often outside North America, and their stories are most influential among faith communities along the East, West, and Gulf Coasts. These regions are more urban and multicultural. The example I am thinking of is a church in Toronto, Canada, a city that rivals New York, Los Angeles, and New Orleans as one of the most cosmopolitan regions of North America. Some years ago, a traditional urban core church reinvented itself as an arts center (galleries and music venues); social service launching pad (local and global); and "Tea Room" (indigenous fellowship for the surrounding cultures). Worship was dialogical; music was performance quality; and Eucharist was both physical and digital. The congregation affirmed LGBTQ people, but was not adversarial toward traditional Christians. It was radically inclusive for women in leadership and people who are economically challenged. An interactive website linked members with like-hearted people around the world. The pastor was bicultural and bilingual. Most meetings were held online.

The *liberal cultural eclectic* members modeled simple living and sought to reduce their environmental footprint as much as possible. They were so successful that the church building closed, participants dispersed, and the church as an institution ceased. They considered leadership disbursement, rather than organizational sustainability, as success. The church is "gone," but ministries and nonprofits across the region became energized. Yet the "cost" to reach the *liberal cultural eclectic* required such change to attitude, tradition, leadership, organization, technology, finance, and property that the denomination and other established churches considered this a "failed experiment."

Experimental

The *liberal cultural eclectic* is perhaps the most experimental and entrepreneurial lifestyle group in America. The combination of limited opportunity, innate talent, and over-confidence makes them high-risk takers. Successful entrepreneurs are idols to be imitated. They are undeterred by the high percentage of failed start-up companies or the dangers of consumerism.

Starting a small business is often *not* their ambition. This kind of entrepreneurship is too slow, too laborious, and too dull. The *liberal cultural eclectic* want to fast-track success and are prone to take shortcuts to pursue their ambitions. They tend to dream big and expect immediate results. For some, that leads to disappointment and stagnation. But for others, that builds character and motivates them to never give up.

Their experimentalism, of course, extends to other activities. They may test the extreme limits of any activity. They may engage in extreme sports, try different and even dangerous stimulants, or explore sexuality. But they may also become radically committed volunteers, go to extraordinary lengths for social justice, and invent micro-charities.

When churches do connect with the *liberal cultural eclectic*, they tend to be extreme churches. People in this group may become involved in divergent church plants, or original and quirky outreach ministries. They may be attracted to megachurches that preach the "theology of success"; or that sponsor a particular outreach ministry that is their current passion. But "current" is the keyword. They are less likely to expand their interest in a church per se, and less likely to sustain their interest over time. The church is simply not experimental enough, daring enough, or sufficiently urgent for their ambitions.

In Debt

The young, urban, socially hyperactive, single, educated, holistic, under-valued, and experimental people in the *liberal cultural eclectic* are extremely anxious about debt. Many have accumulated significant student loans. Although they tend to be urban, some must buy and maintain automobiles for work. Since they often do not receive medical benefits from work, any health-related issue is dauntingly expensive.

People tend to live simply, but this is more of a necessity than a virtue. Only by living simply can they afford to enjoy night life, keep up with fashion and technology trends, and occasionally splurge on travel. They also like to be generous when they have extra money. They will give sacrificially to charitable causes, and particularly for victims of natural disasters, war or oppression, domestic violence, street crime, and so forth.

Many baby boomers of the former cultural left dreamed of wealth and ended up managing wealth. The *liberal cultural eclectic*, however, dream of debt freedom and learn how to manage, eliminate, and avoid debt. In a sense, this makes them less materialistic. They don't collect things, fill their space with family antiques and heirlooms, and maintain large wardrobes. On the other hand, this makes them more materialistic. Their simple lives often include the highest-quality electronics, kitchenware, bicycles, running shoes, and sports gear. The dream of debt freedom, and the resulting simplified lifestyle, leads them to hate waste. They care about the environment . . . and they hate pollution . . . and they intentionally recycle.

Debt freedom is a passion because most of the *liberal cultural eclectic* sense the precariousness of life. They are always living on the edge. They are vulnerable to crises of health, unemployment, crime, and other unpleasant surprises. Many would like to start families if they could only achieve the long-term financial stability that seems to elude them. They often enjoy the present because they fear the future. The "Zombie Apocalypse" is a symbol for their ominous intuitions.

Churches often fail to look behind the veneer of self-confidence, and the appearance of materialism, to see the insecurity and resentment within them. They are very good at having fun, but they can carry significant anger toward society and baby boomers in particular. Churches that include debt management coaching in their stewardship strategy often find that this program opens possibilities of empathy, trust, and (eventually) significant conversation.

PLAYLIST SPIRITUALITY

The evolution and disruption of the music industry provides a helpful metaphor to understand spirituality among the *liberal cultural eclectic.*

The grandparents of this cultural group chose and listened to music *by genre.* Their preference would be substantially loyal to classical or opera, jazz or blues. They bought vinyl records from a store that dedicated specific sections to each genre, occasionally dividing this further into favorite orchestras or musicians. In the same way, their grandparents tended to choose and listen to faith traditions *by denomination.* They participated in an institutional church at a specific location that was different from other institutional churches, even one next door.

The parents of the *liberal cultural eclectic* chose and listened to music *by album.* There were more choices. One could listen to vinyl records, tapes, or CDs, but they were still purchased from stores that now dedicated specific sections to particular musical groups or performers. These people built musical libraries at home, and purchased expensive and elaborate electronics to play music. In the same way, their parents tended to choose and listen to religious leaders, and might even follow them to different locations, or find them on radio or television. They might ignore denominational identity and focus on individual messages.

57

The *liberal cultural eclectic* choose and listen to music *by playlist*. The stores are gone. The genres are blurred between "classic" and "pop," and even that distinction is inconsistently defined by individuals. And there is no reason to waste money on an album, and waste time listening to mediocre songs while waiting for the one you like. You can easily create, order, modify, and/or delete your favorites every minute of every day. There is no physical library that requires expensive equipment, but only a portable library that requires a miniature, low-cost device that you can take everywhere.

In the same way, the *liberal cultural eclectic* create—and re-create—their personal *playlists* of spirituality. A single playlist can be customized with faith traditions the individual prefers; prioritize the preachers or gurus the individual likes; and select the messages with which the individual agrees most at any given moment. That playlist spans religious traditions and cultures; supernatural predilections and moral philosophies; and social concerns and ideologies. Moreover, the playlist can be modified to follow whatever ideas or issues, leaders or gurus, happen to be trending at any given time.

Perhaps the biggest revolution in music is in how it is enjoyed and shared. Music for their grandparents was generally *public* and *polite*. People could only listen to it in concerts or through external speakers that spread the sound across the room and occasionally between apartments. That meant listeners had to be polite to their neighbors. If neighbors elevated the volume in competition with one another, eventually no one would be able to enjoy anything.

Music for their parents was still largely *public*, but much less *polite*. The shift in music from lyric to rhythm meant that some music, from some speakers, could drown out the competition. That motivated the use of cumbersome earphones that would allow listeners who preferred less popular music to still enjoy themselves.

But music for the *liberal cultural eclectic* is either intensely private or extremely public with little in between. On the one hand, listeners can "tune out" the "interference" of the world and listen to their playlist anytime in any activity. They can be so caught up in their music and oblivious to the world that they jog into trees, step out in front of cars, drop out of conversations, or miss urgent communications. On the other hand, listeners can call attention to themselves by forcing everyone around them to hear their playlist whether they like it or not. It is no longer polite.

Again, the shift from religion to spirituality is like the evolution (revolution) of music. For the grandparents of the *liberal cultural eclectic*, faith took the form of religion because it was necessarily public. There were "rules of engagement" that everyone needed to follow to get the most out of their faith. These structures included doctrines and dogmas, liturgies and polities. Religion, therefore, tended to be polite. True, there were some religions that were intentionally confrontational with other religions, but by in large "ecumenicity" meant mutual tolerance and respect.

Faith for their parents was still largely public, and took the form of religion, but the "rules of engagement" changed. If they paid their dues, participated in worship occasionally, voted on church policies, and claimed to belong to a specific denomination in a census or survey, they were faithful. Meanwhile, all the doctrine and dogma, spiritual practice and interactive principles, became private. And woe to any church leader who tried to hold them publicly accountable for what they privately did or did not believe! Faith became less polite . . . and even confrontational . . . whenever the boundary was crossed.

Today, faith for the *liberal cultural eclectic* is intensely private. Not only is religion unnecessary, but the "rules of engagement" for the institutional participation of their grandparents get in the way of spiritual insight. And the "rules of engagement" for the institutional participation of their parents get in the way of spiritual honesty. Public conversation about spirituality actually tends to be *impolite*, unless it is with a small group of intimate friends with maximum trust. Spirituality is a potpourri, a smorgasbord, or an olio, of diverse beliefs or superstitions that may be organized in a playlist of the mind, some of which may be clearly contradictory, and which are not a coherent or systematic theology. Indeed, the *liberal cultural eclectic* tend to resent any attempt to force consistency of faith as an attack on their independence and against the laws of nature. They are quite comfortable with contradiction and paradox as a kind of validation of themselves and their spiritual openness.

There are several paradoxes that shape the playlist spirituality of the *liberal cultural eclectic*.

Skeptical and Gullible: I almost believe it!

The *liberal cultural eclectic* have an approach/avoidance behavior pattern about God. In a sense, this parallels the same approach/avoidance pattern they often demonstrate in their intimate relationships. They prefer to live together, but never marry. They prefer to experiment with spirituality forever, but never commit. It may be that this is a way to avoid ultimate responsibility. If anything happens to radically change the lifestyle of their intimate partner (e.g., physical or mental health, bankruptcy, incarceration, and so on) they can still just walk away. And if anything happens to radically change the lifestyle of God (e.g., death, war, natural catastrophe, or some other inexplicable evil), they can still deny the association.

On the one hand, the *liberal cultural eclectic* are extremely skeptical of all religion and make fun of all religious practices. They debunk miracles and mock saints. They relish contradictions in the Bible or other so-called authoritative texts, and revise "salvation histories" as socio-political movements and cultural creations. They explain away faith as a necessary psychological dependency for some people. They take seriously conspiracy theories dating back centuries to prove that religious traditions are political power plays and religious rites and practices are in fact subtle manipulations.

On the other hand, the *liberal cultural eclectic* is extraordinarily gullible about emerging spiritualties, with a tendency to embrace or invent odd rituals. They are often superstitious and remarkably fatalistic (which makes them predisposed to gambling). They are often open to the paranormal and fascinated by the possibility of ghosts (which leads them to follow television programs in search of Sasquatch). They may be ensnared by cults. They may even take seriously the emerging spiritualties associated with extraterrestrial aliens. Many of their regiments for physical fitness, food preparation and diet, sports, music, and other activities are repetitive priorities for their time, and they can argue about them with intensity that resembles the passion of religious factions.

The *spiritual playlist*, therefore, is an odd mix of individualism and romance. It is an odd mix of earthiness (bordering on crudity) and otherworldliness (bordering on utopian naiveté). Each individual theological playlist contains tracks that both dwell on the sordid and dream of the sublime.

Cynical and Optimistic: I wish I could believe that!

The *liberal cultural eclectic* alternates between extreme cynicism about all institutions and institutional expectations and remarkably naïve wishful thinking. In a sense, this paradox parallels their ambivalence about wealth. They are often minimalists and even paranoid about debt, and yet long for the trappings of success and splurge on their credit cards. Similarly, they are

60

often minimalists about faith (reducing all religion to "love") and even paranoid of religious leaders (condemning them all as hypocrites); and yet long for inner peace and passionately follow the spiritual opinions of superstars and sports heroes.

On the one hand, the *liberal cultural eclectic* exudes negativity. Their life experience is one of constantly broken political promises, disappointment with the measurable outcomes of higher education, exclusion from senior management, and failure to exceed (much less sustain) the upward mobility of their parents. Their negativity extends to the church, because it also has broken promises about happiness and justice, disappointed expectations for change and relevance, excluded vast groups of people in the name of inclusivity, and failed to trust them more than (or even as much as) their parents and grandparents.

On the other hand, the *liberal cultural eclectic* exudes gaiety. They have fun and laugh easily. Their nightlife can often be raucous. Their freedom can be exhilarating. They often live one day at a time and enjoy life one moment at a time. They celebrate a comradery of peers who are instinctively supportive. They do everything with energy and passion, including spirituality (however temporary any given spirituality might be), then pursue it with intensity. However difficult a cause or catastrophe might be, they address sacrificially. As long as any spirituality can take them into deeper self-awareness and change the world for the better, they are enthusiastic participants.

The spiritual playlist, therefore, is an unexpected mix of realism (bordering on nihilism) and idealism (bordering on fantasy). It fluctuates between depression and ecstasy. Therefore, it is an odd-mix of world-weariness and playful fun. Each individual theological playlist contains tracks that condemn religious hypocrisy as a major obstacle to world peace, and elevate spirituality as a solution with a mystical framework for justice.

Secular and Pantheistic: I believe nothing and everything!

The *liberal cultural eclectic* believes nothing, but then accepts the unenviable position of being forced to believe everything. They live in a secular world of materialism and meaninglessness, pollution and climate change, disintegrating infrastructure and cultural dystopia. And precisely because of this they also live in a world that is a bubbling cauldron of spirituality. It is a world in which everything is internally related to everything else, and contains a hidden meaning beyond comprehension. Nature and humanity are intertwined, and we can catch glimpses of utopia through technology, entertainment, and drugs.

On the one hand, the *liberal cultural eclectic* are rationally secular. Many of them live in urban contexts that tend to be dehumanizing. Their world can be grimy and dangerous, dirty and violent, in which "dog eats dog." It is a world of high unemployment and part-time work without benefits. It is more important to be clever than educated, to know the right people rather than do the right thing, and to cut corners rather than achieve perfection. The church fades into the background, much as most church buildings have become dark, sooty, looming monuments amid the neon signs and apartment buildings. Any way you look at it, the church simply does not make sense. It takes up otherwise useful space; and it spends money on useless stuff that could be donated to social service; it makes pronouncements to which no one pays attention; and it gathers people together whose lifestyle is altogether different than their peer groups.

On the other hand, the *liberal cultural eclectic* are intuitively pantheistic. There is a divine spark within every person, making each person a part of a universal spirit. Every person is a potential saint. Every object is a potential talisman. Every activity is a potential sacrament. Spirituality and creation are two sides of the same coin. If you honor natural law and protect the environment, you are fulfilling a sacred duty. The church may have hidden God underneath layers of dogma and manipulation, but somehow God is everywhere and in everything. And we come closer to experiencing the divine through art and music, or through nature, or through sex, or through anything that is about relationship rather than dogma; just as we are *unlikely* to experience the divine through academic theology, a standard church worship service, post-worship refreshments, or anything that supports dogma rather than relationship.

The spiritual playlist, therefore, focuses primarily on the *immanence* of the divine. Unlike ancient stoics or modern theists, however, that immanence is not of the mind. The rationality of humankind is neither proof nor bridge to universal truth. Instead, the immanence of the divine is a relationship of *soul* to *center*, or a participation in a universal process. "Truth" is not a noun, but a verb. It is better to say that human spirit participates in the "truing" of the universe. This action is primarily a matter of the heart (or soul) as it is empathic with all people and all things.

Relativistic and Absolutist: I am absolutely uncertain!

The *liberal cultural eclectic* are usually accused of being radically relativistic. If spirit is about relationship, and truth is a process, then good and bad or right and wrong change as relationships change. Yet their relativism does have limits. Uncertainty and ambiguity are absolutes in themselves, since the *liberal cultural eclectic* cannot imagine an end to the unfolding process. The mind, therefore, is really about control rather than understanding. The mind is a tool . . . or a weapon . . . used to obtain whatever we desire.

If life is a process, then ego is absolute. The *liberal cultural eclectic* tend to be self-absorbed for a reason. The one thing ultimately and consistently significant in life is *me*. These people are always on the move, and in a sense, they take their world with them. They shape their environments to suit their personalities. In this, they are aided by postmodern technology. There is always a soundtrack running in the background (privately walking down the sidewalk with earphones, or publicly driving down the street with resonant bass).

And so, on the one hand, the *liberal cultural eclectic* are radically relativistic. Morality is defined so ambiguously that almost any behavior can be justified. They resist all attempts by the church, or other institutions, to control their behavior or limit their options. Freedom of speech, thought, and action is paramount.

But on the other hand, the *liberal cultural eclectic* can be remarkably absolutist. Ideologies can be unshakeable and confrontational. They do whatever they can to impose their priorities, which inevitably limit the options of others. Freedom of speech, thought, and action may *not* be offered to critics. They can be radically inclusive, and radically exclusive, at the same time.

Ego alone is not enough for more and more of these people. Many are embarking on a new quest for absolutes. The relativist today may become the cultist of tomorrow. The aesthete today may become the monk of tomorrow. The agnostic today may become the fundamentalist of tomorrow. What is interesting is that there is rarely middle ground or much of a transition timeline. This is partly why mainline churches are often bypassed as some people in the *liberal cultural eclectic* go directly to new and demanding religious movements or very conservative evangelical churches.

The spiritual playlist, therefore, can be mellow and strident, lyrical and rhythmic, harmonious and discordant at the same time. Each individual theological playlist will contain tracks that are extremely self-centered and extremely self-sacrificial, but the one common denominator is that the "self" is central: always in control or striving to be in control; or not in control and resentful of being trapped.

Open and Intolerant: Anyone can be included— except conservatives!

The *liberal cultural eclectic* pride themselves on their openness to everyone and any culture, everything and any idiosyncrasy, and every idea and any fantasy. Like their predecessors in the 1960s, they are exceedingly communal, content with simplicity, and able to adjust to almost any social context. They take people at face value, just as they are, without judgment . . . and expect to be treated the same way.

On the other hand, the *liberal cultural eclectic* can behave with remarkable exclusivity. "Openness" is in itself an ideology, and anyone who places limits on "openness" is an enemy. They can find it hard to adapt to organizations that insist on high accountability. They can react violently to any ideology that places any limitations on behavior, mobility, or imagination. They will advocate a cause with passion, but they will also advocate *against* a cause with equal passion.

The spiritual playlist, therefore, is either very passive or very aggressive, and there is not much in between. It is very private. You can listen to whatever music or spirituality that you want. And yet it can be very public. You are forced to listen to what I like. No one has the right to tell me what music or spirituality I follow; but I reserve the right to tell others what music or spirituality is bad or wrong. The boundary between private and public is ambiguous, but the *liberal cultural eclectic*, who are usually open to so much ambiguity, are often unable to cope with this one ambiguity.

What is often missing among the *liberal cultural eclectic* is the willingness to dialogue with their opposite number (which I will describe shortly as the *conservative cultural wedge*). This reticence is, of course, shared by their opposite number. They need other lifestyle segments to help them bridge that gap. Unfortunately, these are primarily lifestyle segments of the *disempowered middle*.

Playlist theology is different from journey theology in both methodology and content. This reflects the transition from the late modern context to the early postmodern context. The late modern context was shaped by cold war, individual mobility, economic boom, progressive civil rights, and churches in slow decline. The early postmodern context is shaped by terrorism, mass migrations, economic recession, regressive civil rights, and churches in precipitous decline.

The context of late modernity made the methodology of journey theology possible. It was all about patience, spiritual exploration, emerging self-awareness, and the optimism that somehow, one day, everything would be understood, justice would be served, poverty would be eliminated, disease would be cured, and society would be whole. In many ways, the philosophy and plot of *Star Trek* typified the methodology. We have left behind social ills, to join a multiethnic crew of explorers, to travel where no one has gone before . . . and the only prime directive was to do no wrong. The quest for God was motivated partly by boredom with the church, and mainly by the search for meaning and purpose. And people had the time, income, and leisure to do it.

The problem was that as we entered the new millennium "journey theology" became "wandering spirituality." The "journey" hasn't arrived at the destination. Optimism is unfulfilled. Time is running out. The quest for God among the former cultural left is now motivated by the dread of aging and sense of guilt for the state of the world they are leaving for their children.

And the context has changed for the heirs of the cultural left, giving rise to playlist theology. This is all about impatience and skepticism. Success is a higher priority than self-awareness. Attitudes toward the future are pessimistic. Everything is a mess, and there doesn't seem to be a way out, nor are there credible leaders to find a way out. We are on the brink of "Zombie Apocalypse," and rather than going out to explore, we are retreating behind walls. The only prime directive is to win. The quest for God is motivated by frustration with leadership, and the need to be cleansed and liberated.

The *liberal cultural eclectic* are driven not by the dread of aging but by the challenge of surviving. Nor do they feel a sense of guilt for the state of the world. Instead, they feel shame for the state of the world. They do not experience an identity crisis but a lack of self-esteem. This is why the *liberal cultural eclectic* intuitively and empathically "feel" the pain of abused, molested, oppressed, and persecuted victims in the world. And they literally "feel" the pain of creation, the extinction of species, and the pollution of the environment. It's more than a problem; it's personal.

The former cultural left (now fragmented as baby boomers have diversified) felt threatened by chronic depression, fearing that their optimism might

65

not be fulfilled. The extreme *liberal cultural eclectic* are no longer optimistic and have become increasingly angry that they have inherited such a dysfunctional world. Baby boomers may have replaced "journey theology" with "wandering spirituality," but the *liberal cultural eclectic* are no longer certain that spirituality is even important.

MINISTRY AMONG THE LIBERAL CULTURAL ECLECTIC TODAY

Most church leaders acknowledge that the *liberal cultural eclectic* are the hardest group of people to reach. This may be hasty. There are still many who are interested in spirituality, although they may not call it that or experience it in the ways of modernity or classic Christianity. I think there are two dimensions to the alienation of this group from organized religion of any sort, and from organized Christianity in particular.

The first dimension is most obvious. Church leaders today seem to naturally think programmatically. They research program expectations, evaluate program realities, make program adjustments, and then manage the stress of change for their existing members. How far is the institutional church willing to adapt in order to reach them? Consider the three key programs that generally define the institutional church.

Worship

There is no doubt that the *liberal cultural eclectic* expect worship to be inspirational (fast paced, loud, image-rich spectacles or "epic" experiences). However, churches consistently draw a boundary between secular and sacred that these people find unnecessary and even prohibitive. For them the boundary doesn't exist. Therefore, there is no distinction between worship and entertainment. Worship should enthrall you. Entertainment should transform you. For them, at least, this does not make worship shallow. It makes entertainment profound.

The *liberal cultural eclectic* also expect worship to be practical. If there is a message to be shared, it is more effective as song and image than as spoken words. If there is a spoken message, they prefer it to be imminently practical rather than theoretical. They are not that interested in the nature of God or God's will for humanity. They are more interested in how God can help them deal with challenges and ambiguities of daily life. Therefore, any message in worship akin to a "sermon" must be dialogical. They will never be a passive audience who write down three heady points to think about the rest of the week. They will be active participants who debate any idea, and download a thought for the day on their way to work.

Many churches have given up trying to "blend" worship styles, and seek to provide multiple options. This is difficult. Most churches and denominations are too poor to hire new staff, retrain volunteers, and acquire new technology; and rely on redeploying existing staff, relying on untrained volunteers, and getting by with refurbished but old technology. The old habits die hard. Preachers, musicians, greeters, ushers, and teachers struggle to change their attitudes, and the changes made are not radical enough.

Education

The methodology, content, and learning environments for the *liberal cultural eclectic* do not fit the patterns of classic Christian education. This group will not routinely sit still in a classroom or a living room, studying curriculum written and approved by a hierarchy, in a group defined by age or gender. They might periodically and unexpectedly pause—in a café, sports arena, theater, or other public place—to discuss a hot or urgent topic, informed by diverse secular and religious sources, among a group of peers.

Yet I observe an even more radical trend. The key to Christian education for the *liberal cultural eclectic* is less and less a small group, and more and more a one-on-one mentoring relationship. Or to say it another way, the *liberal cultural eclectic* can be quite aware of the dangers of pooled ignorance, just as they are already aware of the superficiality of professional and certified teachers. They prefer to connect with a credible person who courageously lives their faith in both intentionally daring and totally spontaneous ways; who speaks from a history of sacrifice for a cause; who is focused on a goal of ultimate significance; and who cares enough about them to pause, talk, and share.

A good example of this trend was visible in the reconstruction of New Orleans after the hurricanes of 2005. The city became a Mecca for individual young adult volunteers and cross-generational mission teams from northern churches, yet established churches struggled to connect with them in the community or include them in their worship. Several Episcopal and Roman

Catholic parishes discovered, however, that their traditions of pilgrimage and communal living were surprisingly relevant. They started hostels that organized volunteers around disciplines of prayer and manual labor, with cells of volunteers guided by credible local lay leaders with reputations of courage saving people (and pets) from the floods.

Today's Christian education leaders have been raised with modern expectations and trained to use modern technologies and methods. They think like professional educators. They tend to assume that informational content and excellent communication are the most important aspects of learning. It is difficult for them to understand postmodern expectations from students and what data is revealing. The single most important aspect of learning is the lifestyle of the teacher. This is why, if they connect with a church at all, they are less likely to talk to the certified and ordained professional pastor, and more likely to talk to a musician, a missionary, or even the custodian. The spontaneous deed and the unrehearsed word reveal the truth to these people.

Outreach

Churches have had the most programmatic success reaching and involving the *liberal cultural eclectic* through social service ministries and opportunities. The best outreach is planned, managed, and evaluated based on the highest standards of accountability for nonprofit organizations. Poorly planned and badly managed outreach ministries that have only modest impact on communities or issues are an anathema.

Moreover, the themes and targets for social service have changed and expanded. Traditional churches tended to focus on "depot" ministries aimed at survival (e.g., food pantries, clothing distribution, and the like). They also tended to concentrate on fundraising to pay other experts (within or beyond the denomination) to do the actual work. There is little interest in this kind of outreach.

A *liberal cultural eclectic* prefers hands-on opportunities for service. They want to have collaborative relationships with people in the community. They want to see change happen before their very eyes. Social service still involves participation in food banks, homeless shelters, and the like. But it also focuses on improving quality of life, developing human potential, advocating justice, addiction intervention, and other aspects of social service.

There is, however, a second dimension to the alienation of the *liberal cultural eclectic* from the established church. No matter how the *programs* of the church change, the fundamental *systems* of church life are unappealing or irrelevant to them.

The "disciple-making process" is the default system of most established churches (mainstream or evangelical). You hear church leaders refer to it all the time. I myself taught it as a church consultant for many years. Yet it is often incomprehensible, or even reprehensible, for many in the *liberal cultural eclectic*.

The traditional institutional church expects worship to lead people into education, and education to move people to mission, and mission to result in more people being invited to worship. It is a classic strategy of church growth, and it is what many church leaders actually mean when they talk about "making disciples." The *liberal cultural eclectic* resist . . . and often resent . . . this strategy. This is why church leaders who have been successful with previous generations are at such a loss with this group.

The *liberal cultural eclectic* perceives worship, education, and outreach as a single activity. Worship *is* mission. It celebrates and motivates social transformation, prays for social justice, plans and advocates human rights, shares the sacrifices of volunteers, and offers tips and tactics to live well . . . and nothing else. Worship flows seamlessly into animated dialogue with mentors and peers in the café; and animated dialogue flows seamlessly into social action. Worship is where the action is. Action is where the worship is. There are no sidetracks for dogmatic pronouncements, friendly chatter over coffee hour, or fundraising to pay for maintenance and personnel. Outreach is the only measurable outcome that matters. There must be tangible, positive change in the world, or worship and education is meaningless and irrelevant.

Churches are generally concerned with bringing people to faith. But the *liberal cultural eclectic* are more interested in bringing people to hope. This helps explain their suspicions about traditional church leadership. If the church is about bringing people to faith, then clergy need to be seminary trained and understand church doctrine, church history, and biblical interpretation. They are professionals. But the *liberal cultural eclectic* are skeptical of their sincerity, their experience with the real world, and their ability to personally overcome the very anxieties and fears that terrify people in this lifestyle group. They do not look for professionals but for role models. They do not look for institutional church leaders or recipients of philanthropic

69

awards, but for genuine heroes of faith whose sacrifices have demonstrably blessed the community.

Recently, a denomination sought my advice to reach the many lifestyle segments of the *liberal cultural eclectic* in the area around Washington, DC. This was a time of especially disastrous climate change with hurricanes or typhoons across the Gulf Coast and in the Pacific Rim, uncontrolled wild fires on the West Coast and in countries such as Portugal, and renewed famine in sub-Saharan Africa, and so on.

I suggested the following: Rather than starting or renewing a church, create a "Center for Catastrophic Intervention" with the purpose of training and sending relief teams and supplies to work alongside victims of climate change. Staff it with an experienced nonprofit CEO who is a role model for Christian virtues and passionate about God's love for all people. Locate the "office" in a Christian coffee house or microbrewery. Rent space for training and warehousing. Arrange emergency transportation with an airline. And directly approach wealthy entrepreneurs (especially those with multicultural backgrounds) to invest. Advertise and recruit among lifestyles of the *liberal cultural eclectic*, especially targeting campuses and surrounding neighborhoods of colleges and universities.

I suggested they rent an auditorium four times a year for inspirational worship and celebration of mission; allow any number of small groups to come and go around mission causes. Model Christian values. Articulate an inclusive Christian faith. But avoid church property overhead, line budgets, preaching clergy, weekly worship, membership recruitment, educational curricula, dogmatic pronouncements, and committees.

My suggestion was met with personal enthusiasm, but institutional pessimism. As much as they would like to do it . . . and knew they could do it . . . they knew that their denomination wouldn't do it. The church still insisted that they measure results by the number of baptisms and confirmations, membership growth, weekly worship attenders, first-time visitors, midweek small groups, Sunday school attendance, balanced budgets, and denominational dues.

There is a postscript, however, to the acknowledgment that traditional institutional churches will likely remain on the sidelines with the *liberal cultural eclectic*. I have already mentioned that a renewed quest for absolutes is taking some of the *liberal cultural eclectic* to more dogmatic and conservative churches. As we shall see later, these former liberals will join a growing radical right. Yet another movement is visible. Some of the *liberal cultural eclectic* are renewing their interest in Eucharistic churches such as the Greek Orthodox Church, Anglican or Episcopal Church, and some Roman Catholic churches in more ideologically liberal dioceses. I would not want to exaggerate this trend, but it is there. These Eucharistic churches often understand the essence of Christian discipleship less dogmatically and more mystically. Ritual and history, aesthetics and solemnity, create a sense of the *immanence* of God. Discipleship for them is less about *allegiance* to a doctrine, and more about *unity* with Christ that is beyond words.

Chapter 3

THE
CULTURALLY RIGHTEOUS

Whatever happened to the cultural right?

The *culturally righteous*, described here, is trending in almost the opposite direction to the *culturally ambivalent*. The baby boomers often associated with the left have splintered in a variety of directions, and there is no longer a sense of generational unity. Values and beliefs have become increasingly individualized and personalized. Emerging generations tend to be more self-indulgent and less committed to the hard work of long-term social change. Lifestyle segments associated with the *culturally righteous*, however, have become more united and more assertive . . . and their ranks have grown to include a number of disaffected former liberals. Values and beliefs have become dogmatized and universalized. Emerging generations tend to be more sacrificial and highly committed to the hard work of long-term social change.

The church is the "canary in the mine shaft" of cultural extremes. It is perhaps the first and most visible institution to feel the impact of this cultural divide. Ecumenism is extinct, and local clergy associations that once brought leaders from all traditions and theologies together have all but disappeared. It is even difficult to achieve cooperation on social outreach as each evangelical, mainstream, and Roman Catholic denomination and church manage parallel and competing programs. Mainstream church leaders make condescending jokes about evangelical Christians from their pulpits, and evangelical church leaders make strident denunciations of mainstream churches from their pulpits.

The *culturally ambivalent* and the mainstream churches that represent their spiritualties have become increasingly individualistic. Faith is a matter of personal choice, and no one is given the right to criticize what the individual believes, or hold individuals accountable for how they behave. Adults refrain from teaching children about faith so that "they can decide for themselves once they grow up." The *culturally righteous* and the evangelical churches that represent their doctrinal nuances have become increasingly hierarchical and more tribal. Faith is a matter of community enculturation, and the church has a divine responsibility to criticize what individuals believe and hold people accountable to objective standards of behavior. To the *culturally righteous*, mainstream churches of the *culturally ambivalent* are pluralistic and permissive. To the *culturally ambivalent*, evangelical churches of the *culturally righteous* are narrow-minded and judgmental.

The shift in terminology from the cultural right of 1990 to the *culturally righteous* thirty years later is significant and requires explanation. Three factors shape the "righteousness" of the *culturally righteous* today: certainty, urgency, and opportunism. The factors that shaped the cultural right thirty years ago were modesty, patience, and optimism.

The shift from "modesty" to "certainty" has more to do with style than content. Thirty years ago the cultural right was certain about an array of values and beliefs. But they were more willing to discuss disagreements and explore ambiguities. They placed themselves in a wider conversation about ethics, meaning, and purpose. The *culturally righteous* today are less willing to discuss disagreements, or even acknowledge ambiguities. Conversations are now lopsided, intent on convincing people to agree or at least conform to specific views.

This might be said, of course, of the *liberal cultural eclectic*, but it is one thing to be utterly convinced about nothing, and utterly open to everything; and another thing to be utterly convinced of something, and intentionally critical of everything. The *culturally righteous* have a solidarity of opinion about ethics, meaning, and purpose in life. The *liberal cultural eclectic* reveal an inherent disunity, because individuals can (and probably should) have different perspectives.

The shift from "patience" to "urgency" reveals the growing sense of crisis that drives the *culturally righteous* to action. Thirty years ago the cultural right felt that time was on their side. Political processes would work efficiently (albeit slowly). Economic downturns would be reversed. Children would grow up, marry, have children, and return to church and accept the values and beliefs of their elders. The *culturally righteous* today feel that time is running out, and that things may well not return to normal. Society is on the brink. The time to simply pray over problems and send petitions to government representatives has ended. Now is the time for advocacy and confrontation.

This might also be said about the *liberal cultural eclectic*. Each has a sense of apocalyptic times. The difference is that the *liberal cultural eclectic* believe "civilization" is threatened by things like global warming, military intervention, racism, wealth inequality, and sexual abuse. Meanwhile, the *culturally righteous* believe that the "kingdom of God" is threatened by things like permissive sexuality, political corruption, mass migrations, and wealth redistribution. Each dismisses the apocalyptic sensitivities of the other as exaggerated or nonexistent.

The shift from "optimism" to "opportunism" reveals the escalating aggressiveness or entrepreneurship of the *culturally righteous*. Thirty years ago the optimism of the cultural right was expressed through institutional loyalty and confidence that the Holy Spirit was working behind the scenes in mysterious ways. The *culturally righteous* today have tempered optimism with initiative. They bypass traditional institutions to establish faith-based non-profits and create partisan political lobbies. The Holy Spirit is working right in front of our eyes in specific ways. They no longer wait for opportunities. They create opportunities.

No doubt the *culturally ambivalent* or the *liberal cultural eclectic* are also opportunistic. They can also bypass traditional institutions to create highly efficient, morally superior non-profits and interventions. The difference is that their opportunism is motivated more by a profound sense of pessimism than an overweening sense of optimism. Hang around with the *culturally ambivalent* and one feels a sense of depression and dread. Yes, their opportunistic venture is right, but it may well (and probably will) fail. Hang around the *culturally righteous* and one feels a sense of anticipation and excitement. They believe their opportunistic venture is not only right but will inevitably succeed.

What has changed? What caused these shifts among the cultural right to transform them into the *culturally righteous*?

The shift has been occurring through the second half of the twentieth century, but it dramatically accelerated with the new millennium. What was once a trickle became a deluge. One can probably point to specific events that accelerated these shifts: Supreme Court decisions in favor of birth control, affirmative action, digital age and loss of privacy, environmental regulations,

9/11 and the threat of terrorism, mass migrations, the recession of 2008, same-sex marriage, job loss to technology, corporate migrations from mid-market cities to other countries, and so on.

The underlying trend, however, is globalization. The lifestyle segments of the *culturally ambivalent* have largely benefited by globalization; but the lifestyle segments of the *culturally righteous* (and increasing those of the *culturally passive*) have not. Globalization for this group has meant job losses; stagnant or decreasing incomes; mobility and fractured families; dual careers and stressed-out marriages; loss of small-town and neighborhood identities; fewer educational opportunities; acceptance of unfamiliar religions and strange customs; and a host of personal pleasures limited or taken away, such as smoking and drinking, fishing and hunting, or a carefree stroll in the park with your loved ones.

Globalization for the lifestyle groups of the *culturally righteous* has generally meant disempowerment and a growing sense of victimization. Their lifestyles have been stereotyped and mocked as they have been shamed in the media. Many have not "succeeded" by the standards of the globalized world, have less self-esteem, and resent it. Some have been very successful by the standards of the globalized world, but refuse to be evaluated by the globalized world. They still hold themselves accountable to the values and beliefs of their roots. They object to elitism and showy pride, disapprove of media and sports idols, and resent confusing bureaucracies and corrupt politicians. Their anger has been growing for some time.

Tex Sample powerfully describes the emerging "blue-collar rage" of the working class.[1] They no longer have a fair share of decision-making power in America. They are different from, and denigrated by, urban and suburban people. They receive less and less from the government for economic, health, educational, and emergency and law enforcement resources. However, these feelings are now shared by a broader constituency than only the working class. Furthermore, Tex Sample convincingly demonstrates why income and education, which are most commonly used to define demographic groups, are no longer useful for defining class consciousness.

The cultural right of the past used to be limited to lifestyle segments that were poorer or less educated. This led lifestyle groups of the cultural left to mistakenly assume that better wages and higher education would naturally

---

1. Tex Sample, *Working Class Rage: A Field Guide to White Pain* (Nashville: Abingdon Press, forthcoming in 2018).

lead to secular habits and liberal attitudes. If you merely label a package of cigarettes as harmful, then surely people will give up smoking. If you prove statistically that gun control reduces the number of deaths by violence, then surely people will support gun control legislation. The same logic is revealed in hundreds of less-controversial ways. It hasn't worked. In the past, the cultural left came to the conclusion that many lifestyle groups of the cultural right must therefore be stupid or belligerent. The *culturally righteous*, in turn, argue that the cause-and-effect logic from the old cultural left is flawed.

The network of lifestyle groups that are included in the *culturally righteous* today is much more complex. Education and wealth are not the determining factors. Two dynamics help us understand them better.

The first dynamic seems to be economically driven and is the combination of occupation, location, and income. These three factors are often visible in the lifestyle choices of the *culturally righteous*. While some people among the *culturally righteous* have careers in executive managerial positions or professional specialities, many are employed in farming, construction, industrial production, transportation, middle management and franchises, food service, security, and health care or personal support occupations. Many rely on hourly wages with limited or no benefits. Fewer and fewer are protected by unions. Many work in jobs highly vulnerable to economic boom and bust.

Economic Influences on the *Culturally Righteous*

It is more accurate to say that lifestyle groups among the *culturally righteous* may not be wealthy, but they are often not poor. There is a margin of disposable income that can be used for entertainment and limited travel, children's educations, and retirement. It is that margin, however, that is threatened as the gap between affluence and poverty widens. Job preservation is not necessarily an issue of survival, but it is always an issue for quality of life. This is most visible in the deteriorating condition of their houses or living spaces, because that has to become a lower priority for disposable income. Yet appearances are important to these lifestyle groups, and inability to sustain the home place hurts their pride.

Occupational demands and income vulnerabilities mean that lifestyle groups among the *culturally righteous* prefer to live in towns or neighborhoods close to the place of occupation. Since many households rely on multiple incomes, they often choose to locate closest to the most vulnerable income earner. There are several reasons. First, commuting and transportation costs often involve long-term debt, so the debt should be applied to sustain the most secure job. Second, proximity to the family home and the support networks of the neighborhood help address temporary layoffs, disability, and long-term unemployment. If there is a spouse commuting, they usually hate it and long to return home.

This dynamic is passed on through the generations. The media stereotype is that young adults leave home as soon as they can to escape the restrictions of family and the limitations of small towns and neighborhoods where everybody knows your name. The reality is usually the opposite. Young adults often choose occupations and accept lower incomes in order to remain at home or in the same location. If they do relocate, they either choose to live in satellite cities or neighborhoods that look like home; or they choose to live in beltway residences from which they can easily get home. Even if all that is impossible, their houses, households, and families model their experience of home. If they ever have a good job opportunity back home, they are very likely to take it even if it means slightly lower income and saying goodbye to their friends.[2]

The second dynamic seems to be more relationally driven and is the combination of family, education, and religion. Again, these are interrelated (and obviously link to the first dynamic). While some people among the *culturally righteous* are single, divorced, cohabiting adults, and single parents, most *value* traditional family life (married male/female partnerships, with multiple children and even multiple generations, living happily together and sharing common interests). They either have it, or aspire to achieve or return to it. Making babies and caring for elders are givens. Many lifestyle groups of the *culturally righteous* readily accept cross-cultural or merged families, but they expect they will resemble traditional family units. The more the family is threatened, however, the more they will look to education and religion to sustain it.

---

2. I think, for example, of lifestyle segments Experian currently describes as F23 *Families Matter Most* (that often include military families); or M44 *Red, White and Bluegrass*.

Lifestyle groups among the *culturally righteous* tend to be *theoretically* intolerant, and *practically* quite generous. I think this is because values are actually more important than beliefs. How one behaves has more impact on family and community life than how one thinks. The *culturally righteous* can include Protestants, Catholics, and Mormons; "Fundamentalists," "Charismatics and Pentecostals" and even the "spiritual-but-not-religious." What matters more are the values taught, modeled, and used for accountability. Those values tend to revolve around family and interpersonal relationships in general. To be sure, these lifestyle groups do not tend to distinguish between beliefs and values. But they are able to make distinctions between essentials and nonessentials, and they are more likely to measure outcomes than appreciate processes.

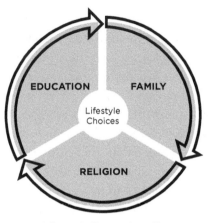

Values Influencing the Culturally Righteous

Family and religious priorities shape educational expectations. Lifestyle groups included in the *culturally righteous* want to learn, and they want their children to learn. One reason most rural lifestyle segments value the church is that their church often is one consistent opportunity to learn and acquire life skills. Almost all of these lifestyle segments value educated clergy, and assume that the clergy know what they are talking about. Despite media reports, controversy about public school education is not really about overturning facts with faith or including the Lord's Prayer in every classroom. The frustration is more about the tendency for public education to exclude faith as an important part of a shared life altogether.

This dynamic preserves educational priorities, family expectations, and religious assumptions that predate the scientific-technical revolution that began around 1940 and have accelerated to the present. In a sense, the very definition of truth changed, and the *culturally righteous* never adapted. Among the *culturally ambivalent* and even among many of the *culturally passive*, "truth" became limited to facts pursued by technology, verified by science, and interpreted by younger generations that were inevitably better informed and more creative. Among the *culturally righteous*, "truth" continued to include insights from tradition, revelation, and intuition. Truth was pursued by community, verified by religion, and interpreted by older generations that were inevitably wiser and more experienced. This is why Catholicism prior to Vatican II and a resurgent neo-Calvinism are vital to the identity of the cultural right. They protect educational priorities for traditional worldviews, classic family structures and parenting models, and religious tradition or divine revelation.

It is very helpful to keep these two dynamics in mind to understand the *culturally righteous* and their perspective on faith. Just as the *culturally ambivalent* have separated "spirituality" from "religion," so also the *culturally righteous* have separated "faith" from "religion." Religion is part of the dynamic that includes family and education, which means that church attendance and adherence to some institutional expectations is included in their weekly spiritual habits. But it would be a mistake to assume that the first dynamic of occupation, location, and income is somehow separate from faith. Such a separation is often true for the *culturally ambivalent* and the *culturally passive*, but not here. Faith penetrates every aspect of lifestyle choice. It shapes what you do for work, where and how you live and raise a family, and even how much income you keep and how much you give to God. The *culturally righteous* have always known what the *culturally ambivalent* are only just discovering, namely, that life and faith (or life and spirituality) can and must go together.

This helps explain some of the oddities about behavior among the *culturally righteous* that perplex the *culturally ambivalent*. They tithe, or give a much larger proportion of net income to the church or faith-based non-profits. They insist that faith be incorporated into public education, and tend to drop out of public education for separate faith-based schools (e.g., "Catholic" or "Christian"). They object to certain medical procedures and clinics. They are reluctant to provide professional services for programs directly related to family morality (e.g., providing refreshments for the marriage of same-sex couples). They are hesitant to pay taxes to intentionally secular governments. They contradict their own unions if a strike goes against their conscience, or refuse to join unions altogether. Such behavior is odd to the *culturally ambivalent*, but perfectly sensible to the *culturally righteous*.

Evangelical and Catholic churches, however, should also take note of these two dynamics, and the separation of all-pervasive "faith" from obligations to religious institutions. Pastors and denominations may well make the mistake of thinking that it is religion that is all-pervasive, and may assume authority to tell people where to live and what to do; define the targets for charitable giving or limit accumulation of wealth; dictate the curricula of education and hire/fire educational leaders at will; and impose rules and limitations on marriage and family. The *culturally righteous* may accept this for a time (usually based on the personal credibility or charisma of the pastor), but in the end they will reject it (and such authority cannot be passed on to the next pastor). In the same way that spirituality is "personal" to the individual for the *culturally ambivalent*, so also faith is "personal" to the family of the *culturally righteous*. Family trumps church.

DIVERSITY AND UNITY AMONG THE CULTURALLY RIGHTEOUS

In order to glimpse the breadth and diversity of the lifestyle groups included today in the *culturally righteous*, it may help to look at two iconic, very popular, long-running television programs that have generated a national visibility and community presence beyond the media itself. This is risky, of course, because all programs come and go, and what is aired and readily recognized by readers of this book today may be over and forgotten by readers tomorrow. Yet the larger organizations these programs have developed are likely to persist at least for the lifetimes of the television personalities involved.

One emblematic program was *Duck Dynasty*, which followed the interrelationship of lifestyle and faith for the extended Robertson family in rural West Monroe, Louisiana, based on a family-operated business that made duck calls. The reality show ended in March 2017 and generated bestselling books and products marketed across the United States and Canada. The personalities involved, and the context of the program, fulfill a major stereotype of rural, agrarian, under-educated, simple-living folk who dress poorly and wear long beards. The lives that unfold and the stories they tell, however, intentionally shatter that stereotype by depicting a remarkably cosmopolitan, talented, intelligent people who have made deliberate lifestyle choices of family over career, faith over doubt, simplicity over technology, and patriotism over cynicism.

The stereotype markets well. They are presented as a snapshot of authentic early Americans with few possessions and strong family relationships. In the modern world they eschew technology and social media and a contract is a handshake. The stereotype, however, is deliberately tongue-in-cheek. Obviously they value television, understand sound marketing principles, and a contract is in writing and specifies obligations and limitations. The values, however, remain the same. They seem to rise above competition with love and forgiveness, and overcome adversity with faith and humility, hard work, and an ability to take God seriously while laughing at themselves.

The family has been controversial. They have been vocal about their conservative views of sexuality; and they have quarreled with their own network about needless censorship of their references to Jesus, which they take as a violation of their rights to religious views and freedom of expression. Despite a much more profound picture of the generosity and compassion of the *culturally righteous*, many viewers from the *culturally ambivalent* and *culturally passive* will still see them as judgmental and exclusive. They still sense (rightly or wrongly) pride beneath the humility and business savvy beneath the piety. I suspect all of the above is true, and that the conservative Robertson family is as flawed as the average liberal family, which suggests that the criticism of what's bad about the "goose" should also be a criticism of what's bad about the "gander."

The second emblematic program is *Fixer Upper*, which follows the inter-relationship of lifestyle and faith for the Gaines family in Waco, Texas, based on their experiences renovating homes and their growing business called Magnolia Market. This reality show has also generated home décor books, magazines, and products marketed across the United States and Canada. In contrast to *Duck Dynasty*, however, the personalities of *Fixer Upper* do not fulfill typical stereotypes from the past.

These personalities are sophisticated and trendy, while remaining down to earth and friendly. They have university degrees. They enjoy urban life, while still appreciating rural life. Joanna dresses well and Chip wears blue jeans, but both are articulate, cultured, and urbane. The same two dynamics are visible in their life and work: family, personal growth, and religion; hard work, roots, and entrepreneurship.

The depiction of the *culturally righteous* in this program is much softer, approachable, and "normal." They do not stand apart, but fit in. They are the kind of neighbors everyone wants to have, and the kind of friends everyone wants to find. Their children behave and play like every parent wants their children to behave and play. Magnolia (their company) invites visitors to come and stay ("Your home away from home") and provides options for accommodation. To be sure, they would like to sell you a property. Yet it seems like this would only be the by-product of a wonderful relationship. Their journal rivals the quality of any journal about home, fashion, and décor in America. Included on the back cover is the "Magnolia Manifesto" that sets out their core values (personal and corporate). Newer isn't always better; nothing matters more than family and friends; balanced living is achievable; failure is another way to learn; professional pride is more important than accumulated wealth. These members of the *culturally righteous* want to go back to basics … but take the best of modernity with them.[3]

There is no explicit reference to faith, but you sense that it is there and if you follow them for a while it becomes clear that their assumptions and values are clearly Christian. They, too, have experienced controversy regarding homophobia, but it is the result of accusation about their church rather than anything individually declared. They focus on respect.

The lifestyle groups associated with the *culturally righteous* today include people formerly associated with the *culturally ambivalent* and the *culturally passive*. It is this softer side of the *culturally righteous* that attracts them. These "cultural immigrants" want to be firm in their beliefs, but avoid confrontation and practice radical hospitality. They want to be accountable to core values, but generous when people make mistakes. They want to be rooted in a tradition, yet intentional about continuous learning. Beliefs are important but open to dialogue. These "cultural immigrants" grieve most over the lack of civility that has come to dominate American culture.

In 1990, Tex Sample identified three distinct groups associated with the cultural right. These represent the traditional "core" conservatives. His criteria was generally based on economic and educational conditions that limited upward mobility.

- The *respectables* were blue-collar, lower-middle-class people who were loyal to the standards of respectability at the time, but especially family unity, identity and belonging, success, self-denial, and upward mobility.
- The *hard living* were poor but managing to survive, marginalized with menial jobs and rootless with low social status, who feel trapped by

---

3. The manifesto is readily available. See, for example, *The Magnolia Journal*, issue #5 (winter 2017), 108.

circumstances, and were distrustful or angry at politicians, corporations, religious organizations, or any institution holding them down.

- The *desperately poor* were the poorest of the poor, and often elderly, ill, with little or no education, and with low self-esteem. They were despairing, distrustful, and often isolated in run-down housing, losing themselves by admiring or fantasizing about media personalities.

They often gravitated to churches included in the *culturally righteous* because the theology is simpler, clearer, and often more practical. They often preferred smaller churches that provide a sense of belonging. Worship provided an inspirational message of hope, or fresh opportunities to experience the transforming power of the God that can liberate them from what entraps them. Their need was not so much to be renewed as it is to be reborn. These tended to be "staff-led" churches that do not rely on committees. They gravitated to spiritual leaders who provide a unique blend of caregiving and CEO leadership, offering personal support on the one hand and administrative skills to organize basic social services for survival.

With more data than income or education, we can describe these participants in the churches of the *culturally righteous* from a lifestyle perspective.

Left Behind and Moved Away: What is the world coming to?

Lifestyle segments associated with the *culturally righteous* are often determined by location. These are lifestyle segments impacted by the decline and aging of rural and small-town populations, the disintegration of small mid-market cities, and accelerating urbanization. Urbanization is experienced in both physical and digital ways. Youth migrate to urban centers, then embrace self-centered values and negative habits that clash with family and friends left behind. Meanwhile, those left behind are inundated by media that import the same values and habits that undermine their assumptions and traditions and create conflict in community organizations like churches, school boards, and municipal government.[4]

The question about "what the world is coming to" is another way of asking and answering another question. Question: Where is the world going? Answer: To hell in a handbasket! These lifestyle segments might escape into

---

4.   For example, consider lifestyle segments currently described by Experian as belonging to N00 *Rural Pride*, including N48 *Rural Southern Bliss* and N49 *Touch of Tradition*.

television soap operas, but increasingly they are listening to radio talk shows, many of which are aggressively conservative and reactionary. They used to attend traditional but declining mainstream churches, but increasingly attend independent or evangelical churches that define their identities through confrontation with culture as they see it.

Fractured Families: The widening gap between ideal and real

Lifestyle segments associated with the *culturally righteous* may also be determined by traditional family expectations and increasing family crisis. As the gap between the ideal and real grows, couples and heads of households feel they are losing control and look for ways to regain it. These are lifestyle segments for which traditional family values have broken down. They experience the shame of divorce, or the grief of parental failure, or the loneliness of single parenthood, or the loss of sons and daughters through violence or war, or the burden of acute or chronic disease without the support of healthcare networks. They see the paradigm of family in America disintegrating (rather than reforming), and associate loss of family values with declining church membership and cessation of regular Christian practices.[5]

The ideal family is a man and woman happily married for over a decade, birthing two or more children, and nurturing them to grow as responsible and productive adults. All arguments are eventually resolved. No addictions ever take hold. Holidays and reunions are festivals of love and appreciation. The children produce grandchildren, and later in life take care of their parents. The ideal is perpetuated by retro television stations that continue to air the family comedies of the 1960s and 1970s.

The perceived reality, however, is very different from the ideal. Couples of either gender, at whatever age, marry or live together, for shorter and shorter time periods. Divorce is more common and increasingly acrimonious. Parents and children are alienated from each other. Arguments are constant and addictions rampant. One adult is struggling to raise children on his or her own, or a newly connected couple is raising children from multiple parents other than themselves. Children are abused and the elderly abandoned. Reality television shows follow the chaos.

---

5. For example, I think of lifestyle segments currently described by Experian as M44 *Red, White, and Bluegrass*; M45 *Diapers and Debit Cards*; or S68 *Small Towns, Shallow Pockets*.

Neither the ideal nor the perceived reality accurately describe what is happening in the postmodern family, but it is clear that marriage and family life are getting more stressful. Yet many lifestyle segments in the *culturally righteous* are not comfortable with ambiguity. Marriage and family are either functional or dysfunctional without much in between. The greater the gap grows, the more aggressively the *culturally righteous* strive to fulfill the ideal. They look for churches that are not only "family friendly" but which actively teach, train, or coach how to be the ideal family. And they look for churches that provide professional help to solve problems within the defined value system.

Overwhelmed by Diversity: Guess who's coming to dinner?

Lifestyle segments associated with the *culturally righteous* tend to be determined by accelerating community heterogeneity. Cultural diversity is especially impacting rural, small-town, and city environments, but also urban core and exurban neighborhoods. It is not just that one ethnic group is replacing another, changing the identity of the community. Multiple ethnic groups are mingling with each other (sometimes harmoniously, often not), thus eliminating the identity of the community. Lifestyle segments that were once quite open to other cultures are overwhelmed and can no longer assimilate them into their churches and other community organizations. They are forced to move away, or live with the reality of being a powerless minority.[6]

Diversity today is both the same and different than in the past. The ground-breaking movie of the 1960s *Guess Who's Coming to Dinner* portrayed cross-racial marriage as highly unusual. Today it is relatively common, but that does not mean that the prejudice has gone away. Indeed, postmodern experience is far more complicated. The global village has brought people from all cultures, races, and languages together through intimate relationships and into every interaction at the supermarket. The assumption used to be that newcomers should learn to speak English, but that is rapidly changing both in large cities and in small towns. Now it is expected that residents should learn a new language other than English, or at least learn to honor customs that are quite foreign.

---

6. For example, I think of lifestyle segments currently described by Experian as belonging to L43 *Homemade Happiness*, I31 *Blue Collar Comfort*, I32 *Steadfast Conventionalists*, or Q64 *Town Elders*.

Many of the churches of the *culturally righteous* are among the last bastions of racial or cultural homogeneity. This is true for white and black, Hispanic and Asian churches. These churches may be too big for everyone to know each other's name, but the membership tends to share key demographic characteristics. Of course, the same might be said of many of the mainstream churches of the *culturally ambivalent* and *culturally passive*. Their denominations, however, tend to be proactive about diversity, placing or calling pastors who look, speak, and behave quite differently than the homogeneous congregations.

These lifestyle segments that traditionally participate in churches of the *culturally righteous* often do include economically challenged or less educated people. They may well be struggling against odds, living hard, or desperately poor. Their major threat to abundant living is a sense of abandonment and dread of the future. Their quest for God tends to be driven by existential anxieties related to displacement and estrangement or fate and death (in contrast to the *culturally ambivalent* whose life threats have more to do with depression and anger). These lifestyle groups among the *culturally righteous* often feel trapped, lonely, discarded and dying; and they are looking for churches that can renew life, offer authentic and truthful relationships, belonging and comfort, and confidence for eternal life.

Note that some of these people have also been represented among the *culturally ambivalent*. They were content with a more ambivalent sense of God's presence, and placed their hope in secular policies, programs, and agencies. Today they feel that their hopes have been misplaced. Government policies continue to favor the wealthy, health care gets more chaotic and unreliable, and social service agencies are overwhelmed and underfunded. Meanwhile, labor unions have lost influence, service clubs cannot solve systemic problems, and liberal churches have fewer resources and become more and more focused on survival than outreach. More and more are migrating to the *culturally righteous* who seem more able to deliver on the promises they make for empathy, trusted and accountable relationships, belonging, and sustainable support.

Note also that it is not necessarily *faith* that motivates this change. As we have seen, some of these lifestyle segments are independent, outspoken, iconoclastic, and hypersensitive to hypocrisy and manipulation. If they feel too much pressure for conformity, they might well migrate back to the *culturally ambivalent*—or perhaps contribute to a new cultural movement. (I will take this up in a later chapter.)

The *culturally righteous* is expanding and becoming more diverse, and this is certainly visible in the growing diversity of conservative churches. Many of these new groups are less likely to join the more traditionally conservative churches that are so helpful to the previous groups. They tend to gravitate to larger churches in which one is anonymous in worship but finds intimacy in small groups. Worship tends to be more theologically nuanced and supported by more contemporary technology. Outreach is less about survival, and more about conversion, spiritual maturity, uncovering human potential, and improving quality of life. Laity provide strong and talented leadership, and the pastor is expected to focus on seeker sensitivity and faith formation rather than caregiving and administration.

Defensive Boomers: People get what they deserve.

The previous chapter noted that some adults who would once have described themselves as quite liberal and progressive have become more conservative and traditional in later life. This has caused a migration of some aging adults from the *culturally ambivalent* to the *culturally righteous*. The demographic search engine that I frequently use (www.missioninsite.com) allows the researcher to explore worldviews that pervade a particular neighborhood or community. This is partly based on Simmons Research variables, one of which is that *on the whole, people get what they deserve.* MissionInsite combines this with other worldviews to get an "impression" of community inclination. Over many years of consulting, I have observed that the view that *people get what they deserve* often correlates with a higher population density for evangelical Christians.

Perhaps it is not surprising that the aging adults who are most likely to feel this way are relatively wealthy and place a high value on security. They may live in gated or otherwise secure retirement communities, or they may have relocated away from urban areas to comfortable retreats in the country with state-of-the-art surveillance.[7] At the time that I write this chapter, California wildfires are common. And it is also common for wealthy adults to

---

7. For example, I think of lifestyle segments currently identified by Experian like A02 *Platinum Prosperity*, C12 *Golf Carts and Gourmets*, or C13 *Silver Sophisticates*; and D15 *Sports Utility Families*, or H27 *Birkenstocks and Beemers*.

pay private firefighting companies to bypass the main fires to protect specific legacy properties.

What kind of worldview agrees that *people get what they deserve*? It does not necessarily mean that adults with this worldview are more likely to endorse policies to limit immigration or continue capital punishment. These adults are still likely to support gender and racial equality. They would not say that the poor deserve to be poor, but they might well say that lazy deserve to be poor and be skeptical of large numbers of people on social welfare. And they probably would say that they deserve whatever wealth and security they have achieved, and they are increasingly anxious about a world in which many forces seem to be trying to take it away.

These aging adults usually have a high value for family, and they tend to believe that generosity begins at home. They want to pass on their wealth to their children and grandchildren for their own well-being and security. They can be very generous, of course, to various philanthropic causes, but especially to universities of which they are alumni and to which they might send their grandchildren, and especially to churches that are prepared to accept them rather than judge them.

The adults migrating away from the old cultural left through ambivalence to the *culturally righteous* tend to look for churches with a clear set of moral boundaries, but which are fairly broadminded within those boundaries. They also look for churches that are willing to be flexible about those boundaries if their own family members seem to have gone beyond them. The church needs to honor their privileges, and not make demands on them that are too high. They rarely tithe because even generosity of 1 or 2 percent of net income is a large sum of money. Therefore, despite their wealth, they tend to support churches that function on remarkably small budgets and are chronically under-staffed.

The motivation to quest for God has changed for these aging adults. Their depression over the state of the world has changed to dread about the future of the state. Once their focus was global, but increasingly it is local, regional, and national. Once their attitude was "both/and," but increasingly it is "either/or." It is easier to see issues as black and white. This may or may not lead to the theological dualism of spiritual warfare, but they are more likely to see the Bible as a rulebook and the church as a bulwark against chaos. They expect the pastor to be guardian, and his sermons to "tell it like it is" rather than "beat around the bush."

Disenfranchised Youngers: Who [stole] my cheese?

A second group from which people are migrating from the *culturally ambivalent* to the *culturally righteous* includes a mix of what others call Gen X and Gen Y younger adults. Some of these may well have grown up with boomer parents or grandparents who are now on the defensive. If their parents felt privileged, these younger people feel entitled. Many others grew up in less affluent circumstances, perhaps in medium-size cities and smaller towns, but in anticipation of upward mobility. They expected higher education to bring good jobs and meaningful careers and were willing to undertake significant debt in order to get it.[8]

Unfortunately, these younger people emerged from university with high debts, or entered the workforce with high hopes, and discovered few opportunities. They are over-educated for the jobs available, and many of these are part time. They submit countless job applications, but suspect that patronage matters more than expertise. They may feel victimized by the Affirmative Action programs that they previously supported. Unemployment or underemployment, therefore, is not an incentive to work harder or continue education, but an indication that something is wrong with you personally or that you don't have the right connections.[9]

Other younger people married and had children seeking personal fulfillment, and building a base of emotional and relational support that would help them move forward and upward.[10] Unfortunately, part-time or contract employment offers no benefits and the health care is spotty and/or too expensive. They got divorced and are single parents, and the public education cutbacks and reduced support for day care puts their children at risk.

This sense of shock and disappointment was evoked in the 1998 book *Who Moved My Cheese?*[11] This is the classic parable of two humans and two mice (Hem and Haw, Sniff and Scurry) who have always gone to the same

8. For example, I think of lifestyle segments currently identified by Experian as G25 *Urban Edge*, O50 *Full Steam Ahead*, O51 *Digital Dependents*, O53 *Colleges and Cafes*, O55 *Family Troopers*, and others.

9. For example, I think of C12 *Boomers and Boomerangs*, F22 *Fast Rack Couples*, or O54 *Striving Single Scene*.

10. For example, F23 *Families Matter Most*; M44 *Red, White and Bluegrass*; or M45 *Diapers and Debit Cards*.

11. Spencer Johnson, *Who Moved My Cheese? An Amazing Way to Deal with Change in Your Work and in Your Life* (New York: Penguin Putnam) 1998.

location in the maze for cheese, and then one day discover it is gone. Hem sets out to find another source of cheese, but Haw is paralyzed by his sense of victimization. Hem eventually realizes that change is inevitable, and that everyone needs to learn how to anticipate, monitor, adapt, and even enjoy change. He leaves messages for Haw to follow in his footsteps, but it is uncertain he will ever do so.

I noted in the previous chapter that many of these people are motivated by anger and join the *liberal cultural eclectic*. But increasing numbers of these people are becoming more conservative and migrating to the *culturally righteous*. The question is whether they do so as Hem or as Haw. Both motivations are probably true. Some migrate to find a new path to a better life; others migrate seeking to regain the privileges of their past life.

Some are migrating to the *culturally righteous* because they have decided that cultural ambivalence is bankrupt and to stay there will mean death. The "cheese" that they seek might be wealth or success, healthy marriage and family life, or other things. But the deeper motivation is a quest for meaning and purpose. However, this migration into the *culturally righteous* may not mean participating in a conservative church. That is most likely to happen if "Hem" is already self-consciously Christian. In the emerging secular world, "Hem" is just as likely to participate in another religion or spirituality that offers the same promise of meaning and purpose.

Others are migrating to the *culturally righteous* for the opposite reason. They feel victimized and are looking for vindication. This may mean simply commiserating with other people who feel similarly victimized by postmodern culture. But it may also mean collaborating to search out and punish whoever stole the cheese. In this case, "Haw" is not seeking meaning and purpose. He is migrating to the *culturally righteous* to find an outlet for his anger. Again, this migration may not mean participating in a conservative church. "Haw" is as likely to participate in a political movement or militant minority.

One of the fastest-growing lifestyle segments today includes disenfranchised "youngers" who have been unable to find jobs and are forced to return home after graduating from their university. These parents may well be among the defensive boomers.[12] They may have different tastes, and have learned to disagree without acrimony, but by and large they share similar

---

12. For example, I think of the Experian segment called C14 *Boomers and Boomerangs*.

values and goals. They often gravitate toward new church starts, large churches with multi-sites, or large churches with multiple options. They tend to seek a pastor who is more of a "life coach" than a "faith tutor," and outreach ministries that are more "hands-on" and involve multiple generations.

Status-Seeking Seniors: Just when we thought we had won, we discovered that we had lost.

A third group is primarily migrating to the *culturally righteous* from the *culturally passive*. These seniors may have lived a long time in the same town or neighborhood, and often in the same house. If they relocate to a senior's residence, it is usually in the same vicinity. They tend to have participated in the same established church all their lives, and have been loyal to a denomination through thick and thin. Their favorite gospel chorus might be "Trust and Obey." These churches may be mainstream or evangelical, protestant or Catholic; their beliefs and worship practices are much the same as their parents and grandparents. These seniors have been extraordinarily sacrificial in keeping their churches open and their social environments friendly.

Some of these people are veterans, or have family members who are veterans, of the Korean or Vietnam wars. Like their parents in World War II, they are proud of their country and church. It is difficult for them to feel that the values and lifestyles, which they thought they had protected, are weakening or disappearing. Some may want to blame someone (e.g., politicians) or something (e.g., postmodern culture). Others may want to fight to restore the privileges or power, in the local and national culture, that they think they lost. Either way, these seniors are becoming more protective about their faith and more assertive about their rights.

Some of these seniors may be retired from senior management in business, law, health, or education sectors. They can bring their skills to create faith-based non-profits, or participate on the boards of parachurches that advocate specific conservative causes. They may have relocated to retirement centers, and they may gravitate to large resource-size churches where their organizational and fundraising skills can be put to good use. Status-seeking seniors may be focused on values, but rather flexible about dogma. Their choice of church may depend more on an ethos that resembles the church to which they were so dedicated back home.

This is often reflected in their choice of pastor. They often prefer a pastor who is a strong CEO and can manage a large staff. The pastor is likely to have traditional Christendom credentials from traditionally conservative seminaries, may have changed denominations during their careers, and may have earned additional degrees in business. They are often excellent motivational speakers, and invest time to network among community leaders.

As in the case of defensive boomers, the quest for God among status-seeking seniors has shifted. Once they were driven by a sense of abandonment, and sought a community in which they could belong. Now they are driven more by frustration and seek a community in which they have influence.

African American and Hispanic Traditionalists: Go with what you know.

One of the realities of radical cultural diversity is that the old categories of race or nationality have morphed and multiplied. Thirty years ago, we still spoke of African Americans and Hispanics as if they were simple homogenous groups with similar perspectives, tastes, and lifestyles. Today there are over a dozen distinct lifestyle segments with high proportions of African American or Hispanic households. The unsettling fact is that emerging generations are distancing themselves from their roots, or perhaps it's better to say reinterpreting their cultures to adapt, mix, and merge with postmodern culture as a whole.

Churches often experience this shift with some anxiety. At one time, for example, younger black families would relocate to safer or more affluent neighborhoods, but still drive some distance to return to the home church. Today every traffic light is becoming another reason to change churches, and every new amateur sport is another reason to postpone church attendance. Or, for example, second- and third-generation Latinos might relocate for better jobs or school systems, but still return regularly to their home church to be with their extended families. Today, every crowded airplane and every new career pressure on children presents another reason to stay home for the holidays.

African American and Hispanic traditionalists are not necessarily elderly. They include younger households for whom the preservation of language, roots, and heritage is very important. They can be alarmed by the behaviors of their own brothers and sisters as they adapt and merge into contemporary culture. For these traditionalists, the church is an important way to preserve the old value and belief systems. Although the old value and belief system result in very different behaviors and convictions depending on cultural roots, they still reveal the two class dynamics of Location/Occupation/Income and Family/Education/Religion.

As the next generations acquire white-collar careers and higher incomes, they tend to move away from the old neighborhoods that reinforced values and beliefs. Among some emerging generations of African Americans, the classic evangelical black church that functions as an extended family, interprets scripture literally, and unites around gospel music and a pastoral role model is replaced by a church that functions as a launching pad for outreach and advocacy, interprets scripture critically, and unites around other music genres and a visionary CEO.

As the next generations acquire advanced education and expand their own families in new community contexts, they not only speak a different language but shift theologically to incorporate new ideas and appreciate new liturgies. Among some emerging Hispanic generations, the classic Catholic parish that functions as a community center, preserves traditional liturgies, and unites around culture, language, and a hierarchical authority is replaced by a church that functions as an agent of social assimilation, experiments with new liturgies and progressive policies, and unites around personal growth and a life coach.

All this makes African American and Hispanic traditionalists worried. Yet their migration to the *culturally righteous* is paradoxical. If culture and location is the key concern, African American traditionalists find themselves entering an awkward partnership with conservative white churches that protect segregation and encourage racism. There are black churches, white churches, but few truly biracial churches. If culture and religion is the key concern, Hispanic traditionalists find themselves entering an awkward partnership with evangelical conservatives that protects Vatican 1 dogmas and traditions and encourages historic distrust between Catholics and Protestants.

Reverse Colonialists: We must save our parents from themselves.

As immigration has increased, Christians who grew up in the global mission movements of major denominations are discovering that their parent denominations have become very different than what they assumed. This might be the result of deliberate policy choices, but it is really more of an unconscious evolution of adaptation and change. The parent denominations worship differently, interpret scripture differently, and manage their churches more democratically. They advocate policies that are contrary to their past worldviews and unacceptable to the former mission churches. The pastors have less authority and influence in their congregations, and are treated with less respect by their peers in other sectors of North American life. The churches converse with secularity, rather than confront secularity. Perhaps most importantly, church members are held to a much lower standard of accountability for spiritual discipline (e.g., weekly worship and daily prayer); personal behavior (e.g., ethical decisions and moral standards); church management (e.g., debt and institutional overhead); and outreach (e.g., reluctance to evangelize or proselytize).

Reverse colonialists include lifestyle groups from all over the world, but this is particularly visible among some Asian (e.g., Korea and Chinese), African (e.g., Zimbabwe and South Africa), Pacific Rim (e.g., Philippines), and eastern European (e.g., Poland and Balkan) countries. Their parent denominations are often Presbyterian, Anglican, Methodist, Baptist, Catholic, Orthodox, and other denominations that were strong leaders in the Sunday school and mission movements of the late nineteenth and early twentieth centuries. They are shocked by the perceived decadent state of their parent denominations in the United States.

Reverse colonialists discover that they are *better* Presbyterians or Methodists or Anglicans or Baptists, than churches of that name in America. The old liturgies are still vital, the ordained clergy are still authoritative, the old spiritual disciplines and practices, the old policies still make sense, and the old fervor to make disciples of all nations is still powerful. Ironically, they find themselves separating from the parent denominations as they now find them, and migrating to the evangelical conservatism of the *culturally righteous* so that they might resurrect them.

The prospects of resurrecting old denominations, however, are less and less likely. Instead, reverse colonialists are splitting off from parent denominations to create a new denomination with nearly the same name. It is tempting to say that one branch is progressive, and the other is reactionary, but that is clearly not how reverse colonialist Christians see it. They see it as the best way to preserve the faith and traditions that were vital in the past, confident that

95

if they are articulated well and followed faithfully they will still be relevant for the future.

All of these new groups that have migrated from the *culturally ambivalent*, the *culturally passive*, and other cultures outside America, toward the *culturally righteous*, do so for different reasons. They also have different expectations. At the moment, they are all united to fight a common enemy (e.g., ambivalence and passivity). In the future their differences may well surface to fracture their unity. This common enemy makes the *culturally righteous* appear solid, but in reality quite unstable.

The End of Dogmatism and the Rise of Boundary Theology

Three decades ago, the theology of churches on the cultural right were rarely systematic. By systematic we mean that a group merges reason, tradition, contemporary experience, and biblical interpretation into a coherent whole. The cultural right was better described as dogmatic, in the sense that biblical interpretation was used to correct reason, replace traditions with a single and simple salvation history, and confront culture . . . but reason, tradition, and culture were not allowed to critique their biblical interpretation. However, the old dogmatism of the cultural right has been replaced by "boundary theology."

Boundary theology (compare with boundary organizational management theory) is about being *proscriptive* rather than *prescriptive*. The dogmatic theology of the past was intended to *prescribe* a rather long list of beliefs (articles of religion) and a limiting series of behavioral patterns that were necessary to be saved. Think of a doctor *prescribing* medicine to make a patient healthy or cure a disease. Boundary theology sees the human situation not as a disease but as a dilemma. It defines limits beyond which you cannot go, but within which you are free to do anything you want. In other words, it simply *proscribes* specific beliefs and practices like a fence contains farm animals. They are free to graze anywhere they wish, but they can't go beyond the fence. Perhaps another way of saying this is that dogmatism as "prescriptive" theology was a fence designed to keep culture out; but boundary theology as "proscriptive" is a fence designed to keep the farm animals in.

So boundary theology does not insist on a long list of beliefs to be understood and affirmed, nor does it insist on a complex evaluation process to measure success. It is extremely pragmatic. Boundary theology simplifies faith to a few essential affirmations. If you do not contradict any of those essentials, you are free to believe whatever you wish. For example, you can believe in angels if you wish, but it is not essential. The only essential is that you believe Jesus to be your Lord and Savior. Similarly, boundary theology does not try to tell you how to behave in minute detail in order to be a good Christian. Again, it is extremely pragmatic. Boundary theology simplifies ethics to essential behaviors that you positively must avoid at all costs. If you avoid those mistakes, you are free to live your life as you wish. For example, you cannot under any circumstances have or encourage an abortion. But if you have the baby, you can raise the child any way you wish.

The churches of the *culturally righteous* are attracting migrants from the *culturally ambivalent* and *culturally passive* because people want to *make a difference*. And the churches of the *culturally righteous* seem more efficient and effective in changing lives and communities because they are so radically pragmatic. *Do whatever works . . . provided only that you don't go beyond certain boundaries.*

This, however, begs the question of measurable outcomes . . . and the vulnerability of the tenuous unity of the *culturally righteous*. Most migrants into the *culturally righteous* want to make a difference. They are tired of the ambiguity among the *culturally ambivalent* and the lack of accountability for leaders and members among the *culturally passive*. However, they are usually unclear about what exact difference they want to make. At the same time, traditionally conservative churches of the *culturally righteous* want to encourage experimentation, provided innovative churches get measurable results . . . but are often unclear about what those measurable results should be. It is here that fractures in the unity of the *culturally righteous* begin to appear.

The emergence of boundary theology is correlated to the shorthand that churches use to describe congregational identity: DNA. The church growth movement at the turn of the millennium compared the "body of Christ" imagery of scripture to DNA and made an analogy to new understandings of biological and genetic research. The first letter from John to an early Christian community refers to God's *sperma* that establishes Christian identity: "Those born from God don't practice sin because God's DNA [*sperma*] remains in them" (1 John 3:9, CEB). St. Paul might have said that the "DNA" of the Christian movement was its affirmation of an original *kerygma* (bedrock beliefs) that is encapsulated in an early Christian hymn preserved in Colossians 1:15-20 (CEB):

97

The Son is the image of the invisible God,
    the one who is first over all creation,

Because all things were created by him:
    both in the heavens and on the earth,
    the things that are visible and the things that are invisible.
        Whether they are thrones or powers,
        or rulers or authorities,
    all things were created through him and for him.

He existed before all things,
    and all things are held together in him.

He is the head of the body, the church,
who is the beginning,
    the one who is firstborn from among the dead
    so that he might occupy the first place in everything.

Because all the fullness of God was pleased to live in him,
    and he reconciled all things to himself through him—
    whether things on earth or in the heavens.
        He brought peace through the blood of his cross.

Paul might have added that the "DNA" of the Christian was also specific measureable outcomes, which is perhaps the intention of his summary of the "fruit of the Spirit": "But the fruit of the Spirit is love, joy, peace, patience, kindness, goodness, faithfulness, gentleness, and self-control. There is no law against things like this" (Gal 5:22-23).

The churches that include migrating lifestyle segments and are expanding the *culturally righteous*, however, tend to simplify and rewrite bedrock beliefs and core values in ways that might be more understandable or agreeable to contemporary culture.

The DNA that represents boundaries (not laws) beyond which church members cannot go, but within which they are free to believe and behave as they choose, are often found on the home page of every church website. Among larger independent churches, the trend is not to list words or phrases but to provide videos that demonstrate values and beliefs "in action." Videos are worth more than a thousand words, and for lifestyle segments migrating away from the *culturally ambivalent* and the *culturally passive*, they provide concrete evidence of a church that is "making a difference."

The images or videos tend to identify particular themes and behavior patterns that set this church apart from others. Themes may include:

- remarkably consistent and generationally inclusive generosity and hospitality;

- remarkable loyalty to marriage, family, and friends no matter how bad things get;

- remarkable enthusiasm and joy in worship that is anything but boring;

- remarkable compassion and self-sacrifice in local, and occasionally global, social service;

- remarkable openness to racial and cultural diversity;

- remarkable piety and spiritual disciplines of prayer;

- remarkable Christocentrism as the vehicle for personal salvation and social transformation;

- remarkable patriotism that merges the Christian movement and the American way.

The point of a video is not so much the activity itself but the fact that it is *remarkable* and *demonstrable*. Taken collectively, the portfolio of images and videos is profoundly *hopeful*. Many who participate in lifestyle segments that are dissatisfied with mainstream or established churches cannot help but compare these scenes of hope with their experience of churches that only offer meager hospitality, loyalty only to cliques, boring worship, limited sacrifice, hidden prejudice, lackadaisical spiritual discipline, esoteric theologies, and constant criticism.

Boundary theology is also revealed by keywords that pepper the visioning and planning, preaching and training, outreach, and fundraising efforts of the church. These keywords are essential, but intentionally left ambiguous. As long as these key concepts—kingdom, mission field, seeker, saving grace, personal relationship with Jesus, discipleship, and "what the Bible says"—are accepted, people among the *culturally righteous* are free to interpret and apply them in different ways.

Kingdom

Kingdom is a metaphorical term that has both present and future significance. It sometimes contains an element of mystery as to who participates in the kingdom today, and who might participate in it in the future. It implies that there is a "divine order" or natural hierarchy of all things: God over humanity, humanity over creation; or Christ over church, pastor over members, and members over seekers. It also implies a divine purposefulness and inevitability in history. Nothing is random (like evolution). Everything is planned, even if the plan is not always clear.

The term kingdom also implies patriarchy and patriotism. God is a father figure, pastors are usually male, men are the natural heads of families, there is an appropriate "glass ceiling" for women that limits how much authority they can exercise or what kind of behavior they should model. America, for all its faults, has been given the mandate to Christianize the world. The acceptance by other cultures of American values is the first and important step to the acceptance of Christian values and beliefs.

Mission Field

The mission field metaphor describes the local, regional, and global diversity of a multitude of lifestyles. It implies compassion for others that is more important than self-interest. It also implies that despite cultural diversity, all people are essentially in the same situation that may be variously described as wayward, fallen, sinful, needy, trapped, or broken. It also implies that the church or Christians in general are in a position of superiority in the world that is primarily a one-way communication. Listening skills are primarily important to find the entry points for the Christian message.

The mission field imagery implies that the culture in general is full of misinformation and upside-down priorities. Christians need to feel a sense of urgency to do something about that. Time is running out. They need to clarify the truth and reset priorities for individuals and families, communities and governments. The concept is in fact a call to action.

Seeker Sensitivity

Seeker is a philosophical term defining the basic position of human beings in their quest for meaning and purpose. It implies that everyone outside the kingdom is a seeker and potential mentee; and everyone inside the kingdom is a "knower" and potential mentor. Among people outside the kingdom, awareness of seeking and their methods of seeking differ. Therefore, churches aim to discern the right place and time for intervention, and provide multiple options for people to enter the kingdom in their own way.

This call is to radical tactical adaptability. The basic boundaries of values and beliefs do not change, and the vision of the kingdom and the mission field do not change. All that matters is the gospel (as defined by these boundaries), and everything else is tactical. It is the "mission to the Gentiles" adapted for today's world and taken to its logical conclusion. Hospitality, worship, education, outreach, infrastructure, financial management, and communication need to constantly change to be absolutely relevant to changing culture.

Saving Grace

The teleological term, saving grace, defines the goal of the church and a means to evaluate success. Salvation may or may not involve actual changes in external circumstances. One *might* be healed or vindicated from injustice, escape poverty, or survive war, but God works in mysterious ways. Saving grace implies inward change. One experiences inner peace or finds strength and courage to overcome difficulties, and is confident that in the end everything will be all right. Saving grace is internal rather than external because grace does not take away freedom. God changes your heart—and your ultimate destiny—but each individual must take responsibility to change their own circumstances.

Saving grace, therefore, implies personal salvation, but does not guarantee social transformation. Grace should inspire compassion for others and lead to good works, but ultimately it is the grace that counts. Often this is accompanied by a sense of personal security. For some this implies the feeling of being okay, and for some this implies the accumulation of growth or a next step up the vocational ladder.

Note that saving grace is not primarily about guilt and forgiveness for the lifestyle segments migrating to the *culturally righteous*. It's about shame and cleansing. It's not primarily about forgiveness for the evil you have done but rescue from the evil of what you cannot help doing. In a sense, saving grace is a kind of addiction intervention. It is divine liberation from self-destructive

101

behavior patterns that you chronically deny or from which you cannot escape by your own efforts.

Personal Relationship with Jesus

Many among the *culturally ambivalent* and *culturally passive* make the mistake of thinking this phenomenological term—personal relationship with Jesus—is a dogmatic or theological term. This misunderstanding is particularly pervasive among many seminary academics, and therefore among many seminary graduates, and the mistake blocks them from really understanding the spirituality of the *culturally righteous*. Academics easily knock down what they think is a "straw man" in popular religion, but seminary graduates often find themselves mystified by and alienated from the *culturally righteous* congregations they serve.

Phenomenology is a potent word to describe how people think about life experienced from a first-person point of view. You might say that it is about experiencing life as "raw," rather than thinking about life in general. There is no critical distance from life allowed, pragmatically. Life is day to day, moment to moment, and in the process of living the lifestyle segments often included in the *culturally righteous* experience both struggle and suffering, and also sublime awe and ecstasy. The question for them is not how to understand life but how to sustain hope. Focusing on "God" doesn't really help. Focusing on "Jesus"—a personal Jesus—helps.

The phenomenon (appearance) of Jesus does not lead to a Christology, per se, and in a sense this means that the *culturally righteous* experience Jesus in much the same way as the first apostles in the Upper Room. They may ask themselves, "what exactly just happened?" Something surprising, glorious, and hopeful. In one sense, Jesus has identified himself with us, and substituted himself for us on the cross to remove our guilt. He gives us confidence that no matter how bad life gets, in the end God will prevail and I will experience ultimate healing, wholeness, justice, and grace. But in another sense, Jesus becomes our connection with the divine on a day-to-day basis. He becomes our companion: a voice at our shoulder; a whisper of assurance in the dark; a touch that tells us we are not alone; a friend (which is to say a *true* friend) in times of need. The fullness of God is at our elbow, as a companion, not just in our minds.

Personal relationship with Jesus is very personal and very practical. The fact that it is personal does not mean there is no social transformation impact to faith. In fact, the church leaders of the *culturally righteous* are discovering that a personal Jesus is a key to social transformation among postmodern people. Transformation accelerates by relationship rather than by policy, and once a network of personal relationships is centered on a relationship with Jesus, there is significant power to change hearts and lives.

The fact that a personal relationship with Jesus is practical does not mean that there is no theoretical framework involved to help us understand God working in culture. It means that ministry is less about teaching than it is about mentoring. Mentoring is a means to pass on perceptions of God and culture from person to person that accumulates and builds on past experience. It becomes a collective wisdom that may not be systematic but which helps people navigate life nevertheless.

Disciple (or Discipleship)

The goal of a personal relationship with Jesus, and the methodology of mentoring, has transformed the word *disciple* from a noun to a verb. To disciple someone is to guide a seeker through stages of self-awareness, biblical knowledge, spiritual awareness, faith affirmation, and hopeful living. Discipleship drives the shift from the traditional dogmatic theology of the original cultural right to the more demographically inclusive boundary theology of the *culturally righteous*. Discipleship is not about teaching principles or propositions to a group of students but about coaching meaning and purpose for an individual in a particular context. Communicating faith is no longer a lecture but a dialogue. Yes, the mentor is still wiser than the mentee—but the mentor is aware of his or her own need for growth.

Discipleship is becoming more and more formal as church plants become church institutions, and as church institutions become megachurch movements. Within the process of making disciples there are bases to run, hoops to go through, levels to be achieved, and outcomes to be evaluated. Christian maturity is once again becoming quantifiable, and as we shall see in the discussion of the more extreme *conservative cultural wedge*, it is also becoming more exclusive and confrontational. What, after all, are the marks of a disciple? For the broad body of the *culturally righteous*, that still remains intentionally amorphous. It is still about how one lives based on fundamental

103

attitudes, behavioral habits, and the ubiquitous "personal relationship with Jesus" that no institution or certified professional has the ultimate right to judge. For some, however, the marks of discipleship have been reduced to adherence to selected moral positions, social policies, and articulated propositions—which has created an even more restrictive kind of dogmatism.

What the Bible Says—or Where the Spirit Leads?

Among churches on the culturally right, tension has always persisted between the ultimate authorities of scripture versus the contemporary experiences of the Holy Spirit. This tension is encouraged by deliberate ambiguity about what a personal relationship with Jesus looks like. That tension increases as dogmatic theology shifts to boundary theology. It becomes more challenging in the post-modern world to define what a true disciple looks like. It is much harder to evaluate faith maturity by mentoring than it is by teaching, because mentors assume spiritual growth is a process, and teachers assume it is an accomplishment.

The tension between what the Bible says and where the Spirit leads is growing. This is revealed partly by the slow decline of traditionally evangelical denominations (Baptists, Nazarenes, and other fundamentalist groups) and the continuing rise of charismatic Christians (Pentecostals, movements initiated by the Toronto Blessing and other spiritual events worldwide, and also among some Catholics). The Bible is authoritative for traditional evangelicals and emerging charismatics and certainly more authoritative than among the *culturally ambivalent* or *culturally passive*, but is used in very different ways and open to new revelations among charismatics and Pentecostals.

Once again, a productive comparison can be observed between the seeker-sensitive contexts and discipleship methods of the post-Christendom world and the religiosities and apostolic methods of the pre-Christendom world. Recall the late second century influence of sects like the Montanists, which lured even intellectual elites like Tertullian, or early attempts by Christians such as Marcion to limit the canon of scripture. These movements largely disappeared after the Bible was codified and the church became institutionalized. The reverse is happening today. As the Bible is de-codified and the church de-institutionalized, elements of the *culturally righteous* are forming new sects and spiritual movements.

Much of this is driven by the migration of lifestyle groups from the *culturally ambivalent* and the *culturally passive* to the expanding *culturally righteous*. After all, participation in the *culturally righteous* is not the only choice they have. Many peers are migrating to other spiritualties, some of which are related to well-known world religions, others to indigenous or aboriginal spirituality, and others to entirely new religious movements.

Church leaders of the *culturally righteous* intuit that there is more at stake here than biblical authority. They are alarmed by the more fundamental and dramatic shift from Christocentric faith to Spirit-centered faith. It appears that Christology is being replaced by *pneumatology*. In Christian context, pneumatology means the priority of doctrine about the Holy Spirit, but in postmodern culture it implies the study of spiritual beings or spiritual phenomena in general. Church leaders among the *culturally passive* see it, but dismiss it as insignificant. They assume the pendulum will swing back to institutionalized Christendom. Church leaders among the *culturally ambivalent* tend to embrace the shift to Spirit-centered faith without understanding the implications for their denomination and its economy. But leaders among the *culturally righteous* are perhaps most aware and most alarmed by this apparent shift toward experience. It is a "slippery slope" from Spirit to spirits.

MINISTRY AMONG THE CULTURALLY RIGHTEOUS

It is difficult to advise specific or definitive tactics for ministry among the *culturally righteous* because they *can* be extraordinarily pragmatic. Do whatever works. What "works" can be described in different terminologies (which metaphors often reveal the age of the believer): save more people, convert more people, bring people to a personal relationship with Jesus, and so forth. The outcomes of ministry, however, are basically the same. I will say more about this later. Ministry among the *culturally righteous* generally matches the pragmatic way in which most of the lifestyle segments included in this group live their lives. Do whatever helps you survive, protect and nurture your family, live in harmony with your neighbors, and focus on a purpose for your life.

The *culturally righteous* can be very pragmatic, but in fact many of them are not. This is particularly true of the blue-collar lifestyle segments and among traditional conservatives commonly associated with the cultural right. These segments tend to be late adopters of technology and are very cautious about innovation. Ministries in their churches are actually quite predictable . . . as predictable as the ministries among the mainstream and liberal churches of the *culturally ambivalent*. Tradition is meaningful, important, and preserved. Worship is predictable. There is orderliness to the service. Even visitors readily anticipate what comes next. The sermon may be at the end, and an altar call may follow the sermon, but it is just as predictable as an Anglican liturgy. There is even predictability among many Pentecostal churches. Expect someone to speak in tongues *here*, or a spontaneous testimony *there*. Predictability is *not* found in some churches where there is an unexpected healing, or in the Pentecostal movement "Catch the Fire" (CTF) that started with the Toronto Blessing.[13] But among the traditional *culturally righteous*, these experiences are often criticized or at least treated with caution.

The essentials of worship are surprisingly similar to that of mainstream Protestant churches: the Bible read and exposited; prayers of supplication, intercession, and/or thanksgiving; a call to respond sacrificially to God's grace; and a command to follow Christ in the world. The choice and explanation of scripture, the method and emotion of prayer, the offering of life and lifestyle, and the signs of following Christ in the world may vary. Lay witness may be as important as pastoral preaching, but that is usually planned rather than spontaneous. The structure is much the same.

The difference between worship among the *culturally ambivalent* and the *culturally righteous* is really observed in the *point* of worship. The *culturally ambivalent* are influenced by the assumptions of modern public education and often assume that faith is a result of education. Worship is an educational experience, and as a person matures they will make a rational decision to believe. The opposite is true among the *culturally righteous*. These people assume that faith is a result of a personal encounter with God, and worship is the link where believers begin to understand the miracle of what happened to them. The altar call after worship is not an invitation for people who have become *convinced* that Christ is the answer. It is an invitation for people to come forward who have been *convicted* in the Spirit. It is this sense of awesome spiritual presence that (surprisingly) brings evangelicals and Roman Catholics

---

13. For an interesting discussion of unpredictability, read Peter Althouse, "Eschatology in the Theology of Paul Tillich and the Toronto Blessing," *Paul Tillich and Pentecostal Theology: Spiritual Presence and Spiritual Power*, edited by Nimi Wariboko and Amos Yong (Bloomington, IN: Indiana University Press, 2015).

closer together. They might not use the terminology, but for the *culturally righteous* worship is fundamentally *sacramental* rather than *educational*. The priority of worship designers is not for worship to make sense but for worship to be *awesome* in the best, and most profound sense, of that word.

Worship among the *culturally righteous* is also a missional event. Educational worship tends to look inward, drawing visitors into members, and members into emerging theologians. But awesome worship tends to look outward, drawing seekers into discipling processes, and sending disciples into the mission field. We can observe this difference most profoundly at Christmas Eve services. Churches among the *culturally ambivalent* and the *culturally passive* anticipate Christmas Eve to be a reunion of the extended family of the church, including former members returning, university students home for the holidays, grandparents and grandchildren, and cousins.

Predictability is also evident in other ministries among the traditional lifestyle segments of the *culturally righteous*. Sunday school tends to be curricular, biblical, and generational (in contrast to experiential education by peer group that is more topical). Fellowship tends to be gender and age based, in large groups. Outreach often focuses on survival or addiction ministries. Church facilities may or may not be ecclesiastical in appearance, but are very utilitarian in their equipment. People are generally encouraged to tithe to a unified budget, trusting the church leader to spend money wisely.

Among traditional mainstream churches that include *culturally ambivalent* or *culturally passive* lifestyles, these choices are not only predictable but often sacred (or at least sacred cows). Among the *culturally righteous*, however, pragmatism is always deeper than predictability. They are often aware that predictability is only about practices that are meaningful to some people but not necessarily to all people. Their traditional churches can be as hard to transform as any other established church, but they are ready to adapt and are willing to stake the resources to do it. They more readily opt for church planting and multisite ministries. The "mother" church may remain the same, but its "offspring" are free within boundaries to find their own way.

In my church consultation work, I often compare a thriving church to a vehicle (car or bus) traveling down the road.[14] The metaphor often raises the anxieties of mainstream church leaders but generates excitement among evangelical church leaders. I say that church growth is a matter of traction

---

14. See my book *Strategic Thinking* (Nashville: Abingdon Press, 2017).

and steering. The "rear wheels" generate traction. This is the synergy of radical hospitality, inspiring worship, and significant conversation about life and faith that follows. The "front wheels" concentrate on steering. This is the synergy of leadership training, outreach, and evangelism that takes a church in a specific direction. Training, outreach, and evangelism generate new people entering the synergy of hospitality, worship, and significant conversation. These people are in turn transformed, and enter leadership training.

The principle of church growth is akin to the definition of "torque" for a motor vehicle. The basic energy principle is:

Clarity of Faith + Accountability in Leadership = Pulling Power.

Visitors are welcomed into church. Seekers encounter God in worship. Mentors help them understand what this means. This principle is not so different from mainstream church traditions. The difference is that the church does not merely assimilate members. It equips leaders. The standard of accountability is much higher. It is about not only giving but tithing. It is about not only volunteering for programs but shaping a lifestyle. It is about not only doing good things but sharing why good things are a result of God's grace rather than human philanthropy. And if church members are unable or unwilling to live up to standards of faith and action, the church leaders do not let it slide. The temptation, of course, is for church leaders to become judgmental (and that is what most people among the *culturally ambivalent* see). The usual practice, however, is not judgment but encouragement. Church leaders come alongside struggling members to help them become more motivated or more capable of living up to the standards.

As important as lay witness and membership maturity might be, churches among the *culturally righteous* are very clear about who is actually driving the bus. The pastor is driving. (Once again there is a surprising connection between the expectation of priesthood among some Roman Catholics and the *culturally righteous*.) The spiritual depth, moral integrity, and skill sets of the pastor are probably more crucial for the *culturally righteous* than the *culturally ambivalent*. If the pastor fails in a mainstream denomination, they wait for a new appointment or merely get another pastor. But if the pastor fails in an evangelical, Pentecostal, or Roman Catholic church, their situation is much more dire. The church stakes its credibility on the credibility of the pastor; and if the credibility of the pastor is undermined, then the church as a whole loses confidence.

The hierarchy of leadership in churches among the *culturally righteous* is a source of potential and peril. The potential is that decision making can be rapid, and the church can exercise its instinctive radical pragmatism and make changes quickly. The peril is that today the credibility of a leader is constantly scrutinized, and momentum for church growth can be lost in a heartbeat. This is especially true for today's independent megachurches (and their multiple sites) and for new church starts. The choice of a leadership successor or a church planter is all-important. Large independent churches have largely abandoned the old system of "preaching for a call," in favor of five-year plans to apprentice the next leader under the tutelage of the current pastor. Evangelical denominations have largely abandoned the practice of hiring enthusiastic but untrained youth leaders to start a new church, in favor of boot camps and intense training (often combined with mentoring from large independent churches).

It is here that the radical pragmatism of the *culturally righteous* has been able to expand the attraction of conservative churches. Most of the lifestyles among the defensive boomers, disenfranchised youngers, status-seeking seniors, African American and Hispanic traditionalists, and reverse colonialists that I described earlier, who are being drawn away from the *culturally ambivalent* and the *culturally passive*, have connected with the *culturally righteous* through large resource-size churches, multiple sites of megachurches, and new church starts.

These emerging churches are quite different from many of the traditional conservative churches. Their staff development and lay training, worship and ministry tactics, technologies and communication strategies, facilities and fundraising is constantly adapting to culture. Yes, this makes many traditionally conservative churches nervous. But as long as they stay within boundaries and show measurable outcomes, they can do whatever works.

Consider How the Church Gets "Traction"

These emerging *culturally righteous* churches do not design a worship service. They shape a "Sunday Morning Experience."[15]

---

15. See *Worship Ways* by Tom Bandy and Lucinda Holmes (Nashville: Abingdon Press, 2016).

These churches are taking radical hospitality to a whole new level. This includes layers of trained greeters chosen to mirror the lifestyle diversity of the community. They are deployed before, during, and after worship; from parking lot to parking lot. Not only do the refreshments equal the typical refreshments enjoyed by the public they intend to bless but the refreshment center environment is made as comfortable as possible. The goal is not to chat with friends but to linger in significant conversation about life and faith.

These churches are offering multiple options in worship. Unlike the mainstream churches of the *culturally ambivalent* or *culturally passive* that repeat the same service and sermon at different times, they offer a service and sermon customized to address the different spiritual needs of the particular publics they are trying to reach (e.g., worship for healing, coaching, education, inspiration, transformation, caregiving, and outreach). Even the Roman Catholic and Anglican churches that are embraced by the *culturally righteous* intentionally adjust their liturgies and customize their homilies with seeker sensitivity.

These churches are supplementing (and often replacing) traditional Sunday schools with midweek small groups. Unlike small groups formed among the *culturally ambivalent* or *culturally passive*, small group leaders are not rotated but trained; and groups are not just about fellowship and learning but intentional spiritual growth. The location, timing, study material, technology, and other tactics are not standardized, but each group is free to do whatever is best for the people in their group.

Consider How the Church Manages "Steering"

Culturally righteous churches do not distinguish between "adherents" and "members" but between "seekers" and "disciples." Decisions about tactics can be made by both, but decisions about essential values and beliefs, public policies and capital campaigns, are only made by disciples. And disciples are held accountable to a higher standard. Members are not taught to be administrators or theologians but trained to be disciples. Membership is not gained and never lost—it is earned through spiritual discipline.

Discipleship changes their attitude toward outreach. The new lifestyles that are attracted to the *culturally righteous* often do not need and/or are not interested in volunteering to serve in the typical survival and addiction intervention ministries of traditional conservative churches. These churches tend to develop signature outreach ministries that gain city-wide, regional, national, and even global recognition. If they are survival ministries, they expand food and shelter ministries to address natural disasters around the world. If they are about addiction intervention, they develop intervention centers and health clinics. Many of these outreach ministries concern human potential with a focus on gifts, discernment and personality inventories, job search and placement, marriage enrichment and parenting, and the like. Outreach may concern quality of life issues such as crime prevention, day care, seniors residences, hospitals, safety, and (yes) environmental advocacy.

Practical outreach is always combined with faith witness. Since "evangelism" is a word with negative connotations among new lifestyles attracted to the *culturally righteous*, many churches focus on the positive elements of sharing faith motivations for generous service. For them, social service is only a short-term solution to a larger problem of sin, and actions do not speak louder than words. Faith is the ultimate cure for social ills, and every good deed needs to be explained as a part of God's plan to save the world.

The churches that are expanding the attraction of the *culturally righteous* are also adapting facilities, financial management, and communication technologies that are relevant to the lifestyle segments they are trying to reach. Church buildings and worship centers are often quite utilitarian. Classic Christian symbols are presented in innovative forms. Ministry sites are often in rented facilities to reduce overhead costs. Communication technologies include web sites and interactive social media platforms that are equal to entertainment sector standards. And since these churches are more rigorous about accountability, they have the financial resources to do it.

The real point of the motor vehicle metaphor in describing the church is to define its potential "pulling power." This is the power to both attract people to the church, and lead programs that transform society. These innovations help megachurches, multi-site churches, and church plants develop greater torque or "pulling power" for personal and social transformation. Compare that with the torque or "pulling power" among many mainstream churches of the *culturally ambivalent* or *culturally passive* who are resistant to innovation. They tend to be ambiguous about faith, and practice low accountability for membership. Therefore, they generate minimal "torque" or "pulling power" to either attract new people or change the world.

I have had the opportunities to work cross-denominationally, cross-culturally, and internationally among most of the lifestyle segments described by Experian.[16] Those lifestyle segments migrating to the *culturally righteous*—defensive boomers, disenfranchised "youngers," status-seeking seniors, African American and Hispanic traditionalists, and reverse colonialists—offer a common refrain: *I just want to make a difference!* And today the most energy and impact for personal well-being and positive social change is among the *culturally righteous.*

LOOKING TOWARD THE FUTURE

There are weaknesses among the *culturally righteous*, which leaders among the *culturally ambivalent* are quick to point out. There are also strengths that they consistently overlook. And there are a number of things they share in common with the *culturally ambivalent* and the *culturally passive* that could become the foundation of future respectful conversation.

There are two major weaknesses among the *culturally righteous*. First, the tendency in folk theology to make faith an "opiate of the people." Tex Sample pointed this out in his 1990 study of American lifestyles and church choices. One implication of this is that gratuitous evil all too easily sabotages faith. Saving grace and a personal relationship with Jesus do not guarantee safety and security. Bad things can and always will happen in life, and even the *culturally righteous* cannot avoid suffering. The real issue, however, is not evil in general but *gratuitous* evil. For gratuitous evil there is neither explanation nor excuse. It cannot be dismissed by an appeal to dogma, and it cannot be assuaged by honeyed words.

There is a second weakness is that leadership is more closely associated with power politics. Boundary theology that relies on a few key concepts that are intentionally ambiguous encourages aggressive or charismatic leaders to take control of a church and dominate the lifestyles of ordinary people in unhealthy ways. Marx was right to say religion can all too easily become the tool of the powerful to enslave the powerless. *Someone* must interpret the concepts, and *someone* must establish measurable outcomes, and *someone* must

---

16. Currently there are seventy-one lifestyle segments identified by Experian in the United States.

evaluate success. Boundary theology also introduces a subjectivity to theology and practice that allows one opinion to dominate others.

On the other hand, there are strengths in the *culturally righteous* that should not be ignored. While the *culturally ambivalent* dither, and the *culturally passive* hide, the *culturally righteous* are now the people who get things done. They are impacting local communities and the global village for positive social transformation in practical, visible ways. They have perfected a method of mentoring and discipleship that appeals to post-modern people. It is relational rather than programmatic; rich in image and song, rather than caught up in words; shared easily in social media, and not limited to preaching. The *culturally righteous* have become the advocates of constant learning and spiritual growth that was once the role of the *culturally ambivalent*; and the *culturally ambivalent* are perceived by many postmodern people as judgmental and dogmatic.

Perhaps the greatest strength of the *culturally righteous* is their ability to adapt effectively and quickly to social change and cultural diversity. The megachurches, multi-sites, and church plants import the same boundary thinking into the decision-making processes. So long as they honor key policies, they are free to innovate tactics in a matter of days, leaving behind traditional church organizations that require endless committees and consensus to change the smallest detail in worship, hospitality, and outreach. Among people yearning to "just make a difference," who are frustrated with bureaucracy and financial overhead, this is enormously appealing. This may dismay some of the classic conservatives, but migrating lifestyle segments can enjoy the fellowship and be fulfilled in outreach without ever taking the dogmatism seriously. They just need to keep going and adapting and growing.

If they would actually admit it, the *culturally righteous* and the *culturally ambivalent* have much in common. They all seek meaning and purpose in a secular world. They all desire a new reformation that brings simplicity, integrity, balance, relevance, and effectiveness to old and declining nineteenth-century institutional churches. They are all patriotic in that they love what their country aspires to be. They are all committed to spiritual growth, and yearning to experience the immanence of God in daily life. They all have spiritual heroes, and their convictions about life and death, God and hope, are remarkably similar.

113

Chapter 4

THE CONSERVATIVE CULTURAL WEDGE

The emergence of the extreme right

The tension between social consciousness and self-centeredness helps us understand how the cultural left shaped what in the twentieth century we called the "mainstream" church.[1] The inability to resolve this tension caused the *culturally ambivalent* to spawn a more radical extension of itself: the *liberal cultural eclectic*. (See chapter 2.) A second and related tension between capitalism and fair play has become more severe in the twenty-first century. This helps us understand how the cultural right shaped a new "mainstream" church among the *culturally righteous*. Evangelical, Pentecostal, independent churches (including most megachurches and multi-site churches), many church plants within formerly "mainstream" denominations, and new Christian sects and religious movements have combined to form a new norm in American society. The growing tension between capitalism and fair play has spawned a more radical extension of the *culturally righteous*: *the conservative cultural wedge.*

Consider two purposes for a "wedge." First, the term can be used as a noun. A wedge is a shim used to prop something up or keep something open. For example, we use a wedge to elevate a table leg to keep it horizontal, or to steady a door to keep it open or closed. Second, the term can be used as a verb. To wedge is to keep two things apart, or to drive two things to become

---

1. As Wesleyans became mainstream during the nineteenth century, they experienced a similar tension between social holiness and personal holiness.

separate things. For example, we drive a wedge into wood to split logs or we use a knife on meat to separate the fat from the protein.

These two uses of a "wedge" can describe the activities of the smaller but more extreme element of the *culturally righteous*. This element is a "wedge" in the sense that it perceives itself propping up an original form of the Christian church, which seems to have lost a leg and is in danger of tipping over; or it perceives itself steadying a door that has been open from being closed (or a door that has been closed from being opened). To this extent, the *conservative cultural wedge* is reactive and understands the mission as defending and stabilizing traditional churches that espouse an older set of core values and beliefs. In their view, the *culturally righteous* lifestyles are in danger of tipping over or losing their way.

This element is a "wedging" movement in the sense that it perceives itself as the driving force to separate the purity of the church from the contamination of culture. On the one hand, they resist the pressure of secularity to close the door on Christian faith. On the other hand, they resist the pressure of the *culturally ambivalent* to open the door to the influence of other spiritualties and faith traditions. To this extent, the *conservative cultural wedge* is proactive and understand the mission as counterattacking the forces threatening to bring their worldview or sense of orthodoxy to an end.

The *conservative cultural wedge* share many of the anxieties of the *liberal cultural eclectic*, but their responses or solutions are the mirror image of the other group. For example:

- They are anti-institutional, but only in the sense that the existing institutions are seriously flawed and need to be reformed. Individualism, unaccountable personal religion, and loose relational networks are not the answer. A new form of communalism, strictly accountable behavior and faith, and strong coalitions of select churches and faith-based non-profits is the answer.

- They are excellent church planters and outreach specialists, but only in the sense that new churches join a specific coalition of power-brokers. Outreach is a first step securing the allegiance of new people, who will bring new energy to a particular ideological and theological agenda. In contrast to planters and outreach specialists of the *liberal cultural eclectic*, the leaders are often excellent managers with an entrepreneurial bent. They focus on sustainable organizations, and less on creative ideas.

116

- The leaders of the *conservative cultural wedge* are relational, and they want to bless lifestyle segments in relevant ways, but with the added purpose of developing a critical mass of personal and financial resources that subsequently reshape social programs and public policies.

The weakness of the cultural left was that their self-interest (personal or denominational) ultimately became more important than their social consciousness. That was hypocrisy to the *liberal cultural eclectic*. In contrast, the weakness of the cultural right was that their sense of fair play, their commitment to civility, ultimately became more important than their mandate to win the spiritual war over compromised values and foggy beliefs. This is hypocrisy to the *conservative cultural wedge*.

If the cultural right once saw itself as a movement, then it appears that the handoff of the torch to the next generation has been bobbled, if not dropped. The traditional conservatives of the *culturally righteous* are no better at understanding the anger of the *conservative cultural wedge* as the experimental liberals of the *culturally ambivalent* are at understanding the anger of the *liberal cultural eclectic*. Each group tolerates their more extreme elements, but are nervous about their behavior and goals at the same time.

It is difficult to clearly identify the lifestyle segments most likely to contribute to the *conservative cultural wedge*. It was easier to draw an "influence map" connecting the *culturally ambivalent* to the *liberal cultural eclectic* because we have had more time to observe it. The *liberal cultural eclectic* began to clearly emerge in the late 1980s and 1990s. The *conservative cultural wedge*, however, became clearly identifiable in the early years of the new millennium. Its political manifestation seemed to have started in 2009 with the Tea Party protests against government intervention in the home ownership mortgage crisis, which was one of many reactions to a wayward culture that could elect a black president. However, this wedge can be spotted earlier, at the turn of the millennium, amid disappointment in the Republican Party's response to Democratic policies, and the terrorist attacks beginning with 9/11 in 2001.

The emergence of the *conservative cultural wedge* in the church follows a similar timeline, although frustration and anxiety amid lifestyle segments of the traditional cultural right (described by Tex Sample in 1990) has been growing since the 1960s, regardless of politics. The high-water mark for church growth in America for most denominations was in the mid-1960s, and thereafter anxiety about the encroachment of secularity on the world-views of evangelical Christians has been increasing exponentially.

As difficult as it might be to identify the lifestyle segments most likely to contribute to the *conservative cultural wedge*, there are some clues that might help draw an influence map. In addition to Tex Sample's original list of the "respectables," "hard living," and "desperately poor," I previously identified eight groups migrating into the *culturally righteous* from the *culturally ambivalent* and *culturally passive*. Several lifestyle groups have gained my attention as potential influencers and contributors to the *conservative cultural wedge*. Let's begin with the groups identified by Experian data: the barely respectable, those overwhelmed by diversity, defensive boomers, and disenfranchised youngers.

Barely Respectable:² Somebody help us!

Tex Sample originally described a group called the "respectables" in 1990, as blue-collar, lower-middle-class people who were loyal to the standards of respectability at the time, but especially family unity, identity and belonging, success, self-denial, and upward mobility. The plight of this group has become increasingly dire in the past thirty years. Consider, for example, the situation of white and black blue-collar workers in Flint, Michigan, and other rustbelt, mid-market cities. As industries downsized and relocated, they left behind enormous economic problems that also impacted key concerns of the *culturally righteous* for education, family, and religion.

Today many of these households are barely clinging to middle-class status. The key factors for stability and upward mobility have been undermined. Unemployment and under-employment are rampant, and meaningful work is almost impossible to define. Working harder, patching together part-time jobs, with no benefits, have created stress on families. Marriages fracture, and children relocate to find jobs or drift into drugs and gangs. Established churches that were once thriving are declining rapidly. Infrastructure investments have dried up, creating by neglect bad roads, crumbling bridges, weak schools, and less food. In cities like Flint, Michigan, people cannot enjoy a healthy environment or even drink clean water from the

---

2. For example, I think of lifestyle segments currently described by Experian as belonging to L43 *Homemade Happiness*, I31 *Blue Collar Comfort*, I32 *Steadfast Conventionalists*.

tap. As their frustration turns to rage, they feed and influence an emerging *conservative cultural wedge* motivated to rebalance the playing field and shut the door on secularity.

Overwhelmed by Diversity:[3] We know who's taking our dinner!

Many in these lifestyle segments are migrating from the *culturally passive* to the *culturally righteous*, and some are going to a more extreme point of view. The old question—*Guess who's coming to dinner?*—has been replaced by an unsettling suspicion: *We know who's taking our dinner!* Sometimes that suspicion is a pleasant surprise; but usually it is experienced as an alarming fear. People in this group are not only blue-collar workers. They also include comfortable boomers and stable seniors.

Comfortable boomer couples who have chosen rural, small-town life can easily shift to the category of *conservative cultural wedge*. They have traditionally been dutiful volunteers, denominationally loyal, committed to harmony in the church; and practiced a more easygoing evangelism. However, they also tend to be opinionated. Many would automatically link the decline of their church to accommodating culture, poor or disreputable leadership, and policies difficult or impossible to justify by scripture. More and more are leaving their former denominations, or are desperately trying to regain control of their congregations.

Stable seniors leading simple, quiet lives in older homes in small towns also worry about the world and the future of the church. They, too, have been brand loyal to established denominations, but are becoming angry at top-down policies that contradict traditional values. On a deeper level, they often link the decline of the "church family" to the growing heterogeneity of their community. So long as the cultural diversity was slow, they could be welcoming and assimilate different people into the family. Now that it is accelerating, they no longer feel the same kinship with church or community. Once in the majority, now they are in a minority. Some will become aggressive to prop out the old ways and shut the door on impinging culture.

---

3. For example, I think of lifestyle segments currently described by Experian as belonging to I32 *Steadfast Conventionalists* or Q64 *Town Elders*.

Defensive Boomers: [4] *People are not getting what they deserve!*

Many defensive boomers are migrating from the *culturally ambivalent* to the *culturally righteous*, and some are adopting a more extreme point of view. The overall attitude toward culture (politics, the legal system, institutional religion, public education, and so forth) is increasingly negative. Their belief that people should get what they deserve seems to be contradicted at every turn. Good people are not getting what they deserve. Bad people are not getting what they deserve. The priorities of public institutions seem upside down.

Some in this group are relatively affluent boomers, retired or near retirement, and often in business management, applied sciences, or professional occupations. They may have already taken a step away from a world they find distasteful by moving to estate homes in the country or gated communities in the suburbs. They are increasingly sporadic in worship attendance, and reactionary to even small changes in worship, hospitality, or ecclesiastical architecture.

Others in this group are middle-aged with older children, at home or in college, who feel financially burdened by university expenses and unreasonably high tax brackets. Family is central to their lives, and the erosion of traditional family structures and family values troubles them greatly. Ordinarily, they are self-absorbed, non-confrontational, low risk takers. But once they get angry they may be aggressive activists. They have always been skeptical of the established church, and are even more alienated now.

Disenfranchised Youngers: [5] *We know who is eating our cheese!*

Many of the younger adults among the *conservative cultural wedge* may well be children of the defensive boomers. They, too, once had positive attitudes toward a life full of possibilities, and now they have negative attitudes, seeing life as a black hole of disappointments. The walls in their low-income

---

4. For example, I think of lifestyle segments currently identified by Experian like A02 *Platinum Prosperity*, C12 *Golf Carts and Gourmets*, and D15 *Sport Utility Families*, D16 *Settled in Suburbia*, or H27 *Birkenstocks and Beemers*.

5. For example, I think of lifestyle segments currently identified by Experian as O51 *Digital Dependents*, O53 *Colleges and Cafes*, O55 *Family Troopers*, and others.

apartments are papered with rejection letters. They no longer wonder who stole their cheese. They know very well who took it and ate it.

Some of the people in this group are enrolled at the university or are recent graduates, and may be living near the university. They may be working part-time jobs because they can't find employment in the field in which they were trained. They feel entitled to better careers and more affluent lifestyles. They may be angry at affirmative action policies, and jealous of women and/or minorities who, they believe, are less qualified for the positions they hold. They often try to *appear* more successful than they are by wearing the latest fashions and owning the most advanced technologies that they can ill afford. Most of these "youngers" have long been alienated from the church and boring worship, but they are looking for heroes of faith as role models. Charismatic leaders can motivate them to action.

Others in this group are the same age, but less well educated. They may be part of military families who have lived so many places that they don't seem to fit in anywhere. But they have also seen the world in a different, more threatening way, and know how important it is to fight for what you believe. They are usually very supportive of the military and law enforcement in general. They tend to see the church as important guardians of moral values, and are troubled by laissez-faire religious leaders who do not protect Western values.

HALLMARKS OF THE CONSERVATIVE CULTURAL WEDGE

The more extreme elements in these lifestyle groups tend to be frustrated with their peers. They don't think that the *culturally righteous* are doing enough, and whether intentionally or unconsciously they gravitate to the *conservative cultural wedge*. Interestingly, this closely parallels the attitudes of the *liberal cultural eclectic* toward the *culturally ambivalent*. The following hallmarks compare the extremes of the *conservative cultural wedge* with the *culturally righteous*:

- While the *culturally righteous* are broadly tolerant and try to be welcoming to outsiders, the *conservative cultural wedge* are remarkably intolerant and exclusive of outsiders.

121

- The *culturally righteous* have the self-esteem to laugh at themselves and enjoy their faith, but the *conservative cultural wedge* take themselves very seriously and overreact on social media to every real or perceived criticism.

- The *culturally righteous* are generally willing to negotiate tactics and collaborate with a broad range of conservatives who may not all agree on everything. The *conservative cultural wedge* prefer confrontation to negotiation, and only collaborate with partners who share the same action agenda.

- The *culturally righteous* are self-conscious of roots in the local community, and with the beliefs and values of their ancestors. In contrast, the *conservative cultural wedge* have left their former communities and ancestral roots to focus on a utopian vision of future conformity.

These points closely match the attitudes of the *liberal cultural eclectic*, the extreme of the parent group *culturally ambivalent*, and it helps us understand why certain groups inevitably clash. In the past, there has always been room for the *culturally ambivalent* and the *culturally righteous* to at least talk together respectfully. The extreme minorities of both cultural groups undermine that possibility.

There are other parallels between the *liberal cultural eclectic* and the *conservative cultural wedge*. My perception is that many of the lifestyle segments represented in both groups have long been skeptical about the trends of culture and are disenchanted with traditional institutional churches in any form. They are more likely to form partnerships with faith-based nonprofits and groups with political influence. They tend to be less concerned about local community vitality, and more concerned about national and global policy. They insist on strict allegiance to particular values, but are often remarkably disinterested in classic Christian faith. They may support any leader who promises to impose the right values, regardless of the depth, or even the presence, of faith. They tend to circle uncritically around heroes or charismatic leaders, albeit with very different worldviews.

The hallmarks of the *conservative cultural wedge* are 180-degree opposites to the hallmarks of the *liberal cultural eclectic*.

Older . . . but Not Necessarily Representative of Seniors

Although there are disenfranchised "youngers" in their midst, the makeup of the *conservative cultural wedge* seems to be older. Older busters and an assortment of boomers tend to dominate the strategic thinking of the group. These may claim to act on behalf of seniors, and some seniors may well influence and/or appreciate their actions, but the *conservative cultural wedge* is not a "gray power" movement.

In contrast, the *liberal cultural eclectic* tend to be younger. They are more individualistic, and are less likely to make claims to act on behalf of those seniors who have traditionally been at the center of community life. They are more likely to claim to act in behalf of marginalized people of any age or culture.

The churches represented among the *conservative cultural wedge* tend to be more intergenerational. They are unlike many established conservative churches in which the average age of membership is over sixty. This significantly impacts worship and technology. Worship tends to be more inspirational, and preaching more motivational, rather than expository or pastoral. Technology is more relevant to children and youth. Music may include classic hymns, but the norm is contemporary.

Mainly Male

Although there are women with influence or in leadership among the *conservative cultural wedge*, they are fewer and seem generally content with the "glass ceiling" that limits their authority. Blue-collar lifestyle segments are increasingly open to dual careers or dual incomes to support the household, but the *conservative cultural wedge* are more likely to emphasize the ideal of traditional male and female roles in home and family.

In contrast, the *liberal cultural eclectic* are assertive about gender equality. Men and women will collectively try to eliminate "glass ceilings" blocking opportunity for women, just as they are more assertive in confronting even the hint of sexual bias or harassment. Among the *liberal cultural eclectic*, males are more comfortable taking traditional roles in home and parenting. It is more common to see males working in trades and their spouses working as professional specialists. The *liberal cultural eclectic* are usually strong feminists, while the *conservative cultural wedge* are usually strong advocates of a family system based on traditional male/female roles.

Senior pastors of churches represented among the *conservative cultural wedge* are usually male. The majority of board members, and in many places all, are male. However, women often share leadership in music, which in these churches also means broader leadership in the order of worship. Couples often are co-leaders of small groups. Males tend to speak authoritatively about faith and doctrine, but women may be some of the most articulate spokespersons for core values and advocates for moral issues.

Married, Dating, or Abstaining

In keeping with the commitment of the *culturally righteous* to traditional family structures and values, people in the *conservative cultural wedge* also tend to be married, dating, or intentionally abstinent regarding sex. But they also tend to be more intolerant. Among the *culturally righteous*, for example, it is not uncommon for households or leaders to condemn homosexuality, but accept a gay or lesbian person into worship provided they remain abstinent; and continue to love and embrace a family member who has declared an alternative sexual orientation. Divorce is discouraged, but is an acceptable alternative in some difficult circumstances. For the *conservative cultural wedge* the attitude is harder. Homosexuality is condemned, and the sinner must repent before being welcomed in worship. Indeed, family members who declare an LGBT orientation are usually ostracized. Divorce is barely tolerated under very special circumstances, remains a blemish on one's life, and is often perceived as the wife's fault. Divorce disqualifies a person for leadership.

Meanwhile, people in the *liberal cultural eclectic* are often single and/or co-habitating. Formal marriage is often delayed for an extended period of time. Abstinence is respected as a personal choice, but generally anomalous to the culture. Homosexuality is recognized (perhaps celebrated) as a way of being and not as a choice. Divorce is unremarkable, and may well occur several times in one's life.

The harsh stance of the *conservative cultural wedge* often places even the most conservative churches and pastors in a difficult place. Many leaders want to be compassionate and leave the door open for conversation and counseling, and they feel pressured to be judgmental and close the door on anyone outside the norm. They recognize the complexities of family dynamics and the challenges faced by young adults growing up in a world of temptations. Most pastors want to approach marriage and sexuality issues in the context of pastoral care rather than church policy.

Small-Town, Rural, Mid-Size Cities and Beltway

The *conservative cultural wedge* does include, and tries to represent, urban industrial working-class people who have lost economic power in the emerging global village. But it tends to associate the depopulation of rural areas, small-town communities, and mid-sized city neighborhoods with the decline of morality, safety and security, and sustainable living in American culture. They have strong values for respect, honor, sacrifice, and mutual support among neighbors that are often associated with smaller communities and tight-knit neighborhoods.

In contrast, the *liberal cultural eclectic* may include young adults living in rural, small-town, or mid-sized cities, but these young adults are often influenced by media that depicts urban life, or are preparing to escape environments that seem to limit their opportunities for self-expression. It mainly includes younger people in urban contexts, particularly in large cities or megalopolis regions (e.g., East and West Coast). It also includes young adults in regions of peri-urbanization, such as major transportation corridors between major cities and the small towns overtaken by urbanization (e.g., the corridors between Chicago and Toronto, Los Angeles and San Francisco, or between Washington, DC and Atlanta.)

Perhaps paradoxically, this tendency has helped feed the growth of large beltway churches. Participants in the *conservative cultural wedge* understand that they need to draw people from a wider region in order to have the critical mass of volunteer and financial resources to pursue their agenda. The norm in America is that people will drive to a spiritual destination that is about as far as they travel to work or shop. But the *conservative cultural wedge* are ultra-committed and will drive even farther. Their destinations, then, are often located at the intersection of major transportation corridors.

Socially Reserved

People included in the *conservative cultural wedge* can certainly be socially active—physically and digitally. However, they tend to socialize more with family and extended family, family church networks, or networks of friends that share long-term history. They may also be active in traditional service clubs like Lions and Rotary. They take time to develop trusting relationships, and therefore feel a deeper sense of betrayal if that trust is broken. They are loyal to people within their circle.

125

In contrast, the *liberal cultural eclectic* often includes people who are socially hyperactive both physically and digitally. They are more likely to say that relationships with friends are more important than relationships with family. They tend to make friends and share intimate feelings quickly, often with the assumption that relationships will shift, change, or end quickly. Consequently, they feel less guilty severing a relationship, and less hurt if the relationship is severed. They can be caring toward people they barely know, but their relationships are less likely to be sustained long term.

Churches among the *conservative cultural wedge* have the luxury of investing more time to educate and train church members. Their people tend to have deeper roots in the community or neighborhood, long-term residencies, and greater discipline regarding church participation. They will stick with a small group for a longer period of time, and "run all the bases" in a discipling process to reach "home plate." However, this also means that in situations of abuse of power or moral breakdown, these members are vulnerable to greater hurt and damage, and it may be harder to forgive and forget.

Aggressively Cautious

The *culturally righteous* are generally cautious about change, but for the *conservative cultural wedge* change evokes strong feelings. They tend to be medium-to-late adopters of technology. For this group, technology can be helpful, but it cannot become symbolic. Use it, but don't make an idol of it. Moreover, use it within limits. They acknowledge that social media can be useful, but intrusive marketing is offensive, and digital technology that allows others (corporations, governments, taxation agencies, and so on) to invade our private lives is frightening.

However, when change becomes necessary, the wedge can become aggressive. Change must be a revolution, not an evolution for the *conservative cultural wedge*. The revolution must have narrowly defined goals, and the goals must align precisely with the group's assumptions and priorities. In these cases, change is positioned as a moral imperative, and anyone who does not completely support that change becomes labeled and dealt with as an adversary.

In contrast, the *liberal cultural eclectic* love change for the sake of change. They tend to be early adopters of technology, and indifferent to privacy concerns. If the *conservative cultural wedge* are aggressively cautious, the *liberal cultural eclectic* are aggressively experimental. Unfortunately, aggression is the one thing both extremes share. They each believe in the absolutely certainty of their viewpoints, the urgency for others to agree with them. And they are quick to identify their adversaries

Churches among the *conservative cultural wedge* usually share their constituency's caution about change. Some have embraced postmodern technology in worship and communication, but it usually comes at a cost in controversy and lost members. When change is necessary, it is usually embraced with revolutionary fervor. Entire congregations can be mobilized to work for a common cause. A single issue can dominate the preaching, teaching, and outreach of a church. Membership may swell because they embrace that issue. However, if the revolution succeeds and the issue is addressed, membership can shrink and new internal controversies can fragment the church.

Educated

It is a serious mistake to assume people in the *conservative cultural wedge* are poorly educated or fit the monicker of "redneck." They are generally better educated than the average person among the broader *culturally righteous*, and certainly better educated than the *culturally ambivalent* might assume. Of course, educational backgrounds are different. Many of the wedge group have been raised in Christian schools, and both clergy and many lay leaders have attended Bible colleges. They may be skeptical of some scientific research (notably evolution and climate change), but many have advanced training in applied sciences, business, and law.

Many among the *liberal cultural eclectic* also have excellent educational backgrounds, and may also have advanced training in applied sciences, business, and law. However, they were more likely educated in public or private schools, have attended secular universities, and graduated from accredited seminaries. Their path might have been more eclectic than those of the *conservative cultural wedge* (e.g., bursts of continuing education between careers, interspersed with travel, and other adventures). People among the *conservative cultural wedge* are often more single-minded, pursuing their education with less interruption, and focused on a clear goal.

Traditional forms of Christian education (e.g., adult Sunday school and midweek Bible study) are more effective with people in the *conservative cultural wedge*. They are more likely to follow a curriculum, do their homework, and come prepared for an educational event. They often take notes during a sermon, watch religious television programs, and listen to Christian talk radio. However, the *conservative cultural wedge* are just as choosy about news broadcasts, publishers, and media outlets that support their views as the *liberal cultural eclectic*.

Marginalized and Defensive

The *culturally righteous* often feel left behind by "progress," and are eager to protect traditional values. The *conservative cultural wedge* go further. They are resentful of supposed "progress," and protective of what they perceive to be their rights and privileges. Ironically, for many "marginalization" is more appearance than reality. Many among the *conservative cultural wedge* actually enjoy significant local, regional, or national power. They are often more affluent, better educated, and upwardly mobile than the typical conservative. They tend to perpetuate a "victimized" mentality, believing that they are deliberately targeted and under attack by outside forces. Their "victimizers" may be imaginary or an exaggeration of reality.

Unfortunately, the same might be said of the *liberal cultural eclectic*. They, too, like to posture as people who are under siege, fighting for their rights and privileges. They too often purport to "victims," but the "victimizers" may be imaginary or greatly exaggerated. But, like the wedge, the eclectic are not as powerless as they claim, also enjoying considerable influence on public policy, municipal planning, public education, and so on. The *liberal cultural eclectic's* adversary, however, is not progress but *regress*. Progress is being held hostage by regressive or reactionary forces. Lifestyle segments among the *liberal cultural eclectic* may feel disenfranchised and angry about limitations on careers and upward mobility, but more generally they feel they are the vanguard of the great wave of secular human progress.

Again, church leaders in ministry with the *conservative cultural wedge* often find themselves in awkward positions. The truth is that their rights are assured, many of their churches are thriving, and they know it. Their confidence in the work of the Holy Spirit and the ultimate victory of God (revealed again and again in daily life) encourages them to be less defensive, and they are less likely to exaggerate their supposed enemies. The pressure from the *conservative cultural wedge* to battle opponents, however, is enormous. This "us versus them" mindset is particularly severe around the selection, evaluation, and potential dismissal of pastors and personnel. The more churches become focused on single issues, the more nervous church leaders become about their jobs and the prospects of a harmonious church emerging from these conflicts.

Closed and Cultic

The sense of victimization and increasingly defensive posture of the *conservative cultural wedge* encourages a gap between church members and true believers. The definition of "Christian" is more narrowly defined. The shared sense of victimization brings a smaller group together, who are passionately committed to each other and prepared to make enormous personal sacrifices of friendships, family, and career for the sake of a single cause. People tend to rally around heroes, but these heroes are *not* pastors. They may be media personalities from talk radio or blogs, or politicians with influential networks. These heroes may come and go, because the slightest misstep can undermine their credibility among the true believers. This means that the unity of the group can be elusive, and internal fights to control the movement can be fierce.

One can see why the word "cult" may surface when describing the churches of the *conservative cultural wedge*, and why these churches are often regarded with considerable caution among churches of the larger *culturally righteous*. A cult is a relatively small group of people with excessive admiration (fanaticism) for a particular idea or leader. Their boundary theology dramatically separates those who are "in" from those who are "out." The group practices intense accountability and punishes mistakes or errors in judgment severely. It is perceived by outsiders as at best unorthodox, and at worst spurious. It self-consciously separates itself from the world, but gathers considerable resources and strength to impose its will on the world.

Now it can also be said that the *liberal cultural eclectic* can be equally intolerant. They often do claim an openness or inclusiveness that is not really true, because they still ostracize or even denigrate people who disagree with their views. However, they do not have a rigid set of rules or behavior patterns that *must* be followed, and their heroes rarely have direct control of their lifestyles. At best they are perceived as unorthodox, but at worst they are perceived simply as odd or eccentric. The biggest difference, however, is that the *liberal cultural eclectic* can be enthusiastically committed to a cause

129

or a project for a *short time*; but the *conservative cultural wedge* sustain their commitment *long term*. They have more "staying power," are less likely to take time out from crusading for a cause for personal agendas, and endure personal sacrifices to achieve a desired result.

It is around causes that church leaders among the *culturally passive* as well as the *culturally righteous* begin to seriously struggle with the methods and aims of the *conservative cultural wedge*. They may have varying degrees of agreement with causes sponsored by the *conservative cultural wedge*. But the *culturally passive* and *culturally righteous* leaders perceive that the methods used by the *conservative cultural wedge* contradict many of the core values propped up by the wedge. Harmony is shattered, families are divided, and other important needs are forgotten. A religious culture of grace is replaced by a cultic, authoritarian culture of works and mandates. Important Christian beliefs are ignored or distorted. The Bible is reduced to a few phrases that become mantras or proof texts, and the richness and nuances and significance of the Bible is set aside. Pastors find themselves competing not with other pastors or churches but with media-savvy personalities setting themselves above the authority of church, tradition, and scripture—and (from the point of view of the *culturally ambivalent*) reason itself.

Acid-Test Religiosity

Earlier I suggested that the "wandering spirituality" of the *culturally ambivalent* was distorted to become playlist theology among the extreme *liberal cultural eclectic*. Something similar has happened here. The boundary theology of the *culturally righteous* has been distorted to become *acid-test religiosity* among the extreme *conservative cultural wedge*. Boundary theology functions like a fence among the *culturally righteous*. Certain core beliefs and values have to be honored, but within that fence faithful Christians are free to do whatever they wish or act according to their own conscience. The *conservative cultural wedge* have not only drawn in that fence to cover a smaller area and reduce the number of people who can be considered faithful Christians, but they have electrified the fence.

The boundary now consists of key either/or questions. Some key questions relate to core values. For example, instead of a broad commitment to "family values," the true believer must answer specific questions like:

Do you believe that abortion is wrong no matter what the circumstances?

Do you believe that homosexuality is a sin?

Other questions relate to core beliefs. For example:

Do you believe every word of the Bible is literally true?

Is Jesus your personal Lord and Savior?

Other examples of key questions might involve health care and wealth management; aging and euthanasia; race or gender equality; war and peace; job creation and climate change; or individual rights and social obligations. Key questions are, in fact, just the beginning of the interrogation. Responses must ultimately be *yes* or *no*, without any qualifications. True believers must believe exactly the same things, in the same ways, with the same moral or theological implications.

One of the hallmarks of the *culturally ambivalent* and *liberal cultural eclectic* is their holistic thinking. They focus on synthesis rather than analysis. They believe that truth is more than the sum of the parts, just as they believe that a human being is more than a collection of arms and legs, circulatory and skeletal systems, brain cells and synapses. Truth is larger and more mysterious than any one religion, tradition, or church can contain. It surpasses the largest library of books. Faith is more than a series of dogmatic affirmations, moral rules, or liturgical practices. The risk, of course, is that absolutes disappear. Every affirmation becomes tentative, every moral position becomes relative, and every liturgical practice becomes a personal preference. For these people, however, this way of living is preferable because it preserves freedom. Holism assumes that authentic living is life without limits, and human beings can and should fulfill their full potential.

The hallmark of the *conservative cultural wedge*, however, is a form of *atomism*. This doctrine is the opposite of holism, with a focus on analysis rather than synthesis. The *wedge* believe that truth really is the sum of all the parts, just as they believe that society is a balance of power and every being has a specific role to play. Truth can be contained in one religion, tradition, or church; and it can be condensed into a single book. Faith really is a collection of specific affirmation, obedience to specific rules, and is best expressed in certain ways. The risk, of course, is that freedom is curtailed by absolutes that are beyond criticism. Every question becomes hesitant, every behavior pattern becomes scrutinized, and religious practices are determined by higher authorities. For these people, however, this way of living is preferable because it guarantees meaning. Atomism assumes that authentic living is life within limits, and human beings must recognize that they are essentially flawed or depraved and can only hope for grace.

Atomism and holism are fundamentally different worldviews. The *culturally ambivalent* and the *liberal cultural eclectic* assume that authentic living is life without limits, in which human beings discover they contain a spark of goodness, and believe hope lies in cultivating human potential. They perceive a world of internal relationships. Everyone and everything is intrinsically, inseparably connected to everyone else and everything else. It's not just that one's existence is tied to the existence of all humanity and the physical world itself (and vice versa), but that the meaning and purpose of one's life is inevitably shaped by the meaning and purpose of everyone else. One's culture is related to other cultures. Living in harmony with creation and living in harmony in the global village are essential to personal fulfillment. One might say that it is a radically *horizontal* world.

Meanwhile, the *culturally righteous* and the *conservative cultural wedge* see a world of external relationships. Everyone and everything is separate from everyone else and everything else. Some are wheat and some are chaff. There is a hierarchy of power or control in the world (which for church people is divinely ordained). One exists independently. The inanimate and animate world (earth and plants and animals) are used to enhance the quality of life for humans. Men and woman are fundamentally different and have different roles to play in society. Meaning and purpose in one's life either is self-generated or depends on a transcendent relationship with God, but it is not necessarily shaped by creation or other cultures. Living with authority over the world, and choosing to live competitively or cooperatively with other people, are essential to personal fulfillment. One might say that it is a radically *vertical* world.

Ironically, atomism is akin to the mechanistic view of the universe associated with modern (i.e., Enlightenment) worldviews of the seventeenth to early twentieth centuries. When it is imported into the church as boundary theology, not only is it used to separate insiders from outsiders, but it distinguishes between roles, religions, and cultures. Society is a construct of various building blocks that can be stacked and ordered, kept in place or moved at the discretion of authority. A collection of clearly defined core values and beliefs is a method to sort people and cultures. The *conservative cultural wedge* take this further, so that a collection of clearly defined key questions sort people and cultures.

Both holistic and atomistic worldviews have existential and practical implications.

The vitality of lifestyle segments that have a holistic attitude and perceive a world of internal relationships is most threatened by a sense of ongoing depression. For one thing, a world without certainties and absolutes fosters a sense of meaninglessness. If everything is relative, then nothing in one's life is normative. If everything is in constant motion, then one's life can never be stable. Freedom comes at a price. History is aimless. One's own life is a speck in the vast interrelatedness of the universe. One's life doesn't matter much. For another thing, a world without transcendent ideals and shared assumptions can be a very lonely world. Long-term, committed relationships are not necessary, and ultimately impossible. What feels good now will probably feel bad in time, and one relationship will be exchanged for another. Institutions don't matter much either. Fundamentally, churches have no more insight into the meaning of life than any other religious institution. Holy Communion and hugging a tree are basically the same thing, and offer the same minimal satisfaction.

The satisfaction of lifestyle segments that have an atomistic attitude and perceive a world of external relationships is most threatened by a sense of underlying dread. Living in a world of absolutes that we may not understand but must obey, or surviving in a world of high ideals that we can admire but never live up to, fosters a sense of fate and impending doom (apocalypse). Limitation comes at a price. History is inevitable and judgment is certain. There is always one power further up the hierarchy of control that is beyond our control. For another thing, a world of eternal truths and high expectations highlights the brevity and weakness of one's life. Reconciliation with that Higher Power is a matter of urgency. Authorities and institutions become important as mediators of grace and representatives of God. One's destiny may hinge on a creed, a rite, or a single mistake.

And what of the *culturally passive* who are caught in between the two extremes? These are the lifestyle segments and their churches who are trying to balance the horizontal and vertical worldviews. They struggle to reconcile internal and external relationships. They are frozen between depression and dread, and paralyzed between anxieties of emptiness and loneliness on the one hand, and fate and death on the other. Inevitably, they feel a sense of abandonment. In comparison to the starkly defined faith of the *culturally righteous* and its conservative extreme, and the remarkably ambiguous faith of the *culturally ambivalent* and its liberal extreme filled with alternative spiritualties, they feel old-fashioned and weak. They feel a sense of abandonment—left behind with old-fashioned doctrines and empty rites. Their discipline flags. They attend worship more and more sporadically. Their clergy know they are under-funded and feel disrespected.

The shift from boundary theology to acid-test religiosity also reveals a shift in the relationship between the church and political sectors. The boundaries of the *culturally righteous* include both core values and bedrock beliefs, but the emphasis is always on the bedrock beliefs. The values flow out of the beliefs. For example, the critique of homosexuality flows out of a more entrenched belief in the inerrancy of scripture. The critique of abortion and women's rights flows out of a more entrenched interpretation of the story of creation. The alliance between church and political leadership was part of this flow. The power of political leaders to advocate specific public policies depended on the theology of the church to give it legitimacy. One might say that among the *culturally righteous*, the "dog wags the tail."

However, with the emergence of the *conservative cultural wedge* and acid-test religiosity, relationship between church and political leaders has reversed. The flow goes the other way. The emphasis is on core values more than bedrock beliefs. Now the conviction about the inerrancy of scriptures demands allegiance to a political policy about sexuality. The validity of the story of creation depends on acceptance of a particular attitude toward gender and family life. In other words, the ability of church leaders to sustain their authority over the life and faith of church members now depends on their willingness to support particular political positions. One might say that among the *conservative cultural wedge*, the "tail wags the dog."

This same shift in the priorities of values and beliefs might give the *culturally righteous* pause to reconsider their classic criticism of the *culturally ambivalent*. Conservatives have always accused the left of being relativistic, although as we have seen the extreme *liberal cultural eclectic* can be remarkably absolutist about specific social values and political policies. Now it appears that despite the theological absolutism of the *culturally righteous*, the *conservative cultural wedge* can be remarkably relativistic about faith. Indeed, they resemble the *liberal cultural eclectic*. Both groups insist on total obedience to specific values and political policies, and zero tolerance for any kind of compromise; but both groups can be remarkably nonchalant about adherence to basic faith convictions and disinterested in a profound spiritual life.

Ironically, the *culturally righteous* and the *culturally ambivalent* share the same political weakness when it comes to controlling their extreme wings. Once faith becomes secondary to politics, they are unable to exercise much accountability over their extreme constituencies. The two extremes can shout accusations, rattle their swords, and prepare for war, and there is little that either the larger body of conservatives or the larger body of liberals can do about it. A parallel can be instructive from the famous historian Barbara Tuchman's analysis of the roots of World War I, aptly captured in the title of her book *In Praise of Folly*. Relatively small but elite groups of extreme politicians with competing political and economic agendas managed to start a war that killed millions of soldiers and civilians, and there was little the more moderate enablers could do about it.

The challenge for the *conservative cultural wedge* is that the key questions and the right answers can vary from group to group, can change over time, and are more likely to be influenced by politics than faith. Acid-test religiosity becomes an instrument of political manipulation. And it tends to flourish only in times of crisis or intense confusion, so that all parties with subtly different acid-test questions can temporarily forget their differences and unite with a common cause. The current context of secularity, the influence of the *culturally ambivalent* and the *liberal cultural eclectic*, and the inaction of the *culturally passive* create a perfect storm for crisis. The church is one of many institutions swept into this storm.

If that perfect storm were to calm down, however, the sense of crisis would fade, and the *conservative cultural wedge* would begin to fragment and lose influence. For example, if secularity became more open to people of faith; or if churches of the *culturally ambivalent* became clearer about faith; or if churches of the *liberal cultural eclectic* could hold their adherents more accountable for their behavior and belief systems; or if churches of the *culturally passive* could be roused to social reform or passionate faith; then crisis would begin to dissipate. The migration of people from various lifestyle segments from the left to the right would slow down or stop; and indeed, the migration might go the other direction as society becomes increasingly urbanized and diverse.

135

Part of the agenda of the *conservative cultural wedge*, therefore, is to encourage and sustain a sense of crisis. Relatively minor trends are exaggerated to be enormous shifts. Small incidents are given universal significance. "Public education is *completely* failing to provide moral instruction to our children." "Allowing one abortion for an abused woman will cause a flood of abortions among all women." "The theory of evolution will undermine *everything* that is true in the Bible." Moreover, the *conservative cultural wedge* can count on the *liberal cultural eclectic* to react extremely and do much the same thing. "Faith education will *destroy* the integrity of public education." "Anti-abortion policies will *enslave* all women." "Teaching alternative theories of creation will undermine *all* scientific inquiry."

Acid-test religiosity is the perfect sparring partner for playlist theology. Together they can keep the cultural left chronically ambivalent, the cultural middle chronically passive, and the cultural right chronically anxious. Both extremes practice "no tolerance" policies that exclude each other. More significantly, their zero-tolerance attitude precludes any attempt at sincere, mutually respectful dialogue. The public is forced to choose sides, even though they don't want to do so. They are afraid to ask questions or share doubts with the other side, lest they be ostracized and harm their careers or lose their privileges.

Chapter 5
THE CULTURALLY PASSIVE

Whatever happened to the cultural middle?

Much has been written and debated about the size, participation, income, and stability of the middle class. Most authorities agree that the number of households and their wages are declining (not keeping pace with inflation or the cost of living), although not for the same reasons. Any study of lifestyle trends in America reveals a growing gap between the very rich and the very poor, and a steady decline of households in the middle with incomes between $35,000 and $100,000.

The middle class can be defined as economically liberal and socially conservative, classically religious, with relatively stable households and realistic optimism for the future. Middle-class households recognize and respect sound leadership and believe that community harmony is good for life and good for business.

They tend to be "economically liberal" in the sense that they are committed capitalists. They seek opportunities and demand the right to make money in responsible ways, and to spend money any way they wish. This liberty tends to make them "conspicuous consumers," and they are often vulnerable to debt. But they usually sustain a high credit rating and manage to save money. They believe in productive careers and expect a comfortable retirement. They want to make profits, but they are not profiteers. They want to rise in social status, but they are not greedy and do not aspire to be billionaires.

They tend to be "socially conservative" in the sense that they believe in basic civility, and at least creatively honor family, community, and national traditions. They pragmatically balance values for marriage and family, parenting, health care and social security; with values for individuality and independence, permissiveness, free choice and personal responsibility; and accept that this balance will occasionally and inevitably be ambiguous. They want to preserve harmony and encourage innovation at the same time.

They tend to be "classically religious" in the sense that they ally themselves with a religious tradition (e.g., Christian, Jewish, Muslim, Hindu, Buddhist, Sikh) that has clear beliefs and expectations for religious practices. They belong and contribute to religious institutions even though they doubt occasionally and attend irregularly. They believe that organized religions contribute to social assimilation and civic virtues, and that disagreements can always be discussed and compromises can always be made. Regardless of how "hard line" the religious authorities might be, they are pragmatically "ecumenical" in their daily lives.

They sustain "relatively stable households" in the sense that they are loyal to their partners, consistently supportive to their offspring, and ready to help their parents in need. The partners may be of the same or different gender; and the offspring may include children from another family; and the parents may be demanding in unexpected ways; but they take their responsibilities for family relationships seriously and consider their commitments to be long term. If households become dysfunctional in any way, they are ready to seek help to remedy the matter.

They are "realistically optimistic" in the sense that they believe continuous education, concentrated energy, personal sacrifices, and teamwork will be rewarded by higher incomes, increased community status, and opportunities for their children to surpass their parents. And they believe this is possible in a context of peace and fair play. They believe that other social institutions will help them rather than hinder them, and that they can shape their lifestyles for their personal advantage.

They want to "recognize and respect" sound leaders in the sense that they believe organizational systems work reasonably well, and hope that leaders will be chosen, trained, evaluated, and held accountable to goals and standards. They believe in good government that is well managed by competent people. They are content to pay reasonable taxes because they believe it is a wise investment to support the well-being of the community, and healthy community is the only way to guarantee the right to make money and create more opportunities to do it.

Finally, they believe that "community harmony is good for life and good for business." They are willing to listen to others, adapt, and compromise. They make lifestyle adjustments to get along with their neighbors. They avoid extremes and seek the middle way. They are prepared to step moderately beyond their comfort zones for a good reason. And they are self-aware to realize that harmony is in their long-term self-interest.

That middle class has been gradually disappearing for several decades. In 1990, perhaps the "middle class" constituted over one-third of the population. Today it constitutes one-quarter of lifestyle segments or less. The decline, however, is not only a result of the growing gap between rich and poor.

The dream of comfortable retirement is fading. People find they must work harder and longer to sustain their current lifestyles. The cultural middle once understood themselves as "managers," "employers," and "owners," but now see themselves as "laborers" and "employees." Small businesses are incorporated into larger franchises, and owners become cogs in a larger corporation. They no longer control their own destinies.

Social norms are changing. Small towns are being overcome by urbanization. Neighborhoods are becoming more densely populated with more diverse ethnicities. It is increasingly difficult to balance harmony and innovation, or community and individualism. The ambiguity inherent in some moral choices seems to have expanded to include all moral choices.

The influence of "classic" religions is becoming less important in the growing secular world and marginalized in the bubbling cauldron of competing spiritualties. The median age of membership in organized religion grows higher and higher. Religious rites are becoming less important to the transitions from one phase of life to another (e.g., births, weddings, and funerals). More importantly, participants in classic religious traditions, and Christian denominations, are less likely to tolerate disagreements or share activities with one another.

Households are increasingly unstable. Adults are less likely to be loyal to their partners or sustain lifetime marriages. Parents are less likely to be present for their children. Peer pressure becomes more important than family tradition. The dysfunctional family is becoming the "new normal" for many households, and they are less likely to have the time or money to seek help.

Individuals are becoming "realistically pessimistic." They find themselves expecting the worst rather than anticipating the best. Higher education is more likely to lead to higher debt, and less likely to lead to career advances and higher incomes. They perceive the context of peace and fair play that was once assumed in the workplace (and in churches) has often been replaced by a context of competition and patronage. Internal politics undermine the ability of other social institutions to be quickly and fully responsive to their needs.

Credible leaders are harder to find. This includes all sectors, especially in government, business, education, health care . . . and yes . . . religious organizations. Leaders are less competent, are rarely evaluated, and frequently escape accountability. Therefore, they are more likely to resent taxes, and also resent financial demands from religious organizations and denominations.

Finally, and perhaps most alarmingly, the certainty of the former middle class that "harmony is good for life and good for business" has weakened significantly. In its place, people are relying more on factional alliances that compete for control of life and work. Rather than adapt themselves, people increasingly expect others to adopt their agendas. Power struggle is more important than compromise. Harmony is actually *not* in their best interests.

If the middle class is declining, then where are many of these lifestyle segments going?

In 1990, Tex Sample described three kinds of people in the cultural middle: the successful, the striving, and the conflicted. "The successful" were upper-middle-class business and professional people in the city—prosperous, materialistic, fulfilling the American Dream. "The striving" were hardworking and ambitious people, gathering resources and education, spending money to validate their upward mobility—pursuing the American Dream. Tex Sample observed that many of the striving were black and Hispanic. "The conflicted" were torn between commitments to family and commitments to career, less willing to make sacrifices or cut corners to succeed, and struggling to sustain compromises between "work time" and "personal time."

Since 1990, some people in the cultural "middle" migrated to the "left" and fit the profile of the *culturally ambivalent*. These include some of the people Tex Sample described as "strivers" who became increasingly frustrated and cynical about achieving success. Many of their children have moved more sharply left to join the *liberal cultural eclectic*.

Those former participants of the cultural middle who migrate left become intentionally relativistic. It means that relativism becomes a daily choice and a lifestyle habit. They are relativistic *on purpose*. Accumulate money any way you can, spend money for whatever is self-satisfying, and give money only to pet projects and personal causes. Faith is a smorgasbord, and religious rites are a matter of taste. Divorce should be easy and parents should be permissive. Pragmatism in leadership is more important than integrity. Minor misdemeanors and white-collar crimes are tolerable. No matter what you have, you always deserve more.

At the same time, many former participants in the cultural middle migrated to the right to become part of the *culturally righteous*. These include many of the people Tex Sample described as "successful," who became increasingly anxious and defensive about sustaining their success into the future. Many of their children have moved sharply right to join the *conservative cultural wedge*.

Those former participants of the cultural middle who migrate right become intentionally dogmatic. This means that dogmatism becomes a daily choice and a lifestyle habit. They are dogmatic *on purpose*. Earn money, save money, and give money only to certified projects. Faith is a creed or a book or a test, and religious rites are prescribed by authority. Divorce should be difficult, and parents should be constant supervisors. Political correctness in leadership is more important than integrity. You deserve what you get; and whatever you have you must truly deserve.

Although there are fragments of lifestyle segments representing the "successful" and the "striving" still in the middle, most of the current cultural middle includes the people Tex Sample described as "the conflicted."

Those who remain in the cultural middle tend to keep their heads down, avoid conflict, and get by. The passivity of the remaining cultural middle is its most notable aspect.

The people who remain in the cultural middle become intentionally indecisive. Indecision becomes a daily choice and a lifestyle habit. They are indecisive *on purpose*. Money is simultaneously a source of pride and embarrassment. Gambling is both an opportunity and a sin. Donate only about 2 percent of net income to any cause, and spread the charity around in small amounts. Faith is a blend of local and denominational tradition, and religious rites must adhere to the expectations of a majority of members. Divorce should be easy, but only for certain reasons, largely determined by current community norms. Parents should set limits but allow anything to happen within them. Leadership that fulfills the wishes of the majority of voters is more important than integrity. By all means vote, but delay the vote as long as possible; and accept the consensus of the majority.

While much of the cultural migration has moved *away* from the cultural "middle," there has been some migration *toward* the cultural middle from the cultural "left."

Two groups of older adults (fifty to seventy years old), once associated with the cultural left, have largely migrated to the cultural middle. In a sense, these participants among the *culturally ambivalent* became either too tired or too bruised to defend their right to be ambivalent, or too disillusioned or frustrated with their new quest for absolutes, that they retreated into the *culturally passive*. These include many households from the groups described earlier as *homebuilders, health conscious, and content* and *adapters, adopters, and multitaskers*. The former were once optimistic, but are now disillusioned. The latter were once enthusiastic, but are increasingly struggling. They have been absorbed into other groups, which means that they are more likely to relate with lifestyle segments who are *not* of comparable age or income.

The net impact of this migration from left to middle renders the cultural middle even more passive, and sharpens the divisions between the left and the right. The *culturally ambivalent* and *culturally righteous* (and their extremes) need bridging lifestyle groups to help them communicate with each other. Unfortunately, those bridge groups are not only fewer but less inclined to be in "the middle" of an argument.

The diminished middle class described as the *culturally passive* has the potential to become mediators between the *culturally ambivalent* and the *culturally righteous*, but so far they have been largely disempowered by both sides to fulfill that role. The *culturally passive* are under constant pressure by the extreme groups—the *liberal cultural eclectic* and the *conservative cultural wedge*—of both the left and right. For example, with the spread of online social media since 2003, whenever a conversation is brokered between the left and right by the cultural middle, it is quickly undermined or sabotaged by their extreme factions.

This sabotage is particularly visible when secular or religious organizations try to set policy regarding ideologically "hot topics" like same-gender marriage, criteria for abortion or euthanasia, affirmative action for women and minorities, multicultural sensitivity, punishment or rehabilitation of criminals, the legitimate use of military intervention, and so on. The debate is quickly polarized by the extremist on either side, forcing the larger liberal or conservative blocs to follow their lead. The elements of the cultural middle cannot broker respectful and productive dialogue. The pragmatism that is the particular gift of the cultural middle cannot gain momentum.

Sadly, the diminished presence of the cultural middle forces them into the role of passive bystanders. They tend to drop out of the debate and passively suffer the consequences of whichever party is ascendant at the time.

CULTURALLY PASSIVE TRAITS

Some lifestyle segments are still self-consciously part of the cultural middle. However, the cultural middle today is composed of large or small lifestyle fragments. These are the lifestyle participants left behind as their counterparts migrated to the left and right; and the lifestyle participants who migrated away from the left and right to avoid conflict. This makes the cultural middle ever more disunited and disempowered. The cultural right becomes the *culturally passive*.

In general, the *culturally passive* avoid extremes. Balanced living and moderation are important goals for people in this group. They prefer stable neighborhoods with older housing built to last. They exercise, but not strenuously. They garden, but not obsessively. And they go to church, but not "religiously." They are committed to percentage giving, but unlikely to tithe. They are hard-working volunteers, but often prefer not to have leadership responsibilities.

They also tend to avoid conflict. Harmony and the appearance of harmony are important. They have a "live and let live" attitude toward their neighbors, and welcome newcomers to the community provided they do not disturb the status quo too much. Slow evolution, rather than sudden revolution, is their preference. This means they often choose consensus methodologies for organizational change. If there is conflict in the community or church, their first inclination is to publicly deny it and privately work things out. The "town hall meeting" and "pot luck supper" are key methods of compromise and decision making.

In 1990, Tex Sample noted that the cultural middle advocated self-discipline, moral responsibility, and social justice. This is still true, but all three values have become ever more vague. Self-discipline has become more of a preoccupation with privacy. An individual must practice some kind of self-control in order to get along with others, but no one has the right to know or judge the private life. Moral responsibility is more about mores. The *culturally passive* person is less focused on moral principles than on family or community customs and conventions. Social justice is more about adjusting the world than changing it. The *culturally passive* have difficulty naming the mission, but simply aspire to "make a difference."

They tend to compartmentalize their lives. Work and weekends, personal lives and public service, home and church, are all in general clearly defined, and do not readily blend into each other. They balance many obligations at once. If asked about their top commitments, they are apt to say that God, marriage, absentee children, and personal health are all number one. Their homes tend to be refuges of peace and relaxation, to which they invite close friends for fun and fellowship.

People in these segments are more likely to associate with a denominational church, or at least a well-established community church, rather than a church plant or fringe organization. The church tends to be a projection of the home, and the ideal is for church members to behave as an extended family. Even if the home or church is in conflict, people will rally to make a common front of unity if confronted by an agency of the state or a hierarchy of the denomination. Today the *culturally passive* are more likely to quarrel over sports than religion, and church members are more likely to quarrel about worship style than doctrine. Even if they drift from church participation, they are unlikely to surrender church membership. Pay attention to them, and they are likely to reinvest their time in the church.

Their preferred pastor is usually seminary trained and ordained; their preferred church building looks like an ecclesiastical destination; and their preferred programs have been tested by time. Fellowship and intergenerational harmony are important priorities. These churches are not particularly radical (neither extremely liberal nor extremely conservative), although their policies tend to be broadly inclusive. They pride themselves on being a "friendly" church that welcomes diversity in age, race, and income; and which encourages both male and female leadership. They are concerned about community migration and immigration, and see the church as an agent of social assimilation rather than social transformation. They are concerned about church decline and aging membership, and see the youth as the future of the church.

There are at least three distinct lifestyle groups within the *culturally passive*.

Balanced, Experienced, and Cautious:[1] *Don't rock the boat!*

People in this group are building careers, but they are also struggling to maintain their standard of living. They often have a lot of experience with different jobs and employers, in different cities and contexts, with diverse groups of people and more than one marriage. In an atmosphere of change, they tend to collect things to preserve memories. They worry about their personal health (especially stress management) and the health of the environment (especially pollution). They are coping with life as best they can. This is why their primary core value is balanced living. The poster of the cat clinging by its claws to a branch and the words "Hang in there!" often describes their state of mind.

Since they are chronically anxious about the future, they expect the church to be a stabilizing force in their lives and a rock in the midst of change. They often complain about "poor communication" in the church. This may reveal a deeper lack of trust in local and denominational church leadership, but usually reveals their need to slow down decision making and control the pace of change.

Jesus's Sermon on the Mount (Matthew 5–7) captures the essence of their faith. They especially resonate with the beatitudes, the advice to pray in secret, and recite the Lord's Prayer. They do not want to judge, and they do want to live by the Golden Rule. They want to be "hearers and doers" who found their houses on a rock that can withstand the vicissitudes of life.

The segments in this group may be increasingly anxious about the changing, shrinking church, and they may quarrel with new institutional policies and practices. However, they tend to be brand loyal. They may drift to the edge of the church, but are unlikely to surrender membership. If the church tries hard to regain their allegiance, they are likely to respond positively. On the whole, they tend to worship with some frequency and are willing to volunteer for church offices and mission teams. They are likely to preserve church memorabilia, value classical hymnology, and try to adapt and reuse old curricula.

In their younger days, many of the people in this group were more active in social causes. They are still keen to support mission projects, especially if

---

1. Many groups may be included (but not limited to) lifestyle segments currently identified by Experian as H00 *Middle-Class Melting Pot*, including H26 *Progressive Potpourri*, H27 *Birkenstocks and Beemers*, H28 *Everyday Moderates*, and to some extent H29 *Destination Recreation*.

they can provide the essentials of food, clothing, and shelter; or improve the quality of life for victims of natural disasters or wars; or improve the lot of disadvantaged people. Environmental issues in particular can motivate them to sign petitions and join a protest march.

Simple, Traditional, and Carefree:[2] Don't panic, everything will turn out all right!

Many people in this group are nearing the end of their careers or already retired, although some are younger couples juggling dual careers and families. Yet they comfortably mingle with each other because they are all nesting. Home life is important to them. They are interested in home renovation and décor. The older people in this group are busy simplifying their lives; and the younger people in this group make simplicity a passion. They will always say that "people are more important than things."

They are content with their standard of living and want to protect their privileges. They are grateful for what they have, and do not feel great urgency to acquire new things, upgrade to new technologies, or make lifestyle adjustments to suit anyone else. Although people in this group are generally conservative in their social, political, and religious attitudes, they rarely go to extremes. They also tend to be liberal in their attitudes about gender equality, open to different cultures, and ready to try something new if it does not entail too much risk or cost.

Their sense of anxiety is periodically acute, but not necessarily chronic. On the one hand, they resonate with Jesus' encouragement to relax and consider the lilies of the field and the birds in the air. On the other hand, they worry about dramatic changes in the world. They may not follow the news daily, but they may overreact to a major event that threatens their peace. On the whole, they believe life unfolds in predictable cycles and God is in control. Spirituality is often tied to the security and comfort of the home, or to the grandeur and beauty of nature. Holidays like Thanksgiving and Mother's Day are important to them.

They are apt to stay brand loyal to the denomination of their youth, but tend to assume that the local congregational customs they left behind should be normative for any new congregation they join.

---

2. Many groups may be included (but not limited to) lifestyle segments currently identified by Experian as L41 *Booming and Consuming* or L42 *Rooted Flower Power*.

They may be willing to experiment with new technologies or music in worship, rotate into a new midweek small group, read about a different theological perspective, or start a new outreach ministry. Yet their default inclination is to preserve the status quo. They like intimacy, consistency, and predictability.

They are most cautious when it comes to church property and stewardship. They often make it a priority to protect church architecture and preserve heritage. They dislike aggressive fundraising campaigns and don't want the pastor to talk too much about money. They can be generous donors to the church budget and outreach ministries, but they like to monitor the finances of the church and prefer to keep the record of giving strictly confidential.

Stable, Diplomatic, and Patient:[3] Calm down and carry on!

This group is generally older. Many have chosen to retire in the same houses, neighborhoods, or communities where they raised their children. They sink deep roots; support local clubs, veteran's groups, and retail stores; and remain brand loyal to their churches. Their lives are stable, barring sudden downturns in the economy. But that's the challenge. Sudden downturns in the economy are becoming more and more frequent.

People in this group are not particularly adventurous and are skeptical about innovation. Yet they generally accept the inevitability of change with good grace. They will do their best to welcome newcomers from different cultural backgrounds into the neighborhood or town, but they may become alarmed by dramatic increases in population density. In the same way, they will welcome new people into the church, but are anxious that the church not become too big. They prefer to know people by first name. The church is seen less like a "rock" and more like an "oasis."

They attend worship regularly, except for vacations. Their children and grandchildren may or may not participate in the church as adults, but they accompany their parents and grandparents to worship in their church on holidays. They are often puzzled and disappointed that their children are not as active in the church as they are. They often think of the youth as the future of the church, and may look to their grandchildren to become that future.

---

3. Many groups may be included (but not limited to) lifestyle segments currently identified by Experian as J34 *Aging in Place*, J36 *Settled and Sensible*, or Q64 *Town Elders*.

They have deep faith in God's plan to redeem the world, and they turn to religion for strength. They generally refer to the church, however, as "my church" and feel a sense of ownership for its programs, buildings, and technologies. Many would be surprised to discover that the denomination owns the assets, not the local trustees.

The facility itself has great symbolic power. It is filled with memories of a growing family and deepening friendships. Memorial funds are important to people in this group, and they may consider leaving bequests to the church. It is difficult for them to make major renovations or technology upgrades to either the sanctuary or the education wings, even though diminishing membership may force the church to mothball a floor of the Sunday school or rent space to outsiders.

The church facilitates quality relationships. It is a center for socializing, and many of their friendships involve mutual service and personal support in the programs of the church. They assume the church will be active in community affairs and represent their interests in the government, health care, education, and legal sectors. Fellowship is emphasized through good food and sit-down dinners; large groups for women and men, singles and couples; and small affinity groups related to hobbies and crafts.

People in these groups trust pastors and church officials to make wise and faithful decisions, but generally believe that most disagreements can be resolved by a "town meeting" or with Robert's Rules of Order. Strategic planning should start with a survey of membership opinions and personal priorities, and then move on to identify needs and opportunities in the community.

GROUPS TO WATCH

There are several groups of people who are considered part of the *culturally passive*, but which bear watching. These are groups that show signs of volatility, and may not remain passive for long. They may become more aggressively liberal or conservative, but they may also aggressively claim the right to be in the middle. These people are rapidly becoming less and less content, and more and more militant. Until now, the potential of the *culturally passive* to become mediators between the left and right has been ignored. These people may insist on it.

Promising, Mobile, and Global:[4] *Keep the door open!*

These younger families, often with preschool children, are determined to get ahead. They tend to have clear goals and they are results-driven. To sustain middle-class incomes, they must go where the jobs are. They are very conscious of their credit rating, the quality of the public-school system, and opportunities for safe outdoor activities. They are devoted to their families and passionate about personal or professional development.

Perhaps when they were single they identified more with the *liberal cultural eclectic*, but now that they are married and growing they have become frustrated with the iconoclasm and relativism of that group. They are also tiring of the polarization that is undermining good government, dividing communities, and hampering global business.

These people often seem self-absorbed, but they are extremely opportunistic. They become alarmed when political correctness, economic restrictions, social prejudice, gender inequality, or other issues block their path. If their child is sick, they believe they have the right to receive the best health care. If their spouse is laid off, they believe they have the right to find meaningful work.

They seem to be looking for God through the eyes of a child. They are concerned about the moral upbringing of their children, but they also tend to see religion as a set of profound experiences rather than a set of rational doctrines. They agree with Jesus that a child is the greatest person in the kingdom of heaven and include themselves as children.

They look for a church that is not too abstract or advanced. They want to experience incarnation, rather than understand it. They want to learn the basics of faith, and are only just now grasping the fundamentals of church membership and leadership. They may still have a hard time discerning the difference between the hope of divine grace and the promise of success. The problem of meaningless evil can really throw them off balance, and they rely on strong spiritual leadership.

Their churches are paradoxical in the same way that their busy, dual-career, child-centered lifestyles are paradoxical. Both can be noisy, messy, and chaotic, and some remarkably odd (and even bad) behavior can be tolerated. Yet there is rigorous alignment to the mission of the church, and high

---

4. This group might include people from lifestyle segments currently identified by Experian like F22 *Fast Track Couples* or F23 *Families Matter Most.*

expectations for leadership in the church. They want a church to be spontaneous and open, but at the same time they expect serious accountability for all paid and unpaid leaders.

This group has the potential to step out of the *culturally passive* to become *culturally courageous*. As church leaders, not only are they younger than most other church leaders but they think out of the box. As church members, they do not feel bound by traditions or dogmas, and resist being manipulated by ideological agendas and charismatic personalities. Moreover, their vulnerability to life struggles motivates them to seek meaning and quest for God. They can select the best and reject the worst aspects of the *culturally ambivalent* and the *culturally righteous*. But can they resist the pressure and manipulation of the extremists from each group and dare to lead?

Working Hard, Protective, and Law Abiding:[5] Remember who you are!

People in this group might once have been labeled working class, but today their incomes and community status place them in a different category. They have positions of responsibility, and they want to do the right thing for their families, the community, and the church. Many of them live in the Midwest and South. They often live around medium-sized cities and small towns, and stay close to home in their own neighborhoods.

They tend to have conservative family values but liberal economic views. They want to remove barriers that stand in the way of entrepreneurs but also protect the benefits and pension plans of hard-working employees. They may be more active in their labor union and cultural organization, or in the PTA and neighborhood association, than they are in the church.

Some people in this group may have related more with the *conservative cultural wedge*, but as their education and community awareness has developed they no longer see issues as black and white. They become alarmed when incivility, intimidation, and manipulation dominate political, educational, and other social institutions.

These people have very pragmatic attitudes. They shop around for the best prices; and they shop around for the best church. Their choice is dictated less by what a church thinks and more by what a church does. Programs must

---

5. This group might include people from lifestyle segments currently identified by Experian like I31 *Blue Collar Comfort*.

be helpful in this place, at this time, addressing real problems in whatever way works. They will only stand for so much preaching and theory; and then they want action and measurable improvements in their lives and communities.

When I have worked among these people in their communities and churches, I have found them readier for innovation than one might expect. If a creative idea is not too controversial or costly, they are willing to experiment. They have discretionary income to support special projects or to make capital improvements and technology updates. Agreement about doctrines and ideologies is secondary to "getting things done" and pragmatically solving social and economic problems.

People in this group may view the local church as part of their social network and extension of their families. But bear in mind that they are quite willing to give up time with their families to advance their careers, increase their incomes, and expand their horizons. And they will resent churches of any ideological persuasion blocking positive change with political correctness or inflexible dogmatism.

This hard-working, law-abiding group has the potential to step out of the *culturally passive* to become the *culturally courageous*. These people might be included in what Tex Sample describes as "working class."[6] They are becoming increasingly resentful over the quarrels that are dividing the *culturally ambivalent* and the *culturally righteous*, and particularly the extremes of the *liberal cultural eclectic* and the *conservative cultural wedge* that contradicts their core values for civility. They may increasingly demand more power in decision making in both liberal or conservative churches, and more resources from respective denominational bodies for leadership, program, and property. They have the inner confidence to stand up to manipulation from either side. But are they willing to stake everything (including "sacred cows" of property, local custom, and the authority of matriarchs and patriarchs) to do it?

Multicultural, Sensitive, and Open Minded:[7] Everyone deserves a chance!

These people often live in large metropolitan areas on the East and West Coasts. They may be blue collar, but they are bilingual with close family ties

---

6. Sample, *Working Class Rage*.

7. This group might include people from lifestyle segments currently identified by Experian like P56 *Midscale Medley*, P59 *Expanding Horizons*, and P60 *Striving Forward*.

in other countries. They work multiple jobs and save their money; and they help support their extended families and try to open new opportunities for them as well. They mix well with people of other cultures and races as long as they live in a context of mutual respect. They appreciate being included, and that generosity extends to others. They tend to be uncomfortable with any church that is exclusive or judgmental for any reason.

Despite long work hours in often heavy labor, they are quite optimistic and eager to advance their careers, improve quality of life, and help their children to a brighter future. They may not have deep neighborhood roots, with average residency less than five years, and are more mobile. They don't tend to join other civic organizations. The church, therefore, can become an important social as well as religious center. It can provide a "safety net" for their families if there are crises of health or unemployment.

They believe that religion should both cherish the past *and* empower the future. It's not always easy to balance the one with the other, but if one side of that equation becomes too dominant, they will focus on the other side to restore social equilibrium. They will preserve their own cultural norms, but do what they can to adapt their traditions to those of their neighbors for the sake of harmony. They are interested in new things and appreciate the openness of social media.

In theory, they strongly support classically Christian values about marriage and divorce, parenting, and family; and classic Christian beliefs about God, sacraments, and judgment day. In practice, they are often open to negotiation and compromise arising from compassion. This combination of principle and pragmatism is what puts them "in the middle" of many arguments, which means that they tend to put their head down, focus on their own affairs, and avoid getting involved.

Yet that may change. The balance of a cherished past and bold future may be hard to sustain, but they will fight hard to do it. Balance in itself is a kind of virtue. When factions and controversies try to drive them to one extreme or the other, they will push back. They are proud of themselves, and of the value of balance, and in the future may lift their heads, pay more attention to external factors seeking to control their lives, and get very involved.

This group also has the potential to step out of the *culturally passive* to become the *culturally courageous*. These people believe in assimilation, cooperation, and conversation. They may treat the church as an extended family, but they insist on greater accountability within the family for respectful behavior. The church is more important to them than many other Americans, and they are more willing to allow family members to agree to disagree, so long as they remain committed to the greater mystery of Christ. But can they overcome systemic prejudice lurking within both the *culturally ambivalent* and *culturally righteous,* and are they willing to risk raising their voices in a culture dominated by people of western or European heritage?

Black, Angry, and Restless:[8] This time, we shall overcome!

Perhaps the most likely group to break with passivity and become a "militant middle" is middle-class African American individuals, couples, and families. A sign of this new militancy may be that many have reverted to the self-conscious identity of "being black." This middle class emerged from the non-violent protest and conciliatory work of Martin Luther King Jr. But there are signs that they are reclaiming the more aggressive attitude and confrontational work of Malcolm X.

The emerging perception is that there never was the social and political will in America to follow through with the accomplishments of the civil rights movement and disempower racism in America. A hidden racism has continued to pervade American culture, and because it was denied or covered a new and overt racism is reappearing. These people sense that the future of their children—and the sustainability of their own lifestyle—is in jeopardy. These people may have grown up working class, but now they are well educated and highly skilled, having gained professional and social status. They have relocated to the suburbs. Personally, they are highly motivated. They are ambitious for their children.

This group is often described as busy workaholics who have overbooked their calendars. They always seem to be rushing from work commitments to family commitments and back again. Parents arrive separately and at the last moment to watch their children in sports, and leave separately at the earliest opportunity to get back to work. Households are efficient, and the food is fast. Hands-free telephone communication is a must on the sidewalk or in the car.

Perhaps it is not a surprise, then, to find that their church connection has often weakened. The best you can say is that, generally speaking, God

---

8. This group might include people from lifestyle segments currently identified by Experian like D18 *Suburban Attainment.*

is among their highest priorities. Initially they may have commuted from the suburbs back to their home churches; but increasingly they are joining new churches closer to home and another rung up the social ladder. These churches are medium-sized (not huge), and have a high profile in the community. Evangelism and social action are two sides of the same coin, and these churches house, coordinate, or partner with a variety of social services. Perhaps it goes without saying that these people are too busy to serve on the church board or chair committees, are often sporadic in worship attendance, and volunteer in short (but intense) bursts of energy.

But there are signs that this pattern is changing. The reemergence of overt racism (and prejudice toward immigrants and other minorities) is giving people in this group a new focus and sense of urgency.

Today you can observe many in this group simplifying their lives; paying more attention to the frequency of racially motivated violence locally and racially slanted public policy regionally and nationally; and including more time for rallies, protests, and advocacy. Previously they tended to be "undecided" about political and religious leaders, but today they seem much more intentionally evaluating and selectively supporting political and religious leaders.

Apparently, this group is not returning to their old working-class black churches but are more intentional about joining, participating, and leading biracial or multicultural churches in the suburbs. They want to place themselves in positions of power, rather than return to mere rage over powerlessness. They are starting to join boards and chair committees; be more selective about pastoral leadership and intentional about staff accountability; and be more critical of denominational policies and practices. They are using the church as a bridge to influence social and political agencies.

It is as if people in this group thought they had succeeded in life and could relax, enjoy, and accumulate wealth like other suburbanites. But now they are more determined than ever to focus, lobby, and gain influence to follow through for racial equality and justice for minorities. They may step out of the *culturally passive* to join the *culturally courageous*. Certainly they are angry enough. But can they resist being coopted by either the left or the right with white people's agendas, and stake out their own cultural priorities?

Some in these groups may gravitate away from the *culturally passive* to join a decidedly liberal cultural left. Unfortunately, they may discover that the cultural left has become so *culturally ambivalent* that there is less commitment among aging adults for social civil rights and religious ecumenism and spiritual growth than they had supposed. Some may move even further to join a more radical left, but discover that the *liberal cultural eclectic* are too unfocused, unpredictable, and self-absorbed to achieve lasting social change and accountable moral behavior.

Others in these groups may gravitate away from the *culturally passive* to join a decidedly conservative cultural right. Unfortunately, they may discover that the cultural right has become so self-righteous that there is less commitment to address systemic discrimination, religious integrity, and spiritual growth than they hoped. Some may move even further to join a more radical right, but discover that the *conservative cultural wedge* are too narrow, inflexible, and self-absorbed to achieve lasting social change and accountable religious toleration.

Perhaps it sounds overly optimistic, but if these three groups could find some common ground and effective ways to communicate with each other, a whole new, and more assertive, extension of middle-class advocacy might emerge from *cultural passivity*.

THE END OF EXPLANATORY THEOLOGY AND THE RISE OF RESIDENTIAL RELIGION

In 1990 Tex Sample described the faith of the cultural middle as "explanatory theology." At its worst, explanatory theology was simply a way to justify the good fortune of the cultural middle at being successful, absolving them of guilt for resulting social evils. But at its best, explanatory theology provided a convincing description of the purpose and activity of God in the world, and our role in it. "The task of explanatory theology is to project a vision of God's reign that can capture the imagination of cultural-middle people because it is a more compelling vision than any vision they know and because it speaks so deeply to the unmet hungers of their own lives."[9]

The "unmet hungers" primarily concern the loneliness that accompanies any separation of private experience from public responsibility, and the

---

9. Sample, *U.S. Lifestyles and Mainline Churches*, 134.

struggle for dignity that is the negative by-product of a society built on success and consumption.

At the end of the twentieth century, whether by luck or divine design, the cultural middle was living the good life and the American Dream. They were grateful. They were also protective. Faith and bourgeois existence went hand in hand. Explanatory theology emerged out of the middle-class experience of stress, fear of failure, and the need to validate one's life by achieving goals such as wealth, fame, and influence. The goal was not just to make faith *reasonable* (making some sense of the chaos of life) but to make faith *rational* (offering demonstrative proofs and logical arguments with guaranteed certainty). There was little room for ambiguity: unexplainable grace or unexplainable evil.

The great expectation of explanatory theology was that the personal needs of church members would take second place to a broader passion for social justice. Explanatory theology and "activist church" went together. For this connection to be made, a church needed a combination of pastoral leadership with credibility and expertise, financial and volunteer resources for outreach, and mutual care and personal support among the members.

In the first quarter of the twenty-first century, however, the cultural middle is struggling to sustain the good life, and the American Dream (as they knew it) is more ideal than reality. Their circumstances have changed dramatically. Their "unmet hungers" are less about loneliness and meaninglessness, and more about aging, fate, and the inevitability of death (despite their desperate attempts to prolong it). The great fear that drives the *culturally passive* today is dread of the unknown. And the great desire of the *culturally passive* is to control their destiny, rather than understand and solve world problems. If one can't explain grace and evil, at least one can try to control and manage it.

In 1990, Tex Sample described church life among the middle class in four ways: good citizenship, safe sanctuary, humanistic evangelism, and social activism.[10] While these modes of congregational life are still operative today, they no longer reflect a bold vision that captures the imagination of the cultural middle.

Churches of the *culturally passive* tend to celebrate virtues synonymous with civic responsibility. Professional pastors often function as civil servants, officiating weddings, praying at graduations, and supplementing social ser-

---

10.   Sample, *U.S. Lifestyles and Mainline Churches*, 125.

vice agencies. They tend to be agents of social assimilation that keep communities running smoothly.

Churches of the *culturally passive* tend to think of themselves as safe sanctuaries. This is less about protecting the human rights of immigrants, criminals, and outcasts; and more about providing a place of non-accountability where members can do whatever they wish. It is not just an environment without judgment but also an environment with low expectations.

Churches of the *culturally passive* tend to practice only mild forms of evangelism. They focus on the love of God and neighbor, but with little consensus about how to express that. They tend to put off baptism and confirmation until children and youth can decide for themselves what to do. They believe that good deeds do not require faith convictions.

Churches of the *culturally passive* tend to practice only indirect activism. They raise money for good causes, sign petitions for good government, support professional missionaries, and occasionally send a team (or youth group) to work on outreach projects. But they do not expect members to do hands-on social service or get personally involved in advocacy, or dedicate more than 1–2 percent of their net income to charitable causes.

This not-so-bold vision of God, the world, and our place in God's plan, has encouraged a rapid decline in worship attendance, financial support for the church, and membership in general. Why bother with church when other educational, social service, and advocacy agencies can accomplish these goals better and with less overhead? The lifestyle segments of the *culturally passive* give more money and volunteer energy to a variety of charities and causes every year, but contribute less and less to the church.

Explanatory theology has given way to "residential religion," which does not require explanations, rather symbols that are vague and comforting. Residential religion correlates with the surge (following the terror attack of 9/11) in television shows on home décor, home renovation, chefs, and cooking. This is an instinctive return to the nest in troubled times. In ways similar to the religious practices of the Jewish diaspora, the faith community is an extension of family, the church liturgy is a family routine, and the church building is an annex to the home (be it living room, recreation room, dining room, or other).

Residential religion contrasts sharply with the wandering spirituality and the playlist theology that characterizes the *culturally ambivalent* and *liberal cultural eclectic*. Faith is not a journey. It is a particular place, at a particular time, in a predictable form. People say they "go to church," and they do it once a week on Sundays, and they expect to see familiar faces and follow a familiar routine.

Residential religion is, quite intentionally, not going anywhere. It has already arrived at where the passive want it to be. The property and the facility are sacred. It is stressful to expand, redesign, or update it. The worship time and liturgy are sacred. It is stressful to change the hour of worship or modify and contemporize the language and music. Even the routine of Sunday morning, the Christian year, and the cycles of life are sacred. It is stressful to upgrade hospitality, or ignore Easter sunrise services, or eliminate children stories and verbal announcements from worship.

Residential religion emphasizes children's education and expects the youth to carry on the traditions of their elders. The goal of adult education is more to satisfy curiosity than accelerate personal and spiritual growth that might lead to change. For the same reason, the *culturally passive* avoid controversy whenever possible. They call, hire, or appoint clergy based on personal needs and comfort zones; and they expect staff to share their tastes and expand participation in decision making.

Therefore, strategic planning is slow, and visioning processes are puzzling for the *culturally passive*. They struggle to define measurable outcomes, and focus entirely on communication processes. The ideal future looks remarkably like the present. If the church building burns down, it will be rebuilt with the same architecture and symbols. If a new church development seeks to build, the structure will resemble the architectural memories of the most vocal participants. The most common articulation of vision among members is that "we just want to make a difference." But it is always unclear just what that difference will be, for whom it will be done, and what will result.

At the beginning of this book, I offered a chart entitled Cultural Habits of Church Participation to prepare the reader for the religious diversity emerging today. Now, having explored this diversity, it might be helpful to provide a snapshot of differences in theological reflection. It might help explain why the traditional Christian academy (seminary) that supported theology has become ever more distant from the realities of church experience and less helpful to clergy trying to communicate the complexity, mystery, and depth of Christian faith in diverse community contexts.

CULTURAL HABITS OF THEOLOGICAL REFLECTION

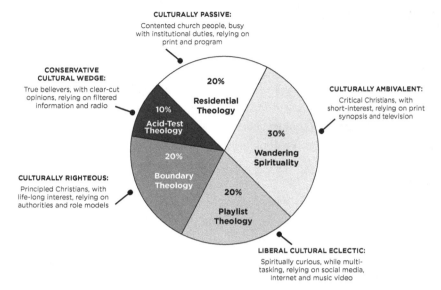

CULTURALLY PASSIVE:
Contented church people, busy with institutional duties, relying on print and program

CONSERVATIVE CULTURAL WEDGE:
True believers, with clear-cut opinions, relying on filtered information and radio

CULTURALLY AMBIVALENT:
Critical Christians, with short-interest, relying on print synopsis and television

CULTURALLY RIGHTEOUS:
Principled Christians, with life-long interest, relying on authorities and role models

LIBERAL CULTURAL ECLECTIC:
Spiritually curious, while multi-tasking, relying on social media, internet and music video

Pie chart labels: 20% Residential Theology · 10% Acid-Test Theology · 20% Boundary Theology · 30% Wandering Spirituality · 20% Playlist Theology

In 1990, Tex Sample and other church leaders believed that the hope of the middle-class church was to become an "activist church." But the diminished need for explanatory theology has diminished the hope for the "activist church." One or more of the three requirements to make the connection between theory and praxis is missing in most churches.[11] The credibility and expertise of pastoral leadership has declined as fewer people enter ministry and standards for ordination weaken. Church and denominational financial resources are exhausted, as the *culturally passive* shift charitable giving priorities away from the church. Church volunteerism is down as older members grow weary and younger members volunteer for agencies beyond the church. The mutual care and personal support among members has been replaced by increasing demands for the clergy to do all the caretaking.

Tex Sample acknowledged that the hope of an "activist" church might not be fulfilled. These churches rely on consensus decision making, and consensus is harder to achieve amid the louder extremes of the *cultural conservative wedge* and the *liberal cultural eclectic*. "Some members want the church to be a sanctuary seeking withdrawal from the world . . . others prefer a civic congregation with an educational rather than an activist approach. The church that does not have such diverse points of view will be rare."[12]

---

11.   Sample, *U.S. Lifestyles and Mainline Churches*, 125–26.

12.   Ibid., 126.

The 20 percent who are activists and the 20 percent who are sanctuary seekers vie for influence on the 60 percent who value civic responsibility but believe that education is the answer. Since 2001, the activists are getting frustrated and leaving for other agencies, and the emerging consensus is a church that simply exercises a "ministry of presence."

There are more positive aspects of residential religion, however.

Residential religion encourages the study of history and liturgy, systematic and philosophical theology, higher biblical criticism and reasonable faith. It expects these studies to be done broadmindedly, collaborating with scholars of other traditions. It is not ideologically driven, and has no preconceived conclusions to validate.

This contrasts sharply with the educational expectations of the *culturally ambivalent* and its extreme *liberal cultural eclectic*. The *culturally ambivalent* and the more extreme *liberal cultural eclectic* are highly selective of the historical events and personages to be studied; narrowly focus theologies of this and that (e.g., theologies *of* the environment, or theologies *of* liberation, or theologies *of* black experience). Biblical studies are also highly selective, setting aside huge swaths of scripture as irrelevant or untrue, and concentrating only on passages that reinforce modern agendas.

It also contrasts sharply with the expectations of the *culturally righteous* and its extreme *conservative cultural wedge*. They are also highly selective of historical events and personages to be studied. Theology is dogmatic, with the goal of universal agreement rather than shared inquiry. Biblical studies are also selective, imposing interpretations of texts to reinforce a different set of modern agendas.

Residential religion encourages ecumenism and interfaith dialogue. Precisely because their religion is so stable and deeply rooted, they feel confident to compare and contrast it with other systems of faith. Residential religion is neither defensive nor offensive in its belief system. Changing trends in culture do not threaten it. Since theology is essentially "reasonable," many among the *culturally passive* do not feel the need to impose it on others. It speaks for itself.

Again, this contrasts sharply with the left and right. The *culturally ambivalent* and the *culturally righteous* both lack the confidence of "reasonable" faith. They are both defensive and offensive, but in different ways. The *culturally ambivalent* are quick to reject abstractions and absolutes, and the extreme *liberal cultural eclectic* often embrace any faith system or spirituality *except* Christianity. The *culturally righteous* are quick to reject ecumenical or interfaith conversation, and the extreme *conservative cultural wedge* insist on the validity of only one faith system that others reject at their peril.

My perception from over thirty years of participation in the American Academy of Religion is that seminary trends in faculty appointments, course offerings, and fieldwork reflect the diminishing priorities for the core subjects of church history, systematic theology, and broadminded biblical studies, catering more and more to the desires of the *liberal cultural eclectic* or the *cultural conservative wedge*. This is one factor that has widened the gap between the seminary education associated with churches and the academic study of religion associated with the universities.

There are more practical advantages to residential religion. Despite the risks and occasional failures, it can provide a stable platform for spiritual renewal and national harmony.

- Residential religion is consistent and easily transferable. A church member can relocate to another part of the country, attend the same brand church, and expect to experience the same thing. If the preaching is excellent, and they can overcome boredom, they carry with them an inner strength and purposefulness through the vicissitudes of life.

- Residential religion can amass huge resources. Natural thriftiness combined with shrewd investment creates huge potential for good. If resources are not wasted on property maintenance, they can be used to address major social ills.

- Residential religion can partner effectively with social service and health-care organizations and educational institutions. Their core values readily match the civic values of other groups, and their professional clergy are peers of their professional leaders. If partnerships are not sabotaged by bad behavior in the church, they can create powerful networks.

- Residential religion can raise standards of leadership and support long-term clergy careers. They can model a high standard of integrity for the rest of society, and sustain excellence in ministry that spans cultural and political boundaries. If they can resist the temptation to lower standards in order to fill pulpits, they can be a powerful voice of reason.

161

Unfortunately, the risks involved to accomplish these things are growing. As the middle class weakens, so also the benefits of residential religion are waning.

MINISTRY AMONG THE CULTURALLY PASSIVE

Ministry among the *culturally passive* is more stressful than ministry among the *culturally ambivalent* and the *culturally righteous*. It is frankly easier to do ministry among people who are either so confused or conflicted that they will try anything; or so rigid and dogmatic that they will only do one thing. Here there is perpetual tension between "renewal" or "transformation." This is true for the congregation and for the individual leaders of the congregation. The church—and the spiritual lives of the leaders—may *need* transformation; but what they *want* is renewal.

These two desires are very different. Transformation is about becoming a completely different person or organization. There is a new vision and there are new measurable outcomes; there is a new board and possibly a new board structure. The agenda of the church is different, and the time management strategy of the pastor is turned upside down. Renewal is about revitalizing what already exists. The individual leader and the church as a whole are better but still the same. The old vision is reclaimed, and the old measurements of success are entrenched more deeply. The nomination's process is modified, but the board membership and structure are essentially the same. The agenda of the church is adjusted, and the time management of the pastor is tweaked.

Every pastor and board and every lay leader and committee struggles with this tension. They want to reach out to strangers without losing any members. They want to blend worship, rather than create different options for worship. They want membership training and education to be exceptional, but keep it optional. They want to attract the youth, but by appealing to the values system of the seniors. They want to impact their community, but minimize risk and balance the budget.

For ministry among the *culturally passive* to survive and thrive, church leaders must acknowledge that they cannot have it both ways. No matter what you do, someone will leave. If you change, some will leave. If you stay the same, some will leave. Ministry planning cannot be done with an attitude of fear but with an attitude of expectation. The issue is never who might leave but rather who might be blessed. It is better for ministry among the *culturally passive* to imitate the attitude of Paul and the mission to the Gentiles than to imitate the attitude of Peter and keep everybody happy in Jerusalem.

The energy for ministry among the *culturally passive* in the recent past has been to minimize the risks of residential religion, rather than maximizing the benefits of residential religion. This reflects the tension in the *culturally passive* congregation between transformation and renewal.

The current tendency is to minimize the risks of residential religion and design ministries for renewal rather than transformation by:

- standardizing ministry practices by imitating success stories from other churches, rather than contextualizing ministries for a particular church;

- making the "Sunday morning experience" of hospitality and worship more homogeneous and attractional, rather than making it more heterogeneous and missional;

- maintaining decaying infrastructure, and protecting diminishing financial resources, rather than renovating facilities and upgrading technologies, while risking manageable mission-driven debt;

- recovering broken partnerships by raising accountability for paid professionals, rather than building new partnerships by raising accountability for unpaid volunteers; and

- recruiting and training clergy and lay pastors from a diminishing pool of recruits, rather than adapting systems and empowering innovators from an increasing pool of restless spiritual leaders.

The strategies for renewal are too slow, too difficult, and ultimately too little to grow churches and impact communities. The church is becoming less relevant even among the *culturally passive*!

Strategies for transformation seemingly take the church in the opposite direction. Paradoxically, in order to be the church of the future, the church stops being the church of the past. The focus should be on radical transformation rather than modest renewal; more about maximizing the benefits of residential religion rather than minimizing the risks. This means that stress management is more urgent among churches of the *culturally passive* than among churches of either the *culturally ambivalent* or the *culturally righteous*.

Today churches of the *culturally passive* need to *contextualize* ministry rather than *standardize* ministry. The habit has been to imitate "best practices." Borrow a strategy that works well in one church, and apply it to another church. It doesn't work because the *context* from community to community is different. Therefore, the first concern of church leaders should be community demographics rather than institutional tactics.

Demographic analysis is not just about trends in age, race, family, income, occupation, and so on. It is also about understanding proportionate lifestyle diversity in the community compared to proportional diversity in the membership. Inevitably there is a difference. Lifestyle segments are over- or under-represented in the church that are much smaller or larger than in the community. This reveals not only *how* ministries must be adapted but also *how much stress* will be involved to accomplish it.

Ultimately, stress management (and church transformation) is a leadership issue. The *culturally passive* tend to prefer that traditional clergy, trained in traditional ways, be caregivers for the members and enablers for the institution. For the church to thrive again, however, what is needed are non-traditional clergy who can be CEOs for a seven-day-a-week church, or disciplers who can guide seekers through a process of mentoring and training through which they are changed, matured, gifted, equipped, and sent back into the world to serve.

Ministry among the *culturally passive* must refocus attention *away* from Sunday morning, and *toward* day-to-day life. Churches today can offer radical hospitality and exciting worship on Sunday and still not grow and still not impact the community. This is because what church members do on Sunday morning doesn't really matter anymore. It's what they do—spontaneously and intentionally, strategically and daringly—during the week that matters.

The *culturally passive* generally yearn for inspiring worship, but in the past this has been blended with educational preaching, wordy liturgies, verbal announcements, and expectations for subsequent Sunday school and Bible study. Today the *culturally passive* still yearn for inspiring worship, but now it is blended with practical lifestyle coaching that helps people live faithfully day by day. Life together is not about expositing scripture, advocating ethical choices, or explaining doctrine. It's about highlighting the daily dilemmas of life, guiding people through ambiguities, and providing helpful tips and tactics to live well. Success is measured by how many people participate in midweek support groups and individual spiritual mentoring.

Yet it is difficult for church members (and traditional pastors) to understand that worship is no longer the primary entry point into church life, and that mere fellowship is no longer satisfying the needs for intimacy among lonely people. Very few people "church shop" anymore, and their choice of a church has less and less to do with the style of music or the quality of preaching. It has more and more to do with the usefulness of religion in daily life.

The new emphasis is not to escape the secular for the sacred but to make the secular sacred. Outreach and midweek fellowship have replaced Sunday worship as the primary doorways for seekers to enter the church and for believers to exit into society. Most churches among the *culturally passive* focus on outreach involving survival (supplying food, clothing, and shelter). The priorities among lifestyle segments in the community, however, are about quality of life (safety, crime prevention, environmental cleanup, and the like); or about human potential (tutoring, skills development, job hunting, and the like); or about intimacy (dating, high-trust friendships, sexuality, and the like).

Moreover, the real key to outreach success is not the program itself but how volunteers behave while working in the program. It is in this daily behavior that radical hospitality and deep spirituality are revealed. Volunteers go out of their way to be inclusive and accepting, and they automatically live prayerfully and share bedrock beliefs that give strength to their lives. "Worker bees" and "tongue-tied Christians" are no longer needed as volunteers. Magnanimous servants and confident believers are required.

The key to effective ministry among the *culturally passive* no longer depends on high accountability for clergy and other professionals. Yes, accountability is important. But it is no longer essential. The real key today is high accountability for laity or volunteers. Outreach and midweek ministries can thrive even if the clergy are incompetent or misbehaving, provided that the volunteers are competent and positive role models. And these are the key doorways in and out of church life.

It is really quite simple. *Culturally passive* churches must learn how to fire volunteers, and they erroneously believe they can't do it. Yet their social service, health care, and other nonprofit partners do it all the time. The secret is that you can't fire a volunteer you have not routinely evaluated; and you cannot evaluate a volunteer you have not trained and coached; and you cannot train and coach a volunteer who is not hired in the first place with a clear understanding of organizational expectations.

165

Moreover, the criteria to hire, train, evaluate, and fire is always the same. You acquire a volunteer because you believe he or she has the right attitude, high integrity, competency, and the ability to work in a team. You train, evaluate, and fire using the same criteria. Any one thing is a reason to fire a volunteer: consistent inability or unwillingness to align one's personal life with the mission of the church; or live up to the core values and beliefs of the church; learn or perfect necessary skills; or behave as a team player. Just like any nonprofit, the church always offers help and reasonable time to change, but when help is unsuccessful, and time is up, the volunteer must go.

Ministry among the *culturally passive* must focus resources on mission rather than maintenance. This is an old refrain that continues to fall on deaf ears. This does not mean giving everything away now, because if the church closes there will be nothing to give away in the future. It does mean reversing a deeply embedded attitude among trustees, finance committees, and administrators. The old habit has been to think that what is good for the church is good for the community. The new habit is that what is good for the community is good for the church. Mission is more practically beneficial to the church long term. Invest in the community, and eventually they will invest in you.

This is admittedly a frightening prospect for the *culturally passive* largely because they have only experienced unreasonable debt for property and personnel. Churches commit to exorbitant debt that cannot possibly be sustained by the existing membership, or by new members who take up to five years to understand stewardship. Reasonable debt is approximately equal to twice the annual budget of any given church, less the "second mile" generosity of members who raise their donations. That sum provides the capital pool for investment in future mission beyond the property, and the training of unpaid volunteers rather than multiplying paid professionals. In short, the churches of the *culturally passive* will only thrive (or even survive) if they have a reasonable, mission driven debt.

Transformed ministry among the *culturally passive* must convert to bi-vocational leadership. Not only is it difficult (and soon nearly impossible) to sustain clergy salaries and benefits, but this practice actually reduces their credibility amid the public. This may mean the multiplication of lay pastors (laity who are "upgraded" with new skills to function as pastors), but this is a limited strategy. It is one thing to train the functions of ministry, and quite another to recognize the identity and peculiar calling of a minister.[13]

Denominations are slowly realizing that guaranteed salary subsidies are neither sustainable nor desirable. But they also recognize that contract work for part-time pastors makes clergy vulnerable to the vicissitudes of life and deters younger leaders with families from ordination. The solution is to encourage bi-vocational ministry, but create capital pools that guarantee health benefits and pensions. And since bi-vocational clergy are more credible to the public, the practice should be required even in large congregations whose financial surplus from personnel costs can contribute to the capital pool for all leaders including those in small, poor churches.

The challenge for the church among the *culturally passive* is that it must do its own strategic thinking. It cannot be prescribed by experts or borrowed from success stories. Every context is unique, which is so obvious from the lifestyle segments actually within your reach. Clear away the fog about vision and purpose; explore thoroughly the diversity of people and needs in your context; and then daringly do whatever works, no matter how costly that might be for changes to attitudes, traditions, personnel, organizational models, properties, technologies, and budgets.

---

13. See Bandy, *Spiritual Leadership: Why Leaders Lead and Who Seekers Follow* (Nashville: Abingdon Press, 2016).

Chapter 6

PERSONAL RELIGION AND CULTURAL CHANGE

What happens when private religion replaces shared religion?

More and more people are identified or identify themselves as "spiritual but not religious." This claim can mean many things, and marketers are tempted to label them as a distinct cultural cohort just as they try to commodify boomer or millennial descriptions with consumer messages. Some are dilettantes who select different beliefs, from diverse sources, that validate their current status and behavior; others are seriously searching for meaning and purpose in life; and still others are radically committed to personal spiritual disciplines. Nevertheless, religion or spirituality in any form or intensity can impact culture in three important ways:

Love: How people empathize with one another

Power: How people influence one another

Justice: How people hold others accountable for their actions

The claim for religion to be "personal" is an attempt to remove one's beliefs from any critique except one's own conscience. Churches and other religious institutions, for example, have no right to interfere with social behavior. Yet religion or spirituality of any kind has social implications. Change the religion. Change the culture.

Even those who think of themselves as thoroughly secular are still driven by beliefs and values that are ultimate concerns, and organize their lives into ritualized activities. The emergence of sports as "religion" is a good example. Sports may be amateur or professional, individual or team based; and involve children or adults. Many who profess themselves thoroughly secular and non-religious actually behave in a manner that shapes love, power, and justice. Sport functions like a religion. Compare, for example, the behavior patterns of classic Christian "fruit of the Spirit"[1] to those of contemporary sports fans:

Christian "Fruit of the Spirit"	Sports' Values and Beliefs
Love	Professional courtesy
Joy	Ecstasy
Peace	Competition
Patience	Momentum
Kindness	Condescension
Goodness	Skill
Faithfulness	Team loyalty
Gentleness	Aggressiveness
Self-control	Obedience

Sport as religion has its own routines to order the week, symbols to focus enthusiasm, superstitions to achieve success, heroes of faith, and referees to adjudicate the rules of the game. The "fruit of the Spirit" adopted by early Christians are quite similar to core values described in Stoic philosophy. Marcus Aurelius and Seneca may have been agnostic about the nature of God, but they were clear that religion itself shapes society in beneficial ways. Given the choice between religion and chariot races, they would choose religion every time because the former contributed to harmony and the latter contributed to riots in the streets.

The personalization of religion (defined in the broadest sense) has been blamed by church leaders for some time as a leading cause for declining participation and attendance. The issues are deeper than this, and reveal major shifts in how the public understands love, power, and justice.

It is helpful to step back and see how *personal religion* is just a part of a larger trend to "personalize" the individual's experience of the world. We observe this trend in all sectors of human experience. For example:

---

1. Galatians 5:22-23.

- Technology and the miniaturization of communication devices;

- Government, the decline of commitment to political parties, and increased numbers of people who describe themselves as some form of "libertarian";

- Education, criticism of public education, and the rise of homeschooling;

- Law and spiralling personal litigation;

- Law enforcement, criticism of police, and adamant assertion of the right to bear arms;

- Business, criticism of corporations, and the surge in entrepreneurism;

- Health care, criticism of doctors and pharmaceuticals, and the rise of naturopathy and other alternative therapies; and

- Entertainment, the decline of theaters and concert halls, and the rise in home theater and personal playlists.

Religion is not immune to the trend toward personalization in America. Not only are participation and attendance down, but there are fewer traditional weddings and funerals, and pastoral care professionals receive less respect than ever. Customizable social media has replaced preaching as a primary source of Christian education. Church *shopping* has been replaced by church *stopping*.

Of course, American culture is grounded in individualistic attitudes and protection of individual rights. Yet the church thrived for 150 years. The current cultural trend toward personal religion cannot be attributed to individual rights. The two back-to-back global wars of the twentieth century encouraged death-of-God theology that began in Europe (the place of greatest pain) and spread to America. Yet the church in America grew exponentially after the wars, and only started its precipitous decline in the 1960s. The current trend to personal religion cannot be attributed to wars.

It is more accurate to say that the personalization of American culture is less about protection of individual rights and more about the chronic (and ever more frequently acute) abuse of human rights. There has been a precipitous decline in the credibility of leaders, institutions, and organizations in all sectors. Every organized social venue has failed to police themselves and hold leaders and members accountable for their actions. It is not only the corruption of systems by self-aggrandizing leaders but also the subversion of organizational goals around the self-interest of members.

The drive to personalize one's life is rooted in the urgency to take control of one's life. People resent outside authorities setting boundaries to limit human potential for their own gain. Today they have both the motivation *and* the means to take control back.

Consider a popular TV commercial that is critical of professional investment counseling. The commercial depicts a well-dressed and rather smarmy professional, and a plainly dressed and anxious client, sitting on opposite sides of the desk. The client is complaining about all the fees deducted from his investments, which have remained static and are starting to decline against inflation. The client says: "It seems that everybody is making money on my investments except me." The counselor responds: "You must understand that there are costs to doing business." The commercial then presents an alternative to self-administrate one's own investments and eliminate the middle man. The client now has not only the motivation but also the means to take control of his own life.

This is the flattened context in which personal religion has grown exponentially. It is not the death of God that has prompted personal religion. It is the death of credibility. God is doing very well. Religious institutions are not. From the point of view of most of the seventy-one lifestyle segments currently identified in America,[2] and among all the emerging generations in America, the church is at best unreliable and at worst corrupt. This corruption is insidious. It is more than a series of bad leaders and strategic mistakes. It is possessed (like so many other institutions) by habits that are self-destructive internally, and abusive externally, that its own leaders and members do not see and chronically deny. In short, the church is comparable to an advanced alcoholic, who is unable to change because their buddies at the bar all say they are okay.

Personal religion is prompted by the same desire to regain control of life that is driving the personalization of culture in every sector. So what is wrong with that? In every other sector, efforts to take back control of one's life seem both logical and beneficial. It may require additional training, but that is readily available (usually for free). There are risks, but they are reasonable and usually manageable, and preferable to the liabilities of entrusting your

---

2. Experian is a corporation that tracks and sorts digital information, and currently identifies seventy-one segments. This is up from about forty segments about fifteen years ago, and culture continues to fragment into more, and smaller, portraits of American life.

life and well-being to someone or some institution who does not really care about you.

Personal religion has many benefits. It reduces stress and encourages holistic health. It restores self-esteem. It motivates personal growth. It helps a person cope with the speed, flux, and blur of change. It encourages social harmony by discouraging religious intolerance. It's far less expensive than the financial overhead of institutions; and it does not leave behind an environmentally damaging footprint that blights urban neighborhoods and rural crossroads. What's not to like?

The problem is that personal religion is categorically different than the personalization of all other sectors of society. Personalization is about taking back control of *the process of living*. Personal religion is an attempt to take back control of *the meaning of life*. Rejection of religious institutions and authorities is often well and good. World history is full of instances when that has happened. But religious institutions and authorities never had that control anyway (even though they may have thought that they did). Control of the meaning of life lies with a transcendent God. This God may well be described in many ways. Yet this God is essentially mysterious and unknowable because this God is beyond human rationalizations and imaginations. As my mentor Tillich would say, this God is a God-above-all-gods.

That is the problem with personal religion. This contemporary rejection of religious institutions and authorities is fundamentally different from other instances in history. In the past, rejection of institutional religion was motivated by the desire to restore the ultimate authority of the God-above-all-gods to control the meaning of life. Today, it is motivated by the desire to take control of the ultimate meaning of life for oneself. The individual self becomes the Ultimate Concern. This means that one is only accountable to oneself—which means that in the end the self is not accountable to anything.

This is not to dismiss the sincerity or significance of personal religion for the self who controls meaning for the self. Individual selves have survived and overcome the trials of living, and some have become martyrs to admirable causes. Personal religion has prompted some to profound philosophical and psychological reflection. Once the self takes control of the meaning of life, however, surviving the trials of life depends more on stamina and stubbornness, and there is really nothing to stop the self from redefining the meaning of life to accommodate persecution. Moreover, there is no criterion that

173

guarantees an *admirable* cause to be a *good* cause, save taking a vote of the people whose personal religion allows them to admire the cause.

Religion is, in fact, *never* personal. And the power of the self to control the meaning of life is not a religion. It is at best a noble perspective, and at worse a terrible bias, depending on what another self considers "noble" or "terrible." So what *is* religion if it is not *personal*?

Religion is the recognition and acceptance that a God-above-all-gods controls the meaning of life and the destiny of creation. This God defies definition and cannot be contained by any cultural form, be it a church, a sacrament, a book, or a particular ecstatic experience. Religion makes faith concrete for the purposes of reflection, discussion, and application, but it cannot pretend to encompass a mystery that surpasses reason, tradition, and denomination. Such a claim would be idolatry: the worship of a cultural form rather than an Ultimate Concern. Individuals will certainly have their own interpretations of Ultimate Concern and perspective on the implications in personal and social life. The key, however, is that every interpretation and perspective is conditional and subject to the God-above-all-gods. In the study of lifestyle and religion, one of my favorite quotations is: "Religious thinking [along with moral codes and social forms] is a 'perceiving' in which [cultural] forms are simultaneously employed and shattered."[3]

The yearning to fulfill oneself through reunion with God, and the reality of always falling short, is a condition of our existence, regardless of which lifestyle segment surrounds us at any given time. The good news is that while we yearn to fulfill ourselves in God, God yearns to reunite with creation. There is a fundamental "restlessness for religion" that does not only emerge from our own self-consciousness, but is constantly being stirred by God in every culture and lifestyle.

Personal religion emerges from the life experience of the individual, and is a form or construct used to interpret that experience. Indeed, you might say that it is a form within a form, because any personal experience of God can only be interpreted from within the cultural framework that shapes that life. But it is always a form—a construct—and while it can be useful it can also be harmful. While it can feel divine, it can also feel demonic. The God-above-all-gods simultaneously employs and shatters every personal religion, just as

---

3. Paul Tillich, translated by James Luther Adams, "The Conquest of the Concept of Religion in the Philosophy of Religion" in *What Is Religion?* (New York: Harper Torchbooks, 1969), 144.

God simultaneously employs and shatters every denomination or religious institution.

What is religion if it is not personal? It is public. This does not mean that it must be institutionalized. It means that it must be shared. The "restlessness for religion" is stirred not just in an individual's heart but in every person's heart whether they know it, intuit it, remember it, or even forget it. The search for God is not an individual quest but a shared desire; and it will require dialogue and cooperation, rather than monologue and personalization to accomplish it.

Love

Religion is public ("shared") because reunion with God is an experience of both the depth and diversity of love. If religion were personal, then love would be merely emotional. I have the power to *choose* my friends and *reject* strangers. I "feel good" about these people, but do not "feel good" about those people. Personal religion generates cliques and cults. In fact, religion is public. It demands to be shared, just as love demands to be shared. One might say that religion is the "ontology of love." This is another way of saying that the God-above-all-gods is the reason that love *is*. The self is not the source of love. One enjoys the possibility of love by virtue of one's existence and not just one's feelings. The essence of religion is the experience of separation and the longing for reunion shared by all.

God's love for us stirs each individual's desire to unite or commune with God. But this same love inspires us to love others. This is not a generic but a very particular love. It is not love for "humankind" or even "creation" but love for that particular individual or lifestyle group over here or that particular lifestyle group over there. God's love must be public, because it requires the collective minds and hearts of all the diverse lifestyle groups represented in cultural diversity, to explore and enjoy.

Religion is inherently public or shared, not personal or private. Those who would make religion *personal* keep it to themselves. It is not possible to compare it or critique it. When God's love is privatized, the shared quest for God is denied. And when the shared quest for God is denied, the individual's own experience of God becomes idolatry. The individual no longer loves God. The individual loves him- or herself only. What happens to empathy with others in society (love), especially with strangers, refugees, immigrants, and anyone outside one's select circle of friends?

First, *agape* (or sacrificial love) becomes charity. Surrender of oneself to a larger meaning, and applying oneself to a larger purpose, is reduced to percentage living and percentage giving. This breaks empathy with other people and creates a false subject/object dualism. True empathy is often described as an "I" and "Thou" relationship. Personal religion artificially limits the degree of sacrifice one is willing to make for the well-being of a stranger.

Second, *eros* (or passion) becomes lust (or *epithymia*). The drive to reunite with God is sidetracked to a passion to control others or manipulate creation. The truth becomes unimportant. My truth becomes all-important. Social relationships become a kind of competition or power politics. Personal religion undermines the ability for social units to negotiate and arbitrate.

Third, *phileos* (or kinship) becomes patronage. The unity of family or friends becomes a hierarchy of influence. We "follow" a leader in life, just as today people "follow" an idol or an expert in social media. Leaders and followers develop an unhealthy co-dependence in which fawning obedience is rewarded by promotion; and status depends on fawning obedience.

When personal religion changes how people empathize with each other, it changes how power and justice are exercised in society.

Power

Amid the clash of cultures, power is the ability to influence one another. This is more than mere compulsion. Power is exercised in many ways, and often without any conscious intention. It is exercised in the context of every decision in daily life, and reveals itself as much (or more) through spontaneity rather than intentionality. The unrehearsed word and the spontaneous deed reveal the truth about who we are, what we seek, and who we want to become.

The word "power" is used with the sense of "powering through" life as it is actually lived from moment to moment. Every individual "powers through" life in different ways, which are profoundly influenced by the lifestyle segments to which they belong. Peer pressure is just one small part of this, albeit a significant one. Power is really an extension of love, if love is defined as desire to reunite with God and live in empathy with other cultures. It is part of a network of lifestyle segments, some of which have more or less power to influence one another, consistently or periodically, evolving as circumstances change. One "powers through" the chaos and complexity of life for both self-affirmation and social acceptance.

Personal religion undermines our ability to "power through" life. It creates a false sense of completion, as if reunion with God has already taken place. Once the individual tries to control the meaning of their life, the self becomes the standard of perfection. The individual is already complete. One feels a sense of complacency. This extends to the lifestyle segment to which one belongs. Their community becomes the best community. Other people, and other communities, may be helpful in collaborating with our goals, but they are not strictly necessary.

Personal religion collapses when faced with unavoidable evil. The first kind of evil is gratuitous evil that befalls us individually, and is evil that is entirely undeserved and unexplainable. Death, disaster, disease, and other calamities occur. The self, as the controller of meaning, cannot overcome it. Philosophers might say that the self cannot "power through" this threat of non-being. The dark side of personal religion is that it generates a sense of desperation. Once challenged by gratuitous evil, people will go to extraordinary lengths to justify themselves. Rather than listening to others, or respecting the influence of others, they resort to fantasy and the technologies that facilitate fantasy.

The second kind of evil is social evil. This kind of evil may also be undeserved, but it is quite explainable. It is the result of power that has been reduced to compulsion, whereby one individual or group exercises power that attacks the autonomy and integrity of another individual or group. The "I" and "Thou" relationship of empathy has been split so that an individual or group objectifies another. *Eros* becomes lust. *Phileos* becomes patronage. Personal religion provides a false sense of privilege and security that tries to lift a person "above the fray" of social injustice. It does not provide the courage to confront injustice but only the instinct to adapt to injustice. Once love is focused inwardly, compulsion can only be used for abuse rather than reconciliation. The possibility of "tough love"—love that uses compulsion for the good of others—is eliminated.

The *culturally righteous* are often accused by the *culturally ambivalent* of abuses of power. In fact, insofar as both groups engage in the personalization of religion, both groups are guilty of the same abuse. This results in the disintegration of hospitality, and the intrusion of xenophobia into society.

177

Both the right and the left attempt to "power through" their own agendas to exclude anyone who does not agree with them.

Justice

The reduction of love to self-love, and the reduction of power to compulsion, changes how cultures perceive and exercise justice. Justice presumes four imperatives.

First, a person should be treated as a *person* rather than as an *object*. A person has intrinsic value as a human being, and not just extrinsic value related to some demographic abstraction like race, income, occupation, or education. Our ability to track digital behavior today, and develop "lifestyle portraits," helps us extend this principle to cultural diversity. A lifestyle segment has intrinsic value as a way of being human, and not just for its contributions to society.

The xenophobia that is allowed to flourish by personal religion undermines justice. In this context justice does not mean public policy but lifestyle behavior patterns vis-á-vis other lifestyle behavior patterns. Personal religion often boasts of being "inclusive." For example, privately spiritual persons who eschew religion often favor policies of racial or gender equality, or purport to unreservedly welcome refugees and immigrants. Yet in the context of daily living, and in the millions of decisions that are made intentionally and unintentionally in the exercise of power, personal religion ultimately becomes exclusive. The more affirmative action advances women, for example, the more men resent their loss of power. The more refugees or immigrants enter a community, the more long-time residents resent their loss of power. Fundamentally, personal religion discourages any true I/Thou relationship, and objectifies others.

Second, all persons are fundamentally equal because they are rational— or have the potential for rationality. This is the one and only common characteristic shared by all humans. It is not that any human choice is justifiable but that any human choice carries within it the possibility of being justified. This is why "justice is blind." It is blind to any circumstance or prejudice that might obscure the justification or non-justification of any demonstration of power.

The patronage encouraged by personal religion allows justice to be obscured and manipulated. This is not to say that justice will always be unbiased but that any bias of justice can be appealed so that bias is eventually overcome. Personal religion often protests against legalism and claims to judge right and wrong "intuitively." *Go with your gut!* But intuition is shaped by personal bias and peer pressure, so that what seems "intuitive" to one person is "counterintuitive" to another—leading to an unresolvable battle between two egos.

Third, all persons are fundamentally free. They are free, or should become free, or should be able to sustain their freedom. It is not that freedom itself is good but that the exercise of freedom should contribute to the fulfillment of love (reunion with God and harmony with others). Justice means that every person should be accountable for their exercise of freedom. The criteria to evaluate the fulfillment of freedom may evolve or change, but that is always a *community* decision rather than a *personal* decision.

The reduction of the ability to "power through" life to the ability to compel others to do what you want eliminates the possibility of accountability. Personal religion holds itself aloof from criticism, claiming a defense of their freedom. In fact, it is defending the power to compel. Personal religion compels others to accept whatever behavior the individual wants to do in the name of personal religion. Another way to say this is that accountability only goes one way. Personal religion condescends to hold others accountable, but does not allow others to hold them accountable.

Fourth, accountability should be adequate or proportionate to the deed. People should get what they deserve. The size of a reward should be proportionate to the accomplishment of the deed. The punishment for a mistake should be proportionate to the harm it has caused. For example, it is unjust that global wealth should be in the hands of a mere handful of multibillionaires who did not earn it; or that poverty should be the lot of people who work the hardest.

Personal religion encourages disproportionate justice, both because there is no norm other than the self to evaluate what is an "accomplishment" or a "failure," and because the individual claims the authority to be simultaneous judge and jury. Personal religion allows disparities in wealth, health, opportunity, and redemption. One sees this accommodation revealed among the *culturally passive*. It is part of the "fortress mentality" of many church institutions. They personalize religion to a "point of view," and fail to ensure justice for anyone "outside the walls."

179

Religion is expressed in society through love, power, and justice. How we empathize with each other has an impact on how we influence each other; and how we influence each other has an impact on how we hold one another accountable. When religion is *public* (shared, transparent, and open to critique), then love, power, and justice are in balance. When religion becomes *personal* (private, opaque, and closed to critique) then love, power, and justice are out of balance.

Perhaps the greatest social failure of personal religion is its inability to tolerate grace. Public (or shared) religion always places love first. Power and justice emanate from this. Personal religion always places power first, and love and justice are restrained and limited by the individual's desire to control meaning. Personal religion has as much trouble coping with gratuitous *good* as it does with gratuitous *evil*. It reacts in three ways.

Most commonly, personal religion tries to *explain* grace. By rationalizing grace, and attributing some unexpected good circumstance to science or psychology, the individual still maintains control of meaning. The mystery can be resolved by education.

A second option is to try to *manipulate* grace. Personal religion tries to bend God to their will by rites, incantations, or even good works, so that grace becomes something deserved. This is not that different from ancient pagans making sacrifices to propitiate the gods.

A third option is to *dismiss* grace as luck. I often call this the "Vegas" option, because making grace entirely random removes any sense of the divine in any good circumstance. And this absolves the ego from any need to respond with particular thanksgiving or gratitude that would reduce its ability to control meaning.

The preoccupation of modern culture with education, manipulation, and luck is encouraged by personal religion, and you can see this among all lifestyle segments whether they are *culturally ambivalent, culturally passive,* or *culturally righteous*. Indeed, these three preoccupations are even more advanced among the two extremes: the *liberal cultural eclectic* and the *conservative cultural wedge*.

Yet there is a more serious social implication over the inability of personal religion to tolerate grace. It severely limits the possibility of forgiveness. Just as the individual controls meaning, so also the individual controls forgiveness. The ego of personal religion can graciously forgive another, but nevertheless it remains in the individual's own power to offer or withhold it. If a stranger or enemy is forgiven and reunited with love, personal religion loses its power to shape society around its peculiar set of beliefs and values. If it is the *state* that forgives those whom the individual ego deems unforgiveable, they can always vote political leaders and change legislation. But if it is God-above-all-gods who forgives, the individual ego has no recourse short of murder.

Unfortunately, that is precisely what we see today in American culture. We see a culture of non-forgiveness. Much of the political strife today boils down to this: one personal religion is vying with another personal religion to control who is accepted in American society and who is not; and who is accepted into "utopia" or "heaven" (depending on whether one belongs to the *culturally ambivalent* or the *culturally righteous*). And the *culturally passive* stand by and watch. Both the established church and personal religion find themselves nurturing a culture of hate rather than a culture of love.

Chapter 7
THE FUTURE OF SHARED RELIGION

Are there signs of a new cultural movement?

It would be a healthy sign to say that there is a great debate today about the relevance of the church, but sadly that is not true for most of the American population. Critique and exchange about cultures and publics continue among seminary professors teaching practical theology and within established church hierarchies. Scoffers might say that the debate is largely driven by lament over loss of power and desperation to sustain institutions and careers. The reality is that for most people (regardless of age, gender, race, income, profession, marital and family status, or lifestyle segment) the debate ended among the publics in the 1990s in the United States, and earlier for the rest of Western world. And, the general conclusion amid the decline is that the church is not relevant.

Yet spirituality *is* relevant—and increases in significance in every public sector. The abundance of "personal religions" has made American culture a bubbling cauldron of spiritualties in the midst of an increasingly disappointing secular world—even as American churches continue to lose leaders and members, resources and influence.

The emerging debate of the twenty-first century between personal and public religion is not just among church institutions. It is a broader cultural debate about spirituality and behavior. The cultural debate reveals the broader tension between *privatized* faith and *shared* faith. *Privatized* faith does not necessarily mean *shallow* faith. Some personal religion is quite profound, particularly as it incorporates ancient and indigenous beliefs, and builds connections between global religious movements. Similarly, *shared* faith does not necessarily mean *church* faith. The irrelevance of *institutionalized* faith for decades to come is for some a foregone conclusion. But the possibility and indeed the imperative of *shared* faith becomes ever more apparent, given the negative implications of *personal* faith described in the previous chapter.

The possibility of a new movement of *shared* faith is driven by two important trends. The first trend is the radical loss of privacy in Western culture. Just when people are trying to take control of their lives, even to the extent of personal control over meaning (personal religion), privacy itself is rapidly eroding. This is one result, for better or worse, of the digital age. People might think their inner thoughts, core values, and fundamental beliefs are private; but in fact they are already being shared with governments, political parties, corporations, universities, hospitals, and also non-profits and churches. The ability to synthesize digital data into lifestyle portraits, and thereby anticipate what any individual actually thinks or believes and how they will behave or react, is growing more detailed every day.

I have lost count of the number of times I have taught lifestyle research and interpreted lifestyle expectations for some organization, and witnessed the shock of people in the room. At first, they are astonished that digital research can reveal exact details about their personal lives. Next, they are amazed that the synthesis of these details can reveal what they think, how they will behave; what leader they will follow, and what political party they will vote for. They are alarmed that all is revealed, their opinions known and evaluated, and their lies and secret convictions available for scrutiny.

The public willingly encourages the dissolution of privacy through the popularity of social media. Most people post comments or send texts to friends or family or followers, without realizing that they are in fact sharing these with the entire world and those with vested interests. Governments and corporations now monitor social media and can track any particular datum of interest. It is an easy thing today for a government to commend one group and persecute another over any profound or trivial issue. It can reward people who eat boiled eggs from the *big* end of the egg, and persecute people who eat them from the *little* end of the egg. Johnathan Swift's satire *Gulliver's Travels* metaphorically describes the journey from gullibility to trivialization to extremism and is all too relevant today.

The positive result of the end of privacy is that some people who are serious about religion accept the inevitability of it being shared, but choose to control with whom and how it is shared. This kind of shared religion has restored a degree of accountability in religion that had been lost. Dialogue encourages the insight that any single human formulation of faith is limited and judged by a higher truth. This kind of shared religion has insisted on empathy or love as primary in the quest for God. It has led to a more balanced distribution of power. And it has restored a sense of justice—and openness to forgiveness and acceptance—that had gone missing in the age of personal religion.

The second trend driving shared religion is the emergence of embodied faith. Embodied faith is evident not only in thought but in action. It is not that what one thinks no longer matters, but that there should be consistency (or integration) between what one thinks and how one behaves. Personal religion is even more vulnerable to accusations of hypocrisy than established churches. It is easier for the church to reform itself than for an individual to reinvent him- or herself. Embodied faith is increasingly visible among younger generations who are disenchanted with dogmatic debates.

Embodied faith is necessarily more humble than personal religion, because it is more aware of the limitations of human control over meaning. Personal religion tends to separate divine immanence from divine transcendence. God is either transcendent and beyond understanding; or immanent and whispering in your ear; but not both at the same time. Embodied faith lives in the paradox of accessible transcendence internally connected with mysterious immanence. The meaning of life is discerned not only conceptually but relationally. Truth is not about being right but about living authentically. This is why younger lifestyle segments care little about institutions and dogmas, but they do yearn to meet "heroes" of faith who live truth even though they don't understand it, and who model core values rather than compel moral principles.

In Christian terminology, embodied faith is an "incarnational" experience. A person has truth within them, but does not "own" the truth. A person perceives the meaning of life, but cannot control the meaning of life. The paradigm of a perfect person is one who both has the truth and is the truth. Such a person is both the ground of truth and the expression of truth. For a Christian, that would be Jesus the Christ. Embodied truth, however, does not necessarily lead to institutionalized religion. The result of incarnational experience does not necessarily lead to institutional church, even though it leads to a shared experience of faith.

185

The church might become relevant to society once again if church leaders can learn the difference between the church and shared religion. The difficulty, of course, is that to discern the potential future *relevance* of the church, they must first be completely honest about the actual and current *irrelevance* of the church. And to do that, church leaders must stake *everything* in the debate. Nothing about the church can be held back. Everything must be examined, including every program, practice, personnel, and property.

Paul Tillich anticipated this twenty-first-century dilemma in the mid-twentieth century in a series of articles published in 1948 as *The Protestant Era*. At the time, he was speaking of the Protestant church in particular, but his insights can now be expanded to confront the dilemma of the church today in all its traditions. Today we are only reaping the whirlwind of cultural upheaval, migration, and diversity that was precipitated by regional and world-wide wars of the twentieth century.

The paradox facing church leaders today is, as Tillich noted in *The Protestant Era*, that "religion must be in protest of itself." The *forms* of religion must be judged by the *substance* of religion . . . and by *substance* Tillich does not mean theological or liturgical content, but rather the import or significance of religion itself.

Already in his day, Tillich observed the exodus of people from the church in search of authorities that could guarantee certainty and success; and the huddling of a minority of church people claiming elite privileges, exclusive perspectives, and inward-looking attitudes. Tillich identified three essential steps to resurrect the relevance of the church.

- Church leaders must put an end to denial and the pretense of institutional health. It must "reformulate its appeal" for a "disintegrating world" and focus on a message of *hope* rather than *harmony*.

- Church leaders must cease their *confrontation* with culture for a *conversation* with culture, and deny the legitimacy of any "cleavage between a sacred and profane sphere."

- Church leaders must "protest every power which claims divine character for itself"—including the institution of the Church.[1]

This last recommendation is the hardest of all. Who says a prophetic word against an institution that is built on the foundation of the protest

---

1. Paul Tillich, *The Protestant Era* (Chicago: University of Chicago, 1957), 228–30.

against secularity, but no longer seems capable of saying no to itself? Where is the *real* faithfulness?[2]

In 1948, Tillich was still optimistic that the first two possibilities were, indeed, *possible*. Today most church consultants and religious observers are more cynical. Denial still seems to characterize the attitude of many churches (and entire denominations), and ecclesiastical energy still seems to prioritize self-preservation over sacrificial service. Churches still seem to rail ineffectively at either the liberal or conservative tendencies of society, without entering a serious and mutually critical conversation with the public.

The third step is especially problematic. The relevance of the church cannot be discerned from within the church amid the membership, but only from beyond the church in conversation with the public. Tillich described the condition under which this might be possible for the reform of Protestantism, but I think that this can now be expanded to churches in general. Accountability is required:

Accountability to interpret human existence and the quest for meaning without the necessity of belonging to any religious organization;

Accountability to reintegrate society without the necessity of belonging to a special philosophical or political party;

Accountability for innovative strategies to intentionally include cultural dialogue and self-criticism; and,

Accountability for any strategy to be adaptable and relevant to the full economic, political, cultural, and religious diversity of the world.

It seems unlikely that any traditional church institution or congregation can practice such radical accountability. It is more likely that small, mobile, culturally diverse "pilgrim bands" will become the primary agents for the revitalization of the Christian movement.[3]

The "pilgrim band" is the informal organizational unit of shared religion. It is informal, in that there is no hierarchy or fixed structure, and no essential policies and processes, but simply a relationship of high trust and

---

2. Tillich, *The Protestant Era*, 231.

3. Ibid., xxv.

accountability. It is a "unit," in that it is a definable group that has coalesced around incarnational experience. Such units of shared religion are already impacting economic, political, cultural, and religious diversity in the world. Think of micro-charities and small nonprofits or protest movements, bloggers and interactive websites, social service and crisis intervention teams, and even creative for-profit organizations that adhere to strict moral principles.

Shared religion is what has transformed an unrelated gaggle of personal religions, competing or colliding in culture, into a growing discussion of spirituality that is truly cross-cultural and interfaith. It starts where personal religion stops. Where personal religion fails to grapple with gratuitous evil and gratuitous good, shared religion uses this boundary between what is known and controllable, and what cannot be known and is uncontrollable, as the beginning of conversation. Shared religion is the common quest to explore the paradox of simultaneous transcendence and immanence.

These conversations are emerging in the shadows cast by the aggressive and confrontational cultural extremes (the *liberal cultural eclectic* and the *conservative cultural wedge*). Such conversations may emerge from within the *culturally ambivalent* or *culturally righteous*, but they are often emerging between these groups as people reject extremism and seek a middle way. It is in the shadow, of course, because this is dangerous territory. If either extreme group becomes aware of such a conversation, they will be quick to punish or ostracize the participants.

Where are these shadow conversations about shared religion happening? It is happening in some parts of the church, in small groups, among clergy accountability groups, but more often it is occurring in coffee houses and pubs, and also in the stands and locker rooms of sports venues. It is happening anywhere that people gather. It is usually face to face, and then expands in a limited and guarded way through the Internet.

Who is initiating these shadow conversations? Certainly not clergy or political lobbyists who constitute the "thought police" among denominations and institutions. The conversations tend to emerge from other sectors of society: business, arts and entertainment, and law; and even people within military service and pure sciences. These are not usually trained through academia or seminary, but initiate conversation from experiences of life.

Many of these conversations are actually facilitated by maverick elements among the *culturally passive*. In earlier discussion of the *culturally passive*, special note was made of particular lifestyle groups that bear watching. People from their midst may become initiators of this new conversation about shared religion.

- *Working hard, protective, and law abiding.* Lifestyle segments include blue-collar workers seeking not only to recover but rediscover essential values and beliefs in the contemporary world. They remember their roots, but they embrace cultural change.

  For example: innovative churches in the urban core of rust-belt cities across New York, Ohio, Indiana, Michigan, and Illinois that are slaying every "sacred cow" of property and technology, matriarchy and patriarchy, ecclesiastical requirements and career ladders to resurrect essentially dead churches and create centers for simultaneous spiritual growth and social action as two sides of the same coin.

- *Multicultural, sensitive, and open minded.* Lifestyle segments include Hispanic/LatinX, Asian, and second and third generations of immigrants and their friends. They believe everyone needs to be included in culture and have a chance to fulfill their potential.

  For example: the emerging network of independent "mosaic" churches across the Southwest, Gulf, and southeastern states. Many of these bi- and trilingual churches honor the customs from Mexico, Cuba, Puerto Rico, Haiti, and elsewhere in South America and the Caribbean. They create a rich dialogue around diverse expressions of faith, and urgently seek to protect the human rights and safety of immigrants.

- *Black, angry, and restless.* Lifestyle segments include the emerging middle class of African Americans, but also younger, less affluent, and less educated generations who are forging a new synthesis of values and beliefs to counter and overcome resurgent racism and xenophobia.

  For example: maverick middle-class black churches in mid-market cities like Peoria, St. Louis, or Memphis that are involved in community organization, police reform, and aggressive ministries to protect children and create options to fulfill human potential, eliminate crime and prostitution, and other outreach. They affirm black identity by encouraging biracial faith communities that can truly share power and work together for justice.

- *Promising, mobile, and global.* Lifestyle segments include young, upwardly mobile couples and couples starting families. They want to fulfill their own potential *and* sustain integrity in life, work, and relationships. They want to keep the doors open for new insights and possibilities.

For example: maverick mainstream churches in the Midwest and Northeast reaching lifestyle segments like those Experian calls "Boomers and Boomerangs" and "Babies and Bliss." They are founding ministries around dinner tables and informal Eucharist, collaborating with schools, nonprofit agencies, and emergency services to address surprising social needs like teen homelessness or spoiled wetlands.

These people are finding new courage to stand up for the right to say "yes *and* no" over against cultures that insist on "yes *or* no." They have the courage to consider "both/and" and refuse to be bullied into "either/or." They are much clearer about the role of religion as the form of love, power, and justice than other lifestyle groups.

Paul Tillich argued that the "boundary-situation" is encountered when human possibility reaches its limit, when human existence is confronted by an ultimate threat.[4] Tillich is not only thinking abstractly here but specifically about the interface between religion and culture. The "boundary-situation" means that humans, regardless of demographic status or lifestyle context, are caught up in existential anxieties that drive the quest for God. Some lifestyles are driven by emptiness and meaninglessness, and are threatened by chronic depression. Other lifestyles are driven by fate and death, and threatened by pervading paranoia. Still other lifestyles are driven by guilt and shame, and threatened by uncontrollable anger. And other lifestyles are driven by anxiety over displacement, and threatened by irreversible abandonment.

The "boundary-situation" between the *culturally ambivalent*, the *culturally righteous*, and the *culturally passive* (i.e., the contemporary expressions of the left, right, and middle of society) can be discerned in a way that opens new possibilities for the relevance of spirituality in general, and the church in particular. There are four fundamental threats to existence: depression, dread, abandonment, and anger.[5]

- The lifestyles of the *culturally ambivalent* are primarily driven by the threat of *depression*. They are beset by existential anxieties related to emptiness and meaninglessness, which robs them of the courage to

4.   Tillich, *The Protestant Era*, 197.

5.   For discussion in several contexts including spirituality, see *Talisman: Global Positioning for the Soul* published by Wipf and Stock; regarding leadership and worship, see *Spiritual Leadership* and *Worship Ways* published by Abingdon Press; and various academic articles including "The Future of the Protestant Era," presented to the American Academy of Religion, 2016.

participate fully in society (e.g., everything from politics to sacrificial service) and compels them to turn inward toward personal religion.

- The lifestyles of the *culturally ambivalent* are primarily driven by *dread*. They are beset by existential anxieties related to death and dying, which robs them of the courage to gain critical distance from authoritarian institutions, dogmas, and leaders (e.g., in all social sectors of government, science, education, and even entertainment) and compels them to turn outward toward dogmatic agreement.

- The lifestyles of the *culturally passive* are primarily driven by *abandonment*. They are beset by existential anxieties related to estrangement and displacement, which robs them of the courage to trust any and all authorities and accept responsibility for leadership for themselves. This compels them to turn aside and protect sacred times and places.

Each of these groups has their extreme edge. These extreme lifestyle groups are primarily driven by *anger* that is expressed in ideological conflict, power struggle, and social exclusion. However, their anger is expressed in different ways. The *liberal cultural eclectic* and *conservative cultural wedge* express their anger through confrontation with each other. They equip themselves with their own media, listen only to voices with which they agree, and manipulate the *culturally passive* to take their side. The extreme edge of the *culturally passive* has yet to fully emerge, but it appears that their anger will be expressed through a form of "tough justice" (in contrast to "tough love"). This is already being expressed through rigorous accountability in all social sectors for human rights, civil discourse, equal opportunity, teamwork, and respect for diversity. Time will tell.

Can the institutional church, even in its decline, make itself relevant to the contemporary boundary-situation?

For one thing, the church can emphasize the fact that the boundary-situation today (i.e., the standoff between the *culturally ambivalent, culturally righteous*, and *culturally passive*) is not simply the product of economics, immigration, technological innovation, or a host of other secular forces that have and still are transforming the world. Nor is this standoff simply about ideology, public policy, and politics. There is something deeper going on. There is a new quest for meaning that is playing out with an urgency that is occasionally violent.

The church has a peacemaking opportunity to stand at the boundaries of cultural confrontation. The independent churches and innovative outreach agencies often associated with *culturally ambivalent*; and the evangelical churches and church plants often associated with the *culturally righteous*; and the mainline churches and denominations often associated with the *culturally passive* can choose to step away from the center where they are feeding factions, and step toward the boundaries where they can build conversations.

This role can be compared to mediators such as the Arbinger Institute, who help corporations and countries shift from what they might call a "heart of war" to a "heart of peace."[6] After all, Jesus the Christ can be experienced by different lifestyle segments in different ways, but the fruit of the Spirit is the same wherever Christ is revealed. Those core values are what churches of all brands and persuasions need to model and mentor on the boundaries of cultural confrontation.

The experience of Christ should lead to a reconciling heart. The Spirit is moving among all lifestyle segments in America, regardless of political or religious affiliation or non-affiliation. The ability of the church to model and mentor the fruit of the Spirit in the public arena can help factions avoid confrontation, and move forward toward reconciliation by helping people find purpose, authenticity, confidence, liberation, healing, justice, and honor.

The word "reconciliation" has been overused and misunderstood in past decades. Churches and denominations of all traditions, perspectives, sizes, and cultures like to boast about being "agents of reconciliation." Most churches claim to be agents of reconciliation for all basic human rights—except one. They will not accept the religious belief systems of other people at face value. They are not respected but denigrated, stereotyped, and even satirized. Their faith is disregarded as unimportant or simplistic or wrong. Churches on the left, on the right, or in the middle may sincerely strive to reconcile people socially, economically, educationally, and even politically—but not religiously.

And yet this is the one human right—the right to be respected in their beliefs—that is more important than all other rights. People can seemingly endure any kind of social injustice *if only their belief system is respected*. Their life situations may differ. Different lifestyle groups may be driven by different life threats (the fear of abandonment, or the dread of death; depression over the state of the world, or anger at abuse). Whatever their faith (even if it appears as un-faith) in response to these threats might be, it is nevertheless authentic. Their faith *deserves* respect because their lives *deserve* compassion.

---

6. Arbinger Institute (Oakland: Berrett-Koeler, 2006).

The essence of the reconciling heart (or as some say, the "heart at peace") is recognition of, and empathy with, the conditions of existence in which people live. This implies respect for, and willingness to dialogue about, the belief systems that directly address the existential condition. Churches among the *culturally ambivalent*, the *culturally righteous*, and the *culturally passive* have got the process of reconciliation backward. They assume that reconciliation on all other levels will eventually lead other people to abandon their faith and adopt theirs. The truth is that reconciliation on all other levels will never be achieved until we respect faith systems that sustain through the vicissitudes of their unique contexts. Reconciliation is impossible without genuine respect between belief systems.

As much as H. Richard Niebuhr helped us understand the relationship between churches and cultures, his typology needs a sixth and different type of relationship *between* Christ and culture. This is not Christ *against* culture, *of* culture, *about* culture, *in* culture, or even as *transformer of* culture. This kind of reconciliation is simply Christ *with* cultures. There is a parity, equality, or partnership here of mutual accountability. The ways in which we experience and talk about Christ, and the ways lifestyle segments behave and express spirituality are all limited and transparent to the Holy. And the Holy (or as Tillich said, "God above gods") simultaneously employs and shatters all rational formulations and cultural forms. The boundary-situation is where minds and hearts meet with both pride in their traditions and humility about their perspectives.

The churches best able to exercise influence in the boundary-situation may not be identified by any particular Christian tradition or point of view. I have often discovered in my travels and consultations that it is often the multiracial and multicultural churches, and the ethnic second- or third-generation immigrant churches that have the most influence for peace. This is often because they have either emerged from situations of violence or conflict, or strongly empathize with people experiencing violence or conflict. In a sense, they are "prone to peace" rather than "pronged for confrontation."

Given the cultural diversity that currently exists, and will grow more complex, it is unlikely that the church can recover the degree or universality of relevance it had in the past. Perhaps the questions church leaders should ask themselves, however, is whether the relevance of the past is desirable, and whether the relevance of the future is a different kind of faithfulness.

193

The church will be one player among many in politics, education, health care, social reform, law, and the other public sectors. The church will not be a *major* player *most* of the time. The power of the church to draw all people to itself, multiply members, maintain buildings, sustain programs, demand a hearing for its preachers, and generally tell people what to think, do, and become has already been broken. Some church leaders have not yet realized the end of Christendom, of course. Many others might realize it, but in the depths of their hearts they still believe that their faith system or beliefs are better and truer than that of anyone else. The overt power of a church and state in partnership to dominate is broken and will not be recovered. The hidden power of condescension among some church leaders is permanently rebuked by other cultures and will not be regained.

And I think that is a good thing. It's about time churches of all kinds (ambivalent, righteous, and passive) realized, accepted, and yes, even celebrated their powerlessness. Only then can their overt or hidden "hearts of war" be replaced by a public and intentional "heart of peace."

CPSIA information can be obtained
at www.ICGtesting.com
Printed in the USA
LVHW02s0951060718
582718LV00002B/2/P